REVOLT IN PARADISE

REVOLT IN PARADISE

K'TUT TANTRI

A **GRIFFIN** **PAPERBACK**

Clarkson N. Potter, Inc./Publishers

New York

PUBLISHED BY CLARKSON N. POTTER, INC.,
DISTRIBUTED BY CROWN PUBLISHERS, INC.,
201 EAST 50TH STREET, NEW YORK, NEW YORK 10022
ORIGINALLY PUBLISHED BY HARPER & BROTHERS IN 1960.

CLARKSON N. POTTER, POTTER AND COLOPHON ARE TRADEMARKS OF
CLARKSON N. POTTER, INC.

MANUFACTURED IN THE UNITED STATES OF AMERICA

LIBRARY OF CONGRESS CATALOGING-IN-PUBLICATION DATA

TANTRI, K'TUT.
REVOLT IN PARADISE / K'TUT TANTRI.

P. CM.—(A GRIFFIN PAPERBACK)
REPRINT. ORIGINALLY PUBLISHED: NEW YORK:
HARPER, 1960.
1. INDONESIA—HISTORY—JAPANESE OCCUPATION,
1942–1949—PERSONAL NARRATIVES, AMERICAN.
3. WORLD WAR, 1939–1945—PRISONERS AND PRISONS, JAPANESE.
4. BALI ISLAND (INDONESIA)—SOCIAL LIFE AND CUSTOMS.
5. TANTRI, K'TUT. I. TITLE.
DS643.5.T36 1989 959.803'5—DC20 89-9442 CIP

ISBN 0-517-57373-3

10 9 8 7 6 5 4 3 2 1
FIRST CLARKSON N. POTTER EDITION

*With the exception of certain people of international importance,
the names of characters in this book have been changed.
The names of Bali villages have been changed.
The incidents in every case are founded on truth.
Of course, the historical events reported are correct.
The book is, in all essentials, factual.*

CONTENTS

ONE

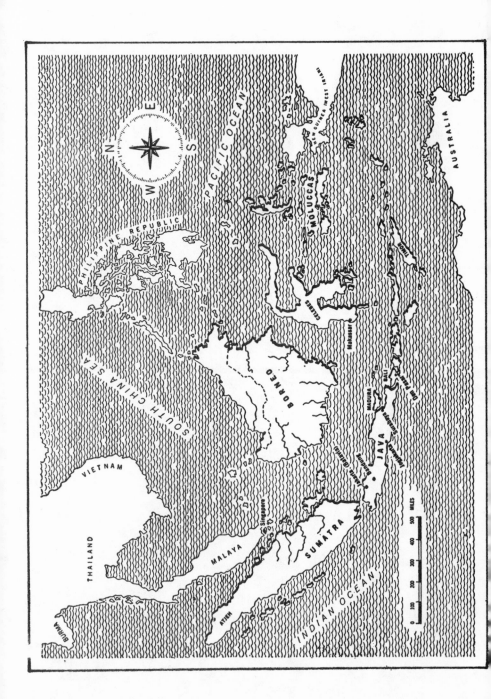

1

THE TREE

This is the story of a white woman who lived for fifteen years in Indonesia—living, not visiting—knowing the country and its people, from the highest to the lowest, and sharing their joys and their sorrows. This woman is myself. Which makes it more difficult for the telling because it is always difficult to be completely honest about oneself.

But I must begin at the beginning, and I am not sure what the beginning is. All lives have many beginnings apart from the obvious one of birth. Let us call mine at the foot of Snaefell mountain on the Isle of Man. One of the earliest stories my mother told me was about a barrel which rolled down Snaefell and did not stop till it reached the bottom. The barrel was filled with spikes. It also contained my great-grandmother. She had been put in the barrel still alive because she was thought to be a witch. At that place, which was a barren waste-land, where the barrel stopped rolling, the Manx people tell that a tree of unusual beauty sprang from the earth. As a child I believed I saw the tree.

In common with everyone else I have many ancestors, but I think they are more important to me than they are to most people, though they are not all witches of course. I was born in Scotland of Manx parents. My father was an archaeologist who left Manxland for Africa before I was born. He never returned, as he caught a tropical fever which killed him. My mother did not accompany him on this final expedition. She had no wish, so she later told me, to have her child born among—as she put it—"cannibals and natives in the Bush and the jungle." She did not share my father's love for these people and this land. She had promised to join him later. But after word of his death was received she married again. My stepfather was a Scotsman.

He adopted me as his own child—insisted on giving me his name and had my birth registered in Glasgow as his own daughter. But I am not a Scot. I am full-blooded Manx, or rather a mixture of blood from the Viking pirates who swept down from the north in the thirteenth century and the kings of the Isle of Man.

We are a superstitious lot, we Manx people. Many of us still believe in witchcraft and in the wee folk. What is called supernatural is not strange to us. We are subject to strong compulsions, not easily explained. We can sometimes foretell the future. When I was young, these powers were very strong in me, and they have returned from time to time. They did so when I was in solitary confinement in a Japanese prison during World War II. But more of this at the proper place. . . . And who is to say that such powers are false? For me, such beliefs are important and I found that they endeared me to the Balinese people, among whom I spent so many years. Their "goona-goona," or witchcraft, was no more strange to me in the Isle of Bali than it had been in the Isle of Man, ten thousand miles away.

I spent the first fourteen years of my life on the Isle of Man, and then I went to school in Scotland. My stepfather was killed in the First World War. After his death my mother decided to go to the United States. We settled in Hollywood.

We soon found a distinct place for ourselves in the Hollywood of those days. I think my mother understood her new American friends better than she understood me and better than she had ever understood my father with his natives and his "cannibals." And yet she was Manx and believed in witchcraft and in the fairies and all the rest.

I myself was really an artist. It was largely through chance that I became successful in another field. I found myself writing interviews and articles about the film stars and the high moguls of Hollywood which were published abroad in British trade and film magazines. I did not enjoy this work, but I made money at it. In fact, success was more than adequate, comfort and security assured. Yet I became increasingly restless. I was discontented. I was unhappy. I often wished that I was an archaeologist and would thus have a real excuse for going to far places. I wanted to paint and do nothing else, but there were so many other things in which I found myself involved. I thought the people I knew shallow and superficial. Their aims, their ambitions, were wholly apart from my own.

Although my mother did not understand me, she was aware that I was unhappy. She suggested once that I might care to return to Manx-land, but this I brushed aside. I had a curious feeling that I would know the place where I wished to be as soon as I saw it.

My mother was always saying, "History will one day repeat itself." At that time I did not know what she meant. I was young then as I now count youth, and there were many things I did not know.

I must come now to the year 1932, which is another beginning for my story—perhaps the one that matters most. It was a rainy afternoon. I was walking down Hollywood Boulevard. I stopped before a small theater showing a foreign film and on the spur of the moment decided to go in. The film was entitled *Bali, The Last Paradise.*

I became entranced. The picture was aglow with an agrarian pattern of peace, contentment, beauty and love. Yes, I had found my life. I recognized the place where I wished to be. My decision was sudden but it was irrevocable. It was as if fate had brushed my shoulder. I felt a compulsion, from which I had no desire to escape.

I began to make my plans. My mother was not in the least surprised. "History repeating itself—I have always known it would happen someday. You and your father—your natives—both of you always preferred strange races."

What race could be stranger than the Manx? I wanted to ask her. But there was no need for argument. After I left I never saw my mother again. She died while I was a prisoner of the Japanese in Indonesia.

Would I do this thing all over again? Yes, I think I would. I survived, that is obvious, and more or less unscathed. The Manx are a sturdy people with a strange resistance to hardship. As I have said, fate brushed my shoulder. The barrel with the spikes had rolled to a stop, and the tree, which few could see, had spread out its branches.

2

PITO

I must set sail from New York, which I did on a bleak morning in November, on a fat little cargo ship bound for the Far East. I was equipped with all necessities, including money, of which I took all I had. As I wanted to paint in Bali, I acquired a two-year supply of canvases, brushes and oils. For my ship Batavia, as it was called then, was the port of call nearest to Bali, and by any reckoning Java was a long sea trek. En route we discharged and picked up cargo in Africa, India, China, Malaya, and Sumatra. There was month on month of this and I was the only passenger.

At last we dropped anchor at a cluster of wharves and warehouses called Tandjung Priok, the disembarkation point for Batavia, some six miles inland. That golden island where I hoped to live, that enchanted paradise of Bali where life would prove uncomplicated and exquisite, was still some distance off, waiting tranquilly between two oceans, the Indian Ocean and the Java Sea.

The dock laborers of Java were not the slow-shuffling coolies typical of Shanghai and Hong Kong with faces hidden beneath brown straw brims. They were lithe, agile brown men, their bare shoulders and strong legs gleaming like metal in the equatorial sun. Lordly Dutchmen and other Caucasians, cool in starched white duck or seersucker, stood aloof from the antlike activities of the natives, and satisfied themselves that all was in order before they signaled for the shiny American-built motorcars, the taxis of Java, to take them home or to their clubs.

To reach Batavia, where I must arrange for my final objective, I drove along concrete-paved, canal-bordered roadways. The hotels in Batavia surprised me. There was the swank Hotel Des Indes, the comfortable Des Galleries, and the Netherlander of older fashion. All excellent. Important guests were received in the great houses whose green lawns surrounded the Koenigsplein, or King's Square, and whose windows looked grandly out on the Governor General's Palace. Java, like all the other islands of Indonesia, was then part of the Dutch East Indies, and Batavia reflected all that was best in colonial elegance.

I had planned to buy a motorcar and drive through Java to the little harbor of Banjuwangi, at the other end of the island, and then cross Bali Strait by native ferry. Dutchmen speaking good English were most eager to help me exchange dollars for guilders and negotiate the purchase of a motorcar until they learned that I intended making my journey alone. In Java, where every car owner has a native chauffeur, it was not considered proper for a white man to be at the wheel himself, and for a woman it was unthinkable! I was implored to abandon my original idea and instead to ship my car and travel in comfort by the Dutch KPM steamship line. I listened politely to this advice, and verified information I had already obtained. There were fishermen at Banjuwangi who could be hired to sail a motorcar across the strait in one of their native praus.

I bought a small drophead car and decided to set out alone that same night. I wished to see the people of Java and the countryside at close quarters, and to me there was nothing frightening in driving alone across Java. I had often driven alone from coast to coast in America. But I am forced to record that this Java drive proved quite a different matter.

The roads were strange and I knew neither the language nor the value of the money. At night I found myself in a veritable jigsaw puzzle of twists and turns with unlighted oxcarts blocking the way. And as for lights, my car lamps proved of limited use. Gleaming surfaces seemed to absorb them and overhanging tree branches blotted the moonlight that crept fitfully through clouds. Java was a motorists' nightmare, and I began to realize why my Dutch acquaintances had been so dissuasive. The air at least was pleasant with a smell of wet earth and the fragrance of strange flowers.

There were many false turnings and fruitless gesticulations of inquiry to natives who couldn't understand me any more than I could understand them. The confusion was particularly trying when I wanted to buy food or petrol with American money. I could see that I had started my drive grossly unprepared, but it didn't matter. I was on my way to Bali and never doubted that I should arrive there.

Then at close to midnight, though it seemed later, I met Pito for the first time. I was destined to meet him three times in my life—always under dramatic circumstances, as this story will reveal. The story of Pito would fill a book in itself.

I was jerked to a stop by a child too close to my path, and there he was. I saw him quite plainly, a smiling, ragged little vagabond thumbing a lift. He had long blue-black hair and a pixy face. He couldn't have been more than nine. And he spoke amusing pidgin English.

This must be a trick, I couldn't help thinking. He might be a decoy for robbers. Or, if I took him into my car I might be accused of kidnaping a native child. For what would such a little fellow be doing alone so late and so far from any village? He offered to be my interpreter and my guide if I would take him with me wherever I was going. There was no question that he would prove useful if I could trust him. And I hadn't come so far for doubt to grip me. My sounder judgment was swayed by his childish appeal. He spoke at surprising length.

"Lady," he said, "you like me? I be your eyes. I be your tongue. I get you right change for your money, and I show you right road. I protect you from evil spirits at night. And I speak English good."

When he learned that I was from America his eyes brightened and his words soared. "American? That is fine! We shall have no trouble. We can fly! All Americans big men—have wings—much treasure. Evil spirits afraid bother Americans. I, Pito, can also protect you."

Yes, this strange little urchin was Pito. When I could interrupt his flow of speech I asked him many questions. Unexplained, he was much too unbelievable. How, for instance, had he learned such fluency in pidgin English, which could not have been his native tongue?

"I pick it up from tourists around the hotels since as long as I can remember."

"And your parents?"

"My father, he taken by Dutch soldiers to the land beyond the moon to die. My mother she die of broken heart, and her jiwa [soul] carried off by leyaks."

"Leyaks?"

"Evil spirits. I told you—they roam at night."

The land beyond the moon, where Pito's father was, has another name. It is New Guinea, a bleak, malaria-infested island to which the Dutch at this time exiled political prisoners. The Indonesians know it as Tanah Merah, which means Red Earth. They lived in fear of the very name.

Pito, who proved an expert navigator, got us by morning to the next town where there was a police station. I was still worried about the boy. I did not trust him wholly, so I stopped at the police station for advice. The potbellied half-caste station commander to whom I spoke roared with laughter.

"The highways are full of these child nomads. Soon you will collect enough children to start a kindergarten! Put him out when you get to Banjuwangi. He's experienced enough and clever enough to find his own way back. He's just another boy and not worth bothering about."

I could not agree with this, but my worry lifted and my mistrust also. So Pito and I continued our journey. There were eight days of leisurely driving to East Java. The boy was an excellent teacher. He knew money values and taught me the Javanese equivalents of yes, no, want, how much, too much, and other simple and useful phrases. I was in luck to have found him.

These days were pleasant adventure, and this child—with no home, no family, and no future apparently—was an amusing companion, quite aside from his practical use. There was, I felt, no need for hurry. At night we stopped in villages at a series of resthouses maintained by the Dutch administration for the benefit of Dutch officials and commercial travelers. Despite the fact that these places were usually run by Eurasians, Pito was always refused admission. His color was wrong. But unperturbed he slept in the car along with the dusty luggage.

I soon found out one thing. It was useless to give him money. It would be taken from him by older boys or, if not, he would gamble it away. He was a born gambler, and took great delight in teaching me odd little native games of chance. Sometimes he would wheedle my permission, and a little money, to make quick trips from the car to the kampongs (native quarters for the peasants) along the way, where he joined Chinese and Arabs. How amazing it was that grown men should gamble with a child—a child who happened merely to be passing by! But Pito was no ordinary child, of course. He had a will and strength beyond his years. In many ways he was far older than I was.

Soon I couldn't bear the thought of parting with Pito. He must come with me to Bali. But when I asked him if he would like to, I was unprepared for his quick and emphatic refusal. He had other plans. The American lady was very kind. But no. A Java boy must grow up in his own land, and find his father in this other land beyond the moon and set him free. He regarded the Bali people as foreigners, knowing nothing of Java's language or religion. I went on coaxing him. His body, starvation thin, needed care and food. These he could have. I would see that he went to school—receive an education. It would be a pleasant life. He was a clever child and would be a credit to his race.

"No," he said, "a Java boy needs no schooling."

It was this that had brought his father to ruin. The gods are angered by too much white man's learning.

When we reached Banjuwangi, I went to see the Dutch controlleur. He was cold and indifferent. More plainly than his guttural accent, his frigid gaze told me that I was an idiotic American woman tarnishing white supremacy. I asked him about Pito.

"Give the boy his fare to the place you so unwisely picked him up, and be glad that you are rid of him."

But I couldn't desert Pito. I decided to cross Bali Strait at night with the boy asleep in the car, and afterward try to persuade him once more to remain with me in Bali.

The first part of my plan was successful. Pito slept soundly while the fishermen, signaled to be quiet, rolled the car into place on the light vessel, a craft so narrow it was impossible either to enter or leave the car while we were on the water. Sails were hoisted silently and the prau, heavy laden, bobbed slowly into the darkness.

All went well until we reached the uninhabited and deserted beach of the island of my dreams. As the car was being unloaded, Pito woke up. I had to tell him that we were in Bali and that Java was five miles across the strait.

For a moment he stood rigid. Then his eyes distended and he screamed. I don't think I have mentioned that his one precious possession was a large dagger which he carried tucked in the belt of his sarong. Looking at the astonished prau men, he took this out. They edged away from him.

"Take me back—take me back!" he shouted. "Bali full of leyaks— I die here—" Then he collapsed into complete hysteria. He wept while the fishermen whispered among themselves.

I managed to soothe Pito by asking his help. "What are they saying?" I asked him.

"That I am right. Bali full of leyaks. And for thirty kilometers a hideout for tigers—a jungle—deserted except for a few Dutch hunters in search of danger. You, a white lady, must take great care. But I—I must go back!" He wept on.

So Bali was not yet attained. It was Pito who suggested that the car be left on the beach while we sailed back across the strait to Banjuwangi. I had desired freedom for myself. I could not take freedom from another.

It was an anticlimax, our arrival in Banjuwangi: the purchase of a train ticket to the village nearest where I had first seen Pito; the giving of a little money, food for the journey, some new clothing; and the writing down of my name should Pito ever wish to come to Bali, with the address of the American consul who might know where I could be found. At the end Pito was calm, silent and somewhat moody. His glances were sidelong and his underlip quivered a little. He removed the new and tightly rolled sarong from around his waist and drew forth an oddly shaped and hammered silver box. From this he took out a small carved wooden figure.

"This is a good luck charm," he said. "Saved me many times from evil spirits. Very powerful. With the money you give me I can buy more strong charms from the doekoen—that is the witch doctor. So you take this, kind American lady, and keep it with you always. I am very happy to be back in Java. The train comes now. I go. I thank you very much."

I watched him board the train. It was the last I saw of him for many years.

"Selamet tinggal!" he shouted as the train moved away. That means, Live in peace.

"Selamet djalan, Pito." Go in Peace.

It is difficult for me to describe how I felt as I stood there, once again alone. My adventure had now begun in earnest.

3

SCENTED WATERS

Having put Pito on the train, I returned to the wharf at Banjuwangi in search of a prau to take me back to Bali, but it was growing dark and my boatmen had gone home for the night. I grew depressed. Even the weather was in harmony with my mood, for the stars had suddenly been eclipsed by clouds heavy and pregnant with rain. I thought of staying overnight at a hotel, but I was too worried to sleep—and there was the problem of my car standing unprotected on the other shore. I was determined to cross the strait again that night.

To my questions about booking a passage, one prau man after another along the wharf shook his head. Wind coming up; tide not right; swells too strong.

Two oceans meet and rush on in opposite directions through a geographical funnel-tip in Bali Strait, thereby producing one of the curious nautical hazards of the East Indies. The Java Sea roars in from the north to oppose the might of the Indian Ocean; and the waters lash at each other in violent mating. But soon again the waves are quieted and the oceans are linked in an ephemeral truce of unpredictable duration. Many a small craft has disappeared in the depths of this interocean barrier.

When some of the prau men had acquainted me with these facts about the strait, I naturally appreciated their reluctance to take unnecessary risks.

Tired of fruitless walking, I paused for a rest at a kopi warong, a small native coffee stall, or hut, patronized by prau men and the native hands from foreign ships loading cargo in the lanes of Banjuwangi. The warong was dimly lit by a small kerosene lamp. Around the primitive counter sat men of the Orient—brown-skinned Indonesians, lighter-hued Chinese, Arabs, and a few turbaned Indians—their passive faces only half revealed in the flickering light. A dozen or more persons were seated in close proximity, yet the place was strangely silent. And although each man seemed absorbed in his own thoughts, I sensed an air of watchfulness, even of tension.

I was dressed in boys' clothing, a cotton lumber jacket and slacks, not as a disguise but simply for ease and comfort in motoring. Nevertheless, it was helpful to be taken for a boy; it made me feel safer and I knew I attracted much less attention. Here at the roadside shop I buttoned my jacket, gave my slacks a hitch, made sure my hair was tucked under my beret, and slipped into place at the counter. I wore no make-up, I had acquired a very deep tan, and my height is such that I was not conspicuous among members of a short race. Unobtrusively I ordered kopi tubruk (native coffee) and shoved a coin across the counter in what I hoped was the hardened manner of a tough seaman.

As I sipped my coffee, the Indian seated next to me inquired politely in delightful broken English whether I came from one of the foreign ships now loading off Banjuwangi. I shook my head and replied that I was seeking passage to the island of Bali.

The Indian told the other men what I wanted. They immediately broke into lively conversation. Their blank faces now beamed with smiles and expressions of interest. The Indian, after a long harangue with the others, turned to me and said:

"Can do, can do. After twelfth hour has passed one fish boat will set sail—take fish—one goat—two Bombay traders—one Chinese man. All want to go to Bali. You go too if pay share."

"Where in Bali will the prau land?" I inquired.

The Indian drew a map of Bali on the counter. "Prau land on beach here," he said. Gesturing with the other hand, he went on: "Chinese bus meet prau, drive seven kilometers to village Djembrana."

My heart sank. The maps I had purchased in Batavia showed that Djembrana was at least thirty kilometers from Gilimanuk, the beach landing where I had left my car.

Noticing my disappointment, the Indian added, "Plenty good taxi at Djembrana—take you anywhere for price." He said that the combined prau and bus fare to Djembrana would be two guilders. I almost smiled at the low fee and was about to agree to it when I remembered the stern teachings of my little guide Pito. Never under any circumstances, urged Pito, should one accept a first offer. No matter how low the initial offer may sound, a period of bargaining is essential—if only to gain the seller's respect.

"Too much," I said. "How about one guilder?" That was just half the amount asked.

The Indian shook his head. "No can do—much too little."

A soft-spoken conference with the others followed, and then he named a sum which was one quarter of the first quotation added to the amount I had offered. I gave ponderous thought before nodding my head in agreement. There had been a saving of face all around. To mark the satisfactory conclusion of an interesting transaction I offered to buy a round of coffee, a gesture that was received with smiles and "trimah kasih, trimah kasih"—many thanks.

As we chatted over our coffee, my new-found friend told me that Bali was the child of India. Of all the islands of the Dutch East Indies, he said, only Bali was Hindu. The Balinese, although surrounded by Moslems on the other islands, had clung for hundreds of years to the customs and religion of India.

Like a practiced raconteur, the Indian began his version of the local saga on the origin of Banjuwangi and Bali, without waiting for encouragement or assent.

Centuries ago, when India was overrun by Mohammedans, a group of Brahman priests decided to flee the country and seek a new home across the seas rather than submit to the conqueror. Taking all their wives, relatives and worldly goods, the Brahmans sailed away, and after much wandering they landed on the shores of Java, where they decided to settle on a beautiful plain called Madjapahit. There they thrived in peace for three hundred years until a great crusading wave of Islam swept across Java. But just as the invading horde was about to overwhelm the Hindus of Madjapahit, a Brahman god named Vishnu appeared and promised deliverance to his people if they would evacuate Madjapahit and proceed to the tip of the eastern shore of the island.

Closely followed by marauding Moslems, the Brahmans—for the second time in their history—suffered themselves to be uprooted. Once again, complete with wives and all worldly goods, they pressed on, this time across mountains and rivers and through jungles laced with vines, until at last their heavily depleted and exhausted ranks stumbled on to the fringe of an impenetrable swamp at a point that was later to be named Banjuwangi. Here the Brahmans waited, as directed, until the god Vishnu appeared and invoked the sacred Hindu bird, Garuda, which miraculously transported all of them, one by one, to safety on the other side of the swamp. The pursuing Moslems came up just in time to witness with rage and incredulity the successful completion of the miracle.

Across the swamp, the Brahmans prayed, rejoiced and feasted in thanksgiving. And while their priests were sprinkling holy water made from the petals of flowers along the edge of the swamp, a second miracle occurred. The vile stench of the swamp disappeared and was replaced by an odor so divinely scented that it seemed to contain the essence of every flower that ever blossomed in that countryside which was called Bali. And then, before the eyes of the happy Brahmans, on the one side, and the distraught Moslems, on the other, the swamp began to give forth fresh spring water; at first trickling, then gurgling into puddles, and later flooding into pools which swallowed the grass and the reeds, and eventually swallowed the swamp.

Soon a great tossing sea separated Moslem from Brahman, and Bali —severed from Java for all time—was safe from invasion. For, lest Islam should consider giving further chase by boat, the waves of the new sea became mountainous, and foamed and boiled furiously.

The Moslems retreated, and though they subsequently established supremacy in Java, never again did they lay claim to the island of Bali.

It was thus, according to my Indian storyteller, that the town at the tip of Java, at the edge of the submerged swamp, got its name. Banjuwangi, in English, means Scented Waters.

Concluding his romantic tale, the Indian told me that on a clear day, when the wind was right, fishermen still claimed that the waters gave off a faint perfume.

I rather regretted having to leave my storyteller, but about midnight—as arranged—I sailed from the quayside. A strong breeze was blowing. In addition to the two Bombay traders—Arabs in fezzes— an elderly Chinese, and myself, there were three Madurese to handle the boat. Aboard there was no place to sit except on deck, where a small woven palm mat had been spread with a tiny lantern in the center.

Ill at ease and frankly frightened, I sat in silence, withdrawn as far as possible from the other passengers. Here was I, a lone white woman, in the company of sinister-looking men of races strange to me. All the money I had in the world was on my person sewed in a belt around my waist. What was to prevent these men from attacking me, robbing me, tossing me overboard? Who would ever know what they had done? Who, indeed, would miss me or worry about my disappearance?

Out in the open sea the wind became bitterly cold and the deck was hard and uncomfortable. The Arabs soon drew out a bundle and unwrapped it, producing an assortment of native sweetmeats and other food cunningly wrapped in banana leaves. Invited to share the meal, I at first declined but when they insisted—and they seemed to have a plentiful supply—I gratefully accepted one of the leaf-wrapped portions. Consisting of rice pressed into a small roll about a meat filling, it tasted delicious but was so heavily seasoned with spices that the tears welled into my eyes. In the months to come I was to grow so fond of this wonderfully hot food of the East that I found all Western food tasteless unless strongly fortified with paprika.

Having cleared the shelter of the shore line, our little craft began to pitch and bob violently on the roughening water. To my amazement the Arabs and the Chinese became seasick. A veteran of more than three months at sea, I had become a good sailor. The rough going failed to upset me and I was soon asleep on the deck.

Within half an hour I was awake again, torn from my troubled sleep by a wild careening of the prau. As I lay on the deck we seemed at one moment to be racing upward toward the sky at an alarming angle and speed. The next moment we were poised on the crest of a wave, and then rushing down into the flailing waters. The boat was entirely out of control—I was sure of that. I have never seen waves heaving and breaking so violently; it seemed that at any instant we might be swamped or sucked under. I clung to the deck boards in absolute terror, hardly conscious of the spray which was drenching me again and again. For an eternity I lay there, tensed, waiting for death to reach out for us, certainly there could be no escape.

The two Arabs were huddled close together, obviously petrified; but the Chinese looked more and more like a sphinx, a graven figure. Now and then the Arabs screamed questions to the crew, but the prau men were too busy handling the sails and bellowing orders across the deck to pay any attention. As the storm raged on, the Arabs became hysterical, fell on their knees and began to chant their prayers. The Chinese sat smoking as though nothing at all were happening. From time to time the chanting Arabs looked hard at me, and over the howling of the wind I thought I heard them mention the word "Amerika" and "Tuan Amerika." Perhaps they were blaming me—a stranger in their midst—for the storm and ill fortune.

I moved closer to the stolid old Chinese. "Not afraid," he comforted me, "storm over soon now." In answer to my questioning looks at the other passengers he added, "Arabs call on Allah for help. Much afraid. Promise gifts of great wealth if reach other side safely. Remind Allah they are not alone on boat—also Amerika young man with much money."

"I have no money," I assured the old gentleman.

"Don't worry about them," he laughed. "Arabs making idle promises to Allah until safe on other side. Then all promises forgotten!"

Gradually the wind abated but the waves remained high. The prau men relaxed their efforts a little, and informed us the worst was over. We had passed the point where the two seas meet. We had been blown off our course and had tacked back and forth most of the night. From now on the sailing would be rough but not dangerous. I lay down to sleep again, as did the Chinese. The last thing I heard was the steady droning of the Arabs at prayer.

When I awoke at daybreak the massive blue bulk of the mountains of Bali lay straight ahead. Clouds clustered about the peaks. Their rose-tinted upper fringes and the clear sky above gave promise of a bright and beautiful day. I was yet to learn that in Bali most of the days begin and end in splendor.

Drawing my thoughts back from the island of my hopes—the land we were fast approaching—I observed that the men were all regarding me in an odd fashion. I turned my head and as I did so my hair came tumbling to my shoulders. My beret had fallen off while I slept. Throughout Java I had been able to conceal my hair beneath it.

Now discovered, I retrieved my beret and hastily gathered up my hair, but it was too late.

"Selamet pagi sobat," I said weakly. Good morning, friends.

The men courteously returned my greeting. "You sleep long, njonya," said the Chinese. He was thus informing me that they were aware I was a woman, for njonya is the feminine of tuan. "Njonya tourist, yes?" he asked.

"Tourist, no," I replied. I was not questioned further. The men were in fact the essence of kindness and good manners. I felt ashamed that I should have doubted their intentions the night before. Truly, I told myself, I had much to learn.

Waiting for us on the beach was a bus. It was an antiquated wreck, but the engine was running. A number of natives were already inside. They had come from Djembrana, I was told, to collect the fish we brought to Bali.

At Djembrana I found a taxi without difficulty and started back toward Gilimanuk and my motorcar.

My first drive in Bali was unforgettable; a long road through deep forest with monkeys playing on every side. At the approach of the taxi they fled into the treetops, screaming and chirping. Now and then a deer dashed across the road ahead of us and sometimes pheasants were to be seen among the bushes. For miles there was no sign of habitation. The lonely western part of Bali, the driver told me, was rarely visited except by the Dutch when they came tiger hunting. Serenity and peace hung like a veil over the beautiful green countryside. Bali was even more lovely and satisfying than I had imagined.

On the lonely Gilimanuk beach I found my car just as I had left it. My suitcases and crates in the rear seat were intact. Nothing had been touched.

I paid the taximan, got into my car, and started the motor. Apparently the man had expected to deliver me to friends at a hunting party. I waved to him and drove on. In my rear-view mirror I could see him staring after me as though I were mad. And as I drove away, it may have been the wind changing or it may have been sheer imagination, but I thought I detected in the warm air the faint and elusive scent of flowers.

4

DEN PASAR

Varicolored butterflies welcomed me to Bali. They danced and flirted around my car as I drove slowly along the jungle road out of Gilimanuk toward Den Pasar, the main town of the island. Like bright confetti flung after me, drifting back and forth, but never falling to the ground, the butterflies floated in pursuit, joyously escorting me on my journey. It was such a pleasant greeting, this vivid shower of wings, and my spirits rose. I felt I was free at last to live naturally and simply—free to find peace.

The road from Gilimanuk plunged into a deep, dark forest; the jungle symphony was music to my ears, and I drove many miles and crossed many narrow flimsy bridges before I saw the golden-skinned, graceful little men and women who are the people of Bali. In manner and dress, the Balinese differ quite sharply from their neighbors in Java. Most striking to a new arrival is the practice among the women of leaving their breasts uncovered—fully exposed.

Everywhere I saw them, along the road or in the rice fields, the women innocently displaying their large firm breasts as they walked in single file, balancing huge loads on their heads.

Much of the way the road to Den Pasar followed winding streams. Frequently I saw natives bathing, washing their buffaloes, and even attending to other bodily functions, all in the same stream. But always modestly. The women carefully concealed themselves up to the waist before removing their sarongs, and the men never exposed themselves fully.

The ancient loveliness of Bali endured almost to the limits of Den Pasar. Then it vanished, and even the people seemed to change. The picturesque temples, the thatch roofs and carved stone walls of the villages were gone, miserable, replaced by shabby Chinese and Arab shops and rows of Dutch houses which were neat and drab and stiff and all alike.

I registered at the Dutch-owned Bali Hotel. I could now bathe and change into a dress. I found the lounge and dining room so crowded with white men and women that it was not difficult to imagine myself again in New York or Hollywood. The people were mostly Dutch, of the colonial administrative type, with a sprinkling of American tourists. There were no native guests to be seen, only native servants.

I sat alone at meals, usually unnoticed. The Dutch did not seem particularly friendly to a stranger. But on the second night a young man with yellow hair and stony blue eyes, self-consciously handsome in his starched white uniform and gold epaulets, introduced himself as the assistant controlleur—"aspirant controlleur"—of the Den Pasar district.

"You are a stranger, are you not?" he inquired affably as he seated himself. I nodded. He made a few observations about the scenery and the weather and then asked me, "How long do you intend to stay in Bali?"

"Indefinitely," I replied. "It all depends—a good long time, probably."

"You understand that there are a number of formalities which the Dutch government requires of foreigners who wish to remain here for more than a few weeks?"

"The Dutch!" I exclaimed. "But this is Bali."

"This is not Bali. This is a little Holland where you and everyone else must conform with all the Dutch laws. Bali is part of the Dutch colonial empire. Possibly you didn't know that. To start with, if you wish to stay here for six months or more you must pay a fee of one hundred and fifty guilders."

"I have paid that already, when I docked at Batavia," I said quickly.

"May I inquire why you came to Bali? It is a long way from America for a young lady to travel alone."

"I came to paint," I replied.

"Oh." He smiled. "An artist? Well, you won't stay long. Foreigners get fed up with the island after a while. I myself have been here two years, and I am sick to death of Bali with its heat and filth. I am praying for the day when I can go home to Holland. But I am a government employee—I must stay. Many artists come here, quickly get tired of the place, and go home."

"Not all of them, Mr. Controlleur?" I asked.

"Well," he conceded, "nearly all. We still have a few crackpots here." He paused and looked at me. "Exactly what are your plans?"

I hesitated for an appreciable moment before I confided my plans to the aspirant controlleur. And then I told him.

"My idea of coming to Bali was, if possible, to follow the pattern of living of the Balinese people. Here in Den Pasar I find no evidence of native life—only the Dutch club, hotel, bank offices, and the Chinese shops of the village. I want to get out into the country and live with the natives themselves—study their culture and come to know the real Bali."

"But that's impossible!" he exclaimed. "You simply can't do it! There are no female artists on Bali—and certainly no white women living alone with the natives. You had better stay in the hotel."

"I'm sorry, but I have made up my mind. You just told me there are other artists here. They don't stay in the hotel, or even in Den Pasar, and I won't either. I intend to live with the natives in their villages."

"You don't know what you are talking about," he replied. "You can't do that here, in the East Indies—not even male artists do that. They don't live in the kampongs but build their own houses. Even so, they are a nuisance to the Dutch government, and they are a most immoral lot." His manner became lighter as he mused on the immorality of the artists. "Let me see—we have a Belgian—he's living with a Balinese woman—set himself up in a lost paradise of his own. Then there is a Swiss, but I advise you to keep away from him. His paintings are crazy, and he is no gentleman. We have another screwball artist who is Dutch. Two Dutchmen in fact. One lives on Sanur beach. We rather expect Americans to be a little odd, but when they're Dutch they're beyond the pale. The other Dutchman I mentioned lives in Ubud with a German artist who also is a musician, a writer, and a collector of butterflies. But in no case do we like it when the whites become intimate with the natives. It is bad for our prestige."

This dissertation on the morals and character of Bali's artists surprised me. Not that I took this young official completely at his word. I had said a little to the hotel manager about my plans, and a word or two must have been passed along. This is why I had been singled out for a lecture. The young official went on.

"If you were to try and live as a Balinese, the effect upon the natives and upon their respect for the white people would be very bad. The colonial administration, I can tell you, would frown upon it. . . . Perhaps we could help you to rent a little house here in Den Pasar."

I had a temper to match my red hair. "Thank you for your advice," I snapped, "but please understand this—if I wanted comfort and luxury and modern living quarters I would never have left America, and if I wanted to live among the Dutch I would have gone to Holland!"

The Dutchman rose. "I make allowances for you because you are a stranger and an American. You are enthusiastic now, but you will soon have your fill of this place. You will become fed up with the dirt, the filth, the unsanitary way of living, and you will long for your clean, comfortable America."

"Mr. Controlleur," I said, "you speak of dirt, filth, and the unsanitary conditions of the kampongs. That doesn't speak well for the Dutch after three hundred years of colonization of the East Indies."

He smiled as he walked away.

Each day at the Bali Hotel found me more restless than the day before. Had I erred sadly in burning my bridges in Hollywood? Would it not have been better to come to Bali for a short visit and then to have made my decision to remain or not? Could I be happy here knowing that the Dutch administration would oppose me at every turn? Would the natives welcome me and ask me to remain if I went to them?

Question upon question clouded my thoughts, filled me with doubt, when suddenly I recalled that first day's drive to Den Pasar. I remembered again the kindliness and friendliness of the natives and the simple sincerity of their smiles. I vowed then that I would go to the Balinese no matter what the authorities said, and I would try to live the tranquil life of a native.

My mind firmly made up, I called upon the head controlleur to show him my passport, and the receipt for the one hundred and fifty guilders landing fee. He treated me coldly, but respectfully.

"It is unusual for a white woman to leave the town without a chauffeur guide," he said. "And it would be out of the question for you to rent a house away from Den Pasar. In fact, there are no houses to rent in the country."

I left the controlleur's office without committing myself in any way. Back in the Bali Hotel, where I asked for my bill, the Dutch manager remonstrated with me.

"Miss, you are really doing a very foolish thing. There are no hotels in the interior, no places to rent—only a couple of small pasangrahans, or resthouses, miles apart, used by the Dutch officials when they are on inspection tours."

"I am here to see Bali, not to live in a de luxe hotel and watch colonials drink and play tennis," I replied.

"You will be back," he said sarcastically. "I'll keep a room for you."

Thus ended my stay in Den Pasar. Whatever lay ahead could surely be no worse. Somewhere on this beautiful island there had to be a place for me, and I must find it.

5

THE PALACE, THE PRINCE, AND THE RAJAH

My plan was simply to fill the car with benzine, drive into the interior of the island, and keep on driving until the car ran dry. I vowed to myself that wherever this happened, there I would stay. Even if it meant sleeping in the rice fields, I would not return to the Bali Hotel. Telling myself that the Bali gods would surely ride with me, and not to worry about events over which I had no control, I started from Den Pasar at a very early hour long before officialdom was astir. It never entered my head that I wouldn't find a place to stay.

Bali was sheer enchantment. Sleepy villages, smiling natives, landscape staggeringly rich in color and design. The benzine tank was fuller than I thought, and hour after hour I passed through primitive villages, up and down mountain roads, across rice fields, and through jungle land.

I stopped once to eat some sandwiches I had brought from the hotel, and at another point high up in the mountains by the volcanoes I stopped at a roadside stall and bought a few coconuts so I could drink the milk.

When the car finally spluttered and died, I found myself in a beautiful, medieval village high up in the hills and outside a high, handsomely carved wall of red brick with an open archway guarded on both sides by four stone figures representing Balinese gods.

Behind the stone wall seemed to be a mysterious-looking temple hidden in tropical foliage. I smiled as I thought surely I must be destined to live with the gods in the Garden of Allah.

Outside this wall was a market square where varieties of goods were being bartered by half-nude mountain women. There were fat green melons, coconuts, strange-looking fruits, primitive cooking utensils, and all kinds of rope—in fact everything a native household in the tropics would need. The natives immediately surrounded me. They looked menacing, but they were only curious.

Hearing weird music coming from within the imposing-looking walls and knowing that the Balinese people have no objection to strangers entering the temples if they do so with proper respect, I timidly entered the courtyard. The startling scene that met my eyes might have been straight from the *Arabian Nights,* or from an illustration for a child's fairy-tale book. It was a tableau that even the moguls of Hollywood could not have imagined in their wildest flight from reality. I stood dumfounded and wondered if I had a fever and were imagining things or if I had suddenly been whisked back to a world that existed a thousand years ago.

A sumptuous Oriental feast was in progress. Temple bells were ringing, and gamelans (native instruments) were softly playing hypnotic melodies from a bygone age. High priests, like Buddhas, were seated cross-legged on bamboo platforms six or eight feet from the ground and surrounded by columns and pyramids of fruit, flowers and carved palm leaves, fantastically shaped offerings to the gods. Behind each priest sat a priestess handing him the different flowers needed for the distilling of holy water. The priests' bodies were bare from the waist up, and around their necks hung several strands of colored beads. They wore tall crimson headdresses, and white loincloths topped with silver brocade sashes. Held in their elegant hands, which had nails five inches long, were golden bells; they tinkled them as they chanted mantras and prepared the holy water to be sprinkled on the heads of the people kneeling before them in prayer.

On other bamboo platforms covered with pale-green matting woven from young palm leaves sat the Rajah with the nobles. At the time I thought they were merely rich worshipers. Their golden bodies also were bare, but from the waist down they wore a kain (a long strip of cloth) of brilliant hue, either in yellow and silver brocade, magenta and black, or blue, green, or purple brocades. Tucked into the back of their sarongs were handsome krisses with gold handles carved in the shape of a Balinese god, and studded with precious gems. Their colorful headdresses were coquettishly tied in front with a bow, and from the bow either a flower or a precious stone was showing. The handles of the krisses were peeping over their shoulders, giving the effect of the gods laughing in the twilight.

The women, looking for all the world like storybook princesses, were seated on platforms covered with silks. Most of them were barebreasted, their lovely bronzed bodies glistening in the soft evening light. They were dressed even more elaborately than the men. Gold snake bracelets studded with star sapphires adorned their slender arms. All were chatting merrily.

Serving maids were flitting back and forth with sweetmeats wrapped in banana leaves, and with artificially colored drinks made from coconut milk. Old men were squatting on their haunches all around the courtyard, massaging large fighting cocks, preparing them for the cockfight which would take place later in the evening.

Suddenly I realized that hundreds of pairs of black eyes were centered on me, projecting the same astonishment that I myself so plainly showed. I smiled in my most friendly manner, but they just kept on staring, until the women started to giggle nervously behind hands held in front of their faces.

Feeling nervous and embarrassed, I started to stroll around the courtyard, stopping now and then to admire a piece of sculpture or a beautiful offering. I watched the priests with their downcast eyes tinkle their golden bells and chant the Vedas. I thought what a beautiful painting this strange scene would make. Once I stopped before a group of children, but they took one solemn-eyed look at me and fled screaming.

I began to feel that something was wrong, that maybe I had been imprudent to enter this temple. I decided to return to the car and see what could be done about getting a little benzine.

Just as I was moving toward the gate a handsome young man of about thirty came up to me saying, "Excuse me, perhaps I could be of some assistance to you. Are you looking for someone?"

I stared at him in amazement, noticing his princely clothing, and then foolishly stammered, "Oh, you speak English."

His large dark eyes danced with amusement as he replied, "Well, is there anything remarkable about the ability to converse in the English language? A few of us have attended universities abroad, you know."

"Of course not," I answered, "but it is a little surprising to hear English spoken in such a remote village, ten thousand miles from the nearest English-speaking country."

He then told me he had been a student at Leiden University in Holland and at Heidelberg University in Germany, that he had always been interested in European languages.

"May I inquire how you came to be in our village, and how you found your way into the palace?" he asked.

"Palace!" I exclaimed. "This is a temple, is it not? I entered because I heard temple bells ringing, and saw a temple feast in progress, and I have heard that the Balinese people do not object to strangers entering their temples. I came in to hear the lovely music and to admire the beautiful offerings. It is like entering fairyland or the abode of the gods."

The young man threw back his head and laughed heartily.

"It gives me great pleasure to hear you refer to the puri as an abode of the gods. You have in fact entered the palace of my father," he said, "but being a stranger you would not be expected to know the difference between the palaces of the rajahs and the Brahman temples, for they are very much alike in appearance, especially from the outside.

"May I introduce myself? My name is Anak Agung Nura. I am the only son of the Anak Agung Gede. I bid you welcome to my father's palace. The feast in progress is a marriage feast, for this day my cousin Anak Agung Anom has married."

I shyly stammered my name, and told him that I was an artist from Hollywood. Then I offered my apologies for having entered his father's palace in such an unceremonious manner.

"Think nothing of it. We are delighted to receive you, although it is a bit of a surprise to find a young lady all alone in our village, and so far from her own countrymen. I am most curious to hear how you found your way here, for you are an American tourist, are you not?"

"No, Anak Agung Nura, I am not a tourist. I came to your lovely island with the intention of staying for the rest of my life, hoping to be able to paint and follow the peaceful, contented way of your people."

I explained how I could not endure living in the Dutch tourist hotel another day, how I had started for the interior of the island, vowing that with the help of the gods I would stay wherever the car ran out of petrol. "The car spluttered and stopped dead outside your palace gates."

I was wondering how I could excuse myself gracefully and return to the car when Anak Agung Nura smiled and said, "It seems to me that your fate has been decided by the gods you so wisely invoked—it is evident that you are destined to stay at my father's palace."

"Oh no, Anak Agung Nura," I replied. "Under no circumstances would I dream of imposing on your family, but I should like very much to stay in your charming village. Perhaps you could direct me to a pasangrahan. I could stay there for the night, and make fresh plans tomorrow. If there is not a pasangrahan, maybe I could stay in the kampong."

"Certainly not," he quickly replied; "you haven't any idea what a kampong is like. It is very primitive. You couldn't possibly stay there, and besides the kampong people would be afraid of you, especially with your long red hair. They are very superstitious. Furthermore," he added, with a twinkle in his eyes, "it is unwise for one to set oneself against what the gods have predetermined. If it had been your fate to stay in a kampong, your car would not have brought you to my father's gate. We Balinese people are strong believers in destiny, and in reincarnation. Who knows but that in some former life you were a Balinese maiden, and now after a thousand moons of wandering you return to the land that is your rightful home. Come, I shall introduce you to my father. He is an even greater fatalist than I. He will be amused at hearing about your flight from the Dutch officials, and he will love to learn something of your fabulous Hollywood."

He took my arm, led me to the veranda where his father was seated with his nobles, and whispered to me, "Quismat" (Kismet).

I shivered with premonition of things yet to come.

The Rajah's sweet old face wrinkled up in smiles as he heard his son tell him the story of my defiance of the Dutch officials; and the nobles laughed heartily at the account of my predawn escape from the Bali Hotel at Den Pasar. After Anak Agung Nura had finished the story of my adventure, the old Rajah studied me thoughtfully. After a few moments he said, "What is written in stars must be. The way of the gods is sometimes difficult to interpret, but once understood, not even a moon-calf would ignore the omen. I think that you did not come to my puri by chance. It was written thus long ere you were born. I bid you welcome, daughter."

6

FOURTH-BORN

I could not provoke the gods. The Rajah's offer must be accepted. I must stay at the palace as a daughter.

I said yes, with many thanks, and at once was taken by father and son to another part of the courtyard where I was formally presented to the Rajah's first wife, known as Isteri Satu. She was a sweet woman, but very shy. With her were her two daughters, charming young girls in their teens, both unmarried and as shy as their mother.

The Rajah's broad smile needed no translating. His speech was always translated by his son.

"Now I have three daughters and one son." The old man spoke so gaily that I was inclined to think the entire matter had turned to jest. But then his tone turned serious. "We shall call you K'tut, which is Balinese for fourth-born child. Soon I shall summon the high priest and, after the custom of our ancestors, we shall give you another name which will be the name of your destiny."

A month later I found myself playing the star role in a ceremony, part medieval and part pagan, in which the name K'tut Tantri was bestowed upon me. I have kept the name ever since.

If I had realized what my destiny held I should probably have fled from Bali while there was yet time. But I had no such intimation, and for the present everything was so gay and happy.

What did disturb me, however, was the way the servants groveled on the floor when they served me or fell on their knees when I passed. The Rajah and I had some lively arguments about these matters which highly amused the prince. I was born and bred a white woman and then . . . quite deeply . . . I became a Balinese. The cross-currents have always . . . at least subconsciously . . . fought in me.

All this came later. I must return now to that first day at the palace. The Rajah, having introduced me to his family and welcomed me, excused himself to attend to certain guests. The prince then took me to a farther courtyard, to a small bungalow which had intricately carved wooden doors and roof beams overlaid with gold leaf.

"This will be your home," he told me casually. While I stood admiring the carvings he explained that his father had done them himself. "We of the younger generation can no longer do this traditional carving."

When we opened the doors I was even more astonished at the magnificence of the room within. There was a great bed with silken canopies and the rest of the furniture was en suite. The ceiling was beamed, the beams carved with little godlike figures covered with gold leaf and rubbed down with Chinese red and blue. The walls of this room, and also the walls of a veranda, had paintings depicting a variety of incidents in the lives of the gods. The white walls of an enormous bathroom served as background for scenes, as I learned, from the epic poem the Ramiyana. The entire effect was overwhelming.

Outside the palace once more, the prince was greatly amused when he saw my dust-coated car still laden with roped-up luggage. He never quite recovered from the shock of learning that I had taken the long drive from Batavia.

As servants unloaded the car, he observed my art materials. "Painting is the one thing I myself like to do," he told me. "But I can't paint in the traditional Balinese manner. I have my own way. Incidentally, it will be impossible for you to paint in your living quarters. There isn't enough light. I shall have to find you a studio. Come— I think I know—"

I realized suddenly that I was very tired and had seen for the moment as much as I could bear. But the prince conducted me to yet another building, much like my little house in design except that it was without furniture.

"The roof is too low for good light," he said, "but I shall have workmen take out the tiles and put in a skylight."

I told the prince that I was very tired from my day's drive and should like to rest awhile in my lovely little house. He apologized for his thoughtlessness, and took me back there. Food was brought and eventually I was alone. I was soon asleep.

A faint tinkling of bells ushered in my first morning at the palace. It was a sound wholly unlike the gamelan music of the courtyard. Its strangeness didn't matter somehow. My mind was curiously at ease. My rest had been deep and long—the first refreshing sleep since my arrival in Bali. The light singing of the bells continued as I bathed in the cool waters of my exotic bathroom. The bag I most required had been quite magically unpacked for me. I found clean clothes, and then—with equal magic—breakfast was ready on my veranda.

As I sat there enjoying the newness of the morning, the prince joined me with his sisters Princess Ara and Princess Ksiti.

"Good morning, good morning," he greeted me cheerfully, "I hope you had a fine rest."

"It was perfect," I assured him. "Tell me—what are those strange bells? I keep hearing them."

"Oh—those! I'll show you."

He produced two small strips of wood, placed them between his fingers and rattled them like castanets. In answer to this staccato rat-a-tat, the tinkling of the bells swelled and a flock of doves landed at our feet.

"This is my private orchestra," Prince Nura said laughingly. He tendered his arms as perches for the fluttering birds. "See the tiny bells fastened to their feet? And those without bells have wooden whistles or flutes carved in bamboo. They are intelligent birds and come to feed at the call of the castanets. All over Bali and Java you will find these bird orchestras. The bells and the flutes are too light to interfere with flight. And the music the doves make, especially at daybreak and when they return to their roosts at night, is beloved by all."

The anticipated food was brought and soon the birds were scrambling for it. Then about nine the two young princesses hurried away. Their brother explained that they went every day to a school across the square where the children of the village were taught to speak Malay.

"Malay is so simple," the prince said. "It is the lingua franca of the East Indies. We will teach you it in no time at all! But first you must learn Balinese. And—with your permission—I shall be your instructor."

Official duties occupied the Rajah during the daytime. He had been appointed by the Dutch as regent for the district. But the prince appeared to have plenty of time to give to me. He explained the many things that were unfamiliar to me, invited me for a stroll through the village, and took me later for a tour around the country-side.

Strangely, I never for a moment doubted his intentions, which would have been natural under the rather peculiar circumstances. He was young, good looking, had been everywhere, and was in a position of considerable authority. Some women would have thought him dangerous. I did not, and time proved me right. He had a gentle-ness, a refinement, and a sort of simplicity which was not in any way childlike. Moreover, he was highly intelligent, as are most of the educated Balinese, and bred to a culture very different from our own but based on moral standards extraordinarily high by any reckoning.

The day we were to visit the village a messenger came and de-livered to the prince an official-looking document. He glanced at it and then said, with some surprise, "This is for you!"

I opened the envelope. "It's in Dutch. Can you tell me what it says?"

He read the contents to himself, then turned to me. "It didn't take long for the news to spread. The controlleur of Klungkung already knows that you are here. He asks that you present your passport at his office as soon as possible."

"But I showed my passport to the controlleur of Den Pasar before I left the town!" I was very annoyed. "This is an unwarranted in-trusion—chasing after me. I shall ignore it. I am not going to drive twenty-five miles to Klungkung!"

The prince looked at me in surprise. "I'm afraid it's not quite so simple as that."

"What do you mean?"

"I mean that the Dutch have the final authority. You can't merely ignore them. My father and I have learned that it pays to be dip-lomatic. They might make trouble—both for you and for us. The Dutch do not approve of a white woman associating too closely with the Balinese."

"Yes, so I have been told."

"I'm sure you have. In fact, I have wondered a little about how you have managed so well, and so has my father. I'm afraid you'll have to go."

"If I go, it will be only because you have asked me to go."

He smiled a little uneasily. "Yes, I do ask you."

"Will you come with me?"

"I think it would be best for you to go alone. If the controlleur sees us together, he would make it much more difficult. In fact, he wouldn't like it in the least."

I was confused but could see that I had no choice. I refueled my car from the palace stocks and drove unwillingly to Klungkung. I did not know what I should find there. Perhaps my stay at the palace was a beautiful dream.

7

A BRUSH WITH THE CONTROLLEUR

Since my ship dropped anchor at a port in the Dutch East Indies I had been subjected to a great deal of advice from many sources. There was the handsome blond youth who sat down uninvited at my dinner table in the hotel at Den Pasar. He was the "aspirant," or assistant, controlleur. He had asked me a great many questions and told me quite firmly that I couldn't remain in Bali as I had planned. There was the Dutch controlleur at Banjuwangi with whom I had discussed the little boy, Pito. There was the head controlleur at Den Pasar to whom I had shown my passport and my receipt for its payment. And others, I am sure, whom I have forgotten to list.

Their songs all had the same refrain. I could not remain. It was dangerous. It was not done. It imperiled white supremacy. Some of them regarded me as insane, some as merely foolish, but none were quite as unprepossessing as the controlleur of Klungkung. None of them had made me quite so angry. He was rude and stupid. He tried to frighten me. He tried to browbeat me. But he didn't know how.

He didn't keep me cooling my heels. I was granted an audience almost at once. The preliminary courtesies were of the briefest. He was anxious to come to the point.

"Young lady," he addressed me, "you have been called to this office on the orders of the controlleur of Den Pasar. He has informed you that the Dutch colonial administration would take a most dim view of your leaving the vicinity of Den Pasar to live with the natives in the interior of the island. We Dutch rule these people by keeping them in their place. What will happen to that, do you think, if once they get the idea that the white people regard them as equals? You—a white woman—accepting the hospitality of a native family . . ." He spluttered at this. For the moment he seemed to have run out of petrol.

He obviously ate too much and drank too much and had high blood pressure. A really long diatribe was beyond his capacity.

"I find the Rajah and his family cultured and civilized," I told him. "And I do not think that I am in any sense lowering myself or injuring the dignity of the white race by accepting their delightful hospitality."

"Don't you know," he asked, "that all the Balinese rajahs have several wives and numerous concubines? Why—the Rajah of Karangasem had forty wives at least! Aren't you afraid that you'll have to join the harem?"

"I believe that my host has two wives. I have met one of them, a most charming lady. They regard me as a daughter, I assure you."

"If that's so, it's lucky for you. Have you heard of goona-goona?"

"Black magic? Yes, I've heard of it."

"If any native woman becomes jealous of you, you'll die very quickly. They have ways—devilish, undetected ways. It's up to us officials to warn you—to avoid any possibility of such a thing happening to any white person on this island. You're putting yourself in a very dangerous position, living in the puri—I mean the palace— the women there are especially skilled in the use of goona-goona. You don't understand the customs nor speak the language—"

"I can learn."

"You can't learn overnight."

"I shall never give any Balinese woman cause to be jealous of me. I know how to deport myself with decorum."

"In America perhaps, but here it's different. You don't know how they can dispose of those whom they regard as rivals. You get ill—then helpless—your mind goes—you suffer torture—real torture—and then you die. And it's all kept secret." He started to go

into some rather gruesome details but I didn't listen. "There was
an English officer poisoned by his native paramour's husband. . . ."
As it was clear he was not frightening me he tried another tack.
"What respect do you think these natives will have for you if you
accept them as equals?"

I had been looking at the man rather closely. The conclusion
I had reached was unavoidable. Indonesian blood was dark in his
veins. Perhaps if I hadn't been so angry I would not have mentioned this. But I could not resist it. "I'm surprised at you, Mr.
Controlleur, being so down on the natives. Haven't you any respect
for your own native blood? I should think it was something to be
proud of—not ashamed."

I thought he would have an apoplectic fit. Very few Indo-Dutch
admit that they are half Indonesian. Nothing upsets them more
than being reminded of it. For the moment I was afraid that,
without benefit of goona-goona, I would be responsible for a major
disaster. But he recovered. He suddenly became calm.

"You say you are being treated as a daughter. I presume you have
met the Rajah's son? A very proud young man indeed, who fancies
that as he has attended the University of Leiden in Holland he is
the equal of any Dutchman. That's what comes of education! I have
had to put him in his place more than once. I suppose he tried to
impress you?"

"He has been most kind. I think him a very well-bred young man,
the most civilized person I have met so far in Bali, though all the
members of the Rajah's household I have found charming. I am
very happy and proud to be a guest at the puri, and I have no intention of leaving. I think you have ignored the fact that I am not
living in the kampong of a poor uneducated native, although I
would be happy to do so. It is shameful to speak of the natives as
though they were a race of murderers. What dignity I have seen so
far on this island comes from them."

"We have always found America's idea of democracy strange," he
said. "For the Dutch it is ruinous. So why don't you be sensible
and leave? You could leave now without . . . without . . ." He
hesitated and I supplied him with his words: "Without being deported as an undesirable alien?"

He let that pass. "Look. There's something I must know. How
did you get into the puri in the first place? You have no connections

in Bali that we are aware of. Of course you might have run across the Rajah's son somewhere in Europe—it's a possibility—"

"I never laid eyes on Prince Nura before yesterday."

"Then how?"

"The Bali gods led me," I said sweetly.

"Bali gods! What do you mean—Bali gods! Don't be funny."

I knew that sooner or later I would have to explain how it happened that I became a guest in the Rajah's palace, so I told the simple truth.

The controlleur listened attentively. When I was through, he jumped up from his chair. "I never heard such a preposterous and fantastic story in all my life!" he shouted. "Just wandering in—a strange white woman. The Rajah and his son know what's what, even if you don't. I don't believe your story—I don't believe a word of it!"

"You mean I'm not good enough to stay at the puri? I thought you considered me too good, because I'm white—thought I was lowering the dignity and the prestige of the entire white race."

He glared. "So you persist in this mad idea?"

"I most certainly do!"

"I suppose you know that you'll be ostracized by all the Dutch on the island? No white person, outside a couple of artists perhaps, will speak to you. Nor will you be received in any European home. Furthermore— Well, you did mention it yourself."

"Mention what?"

"Deportation as an undesirable alien."

I had a faint feeling that I was getting the upper hand. I went on with what I had to say. "I shall continue to be a guest at the puri, and I assure you that I shall act with the greatest decorum. Therefore, Mr. Controlleur, I advise you not to make any trouble for me—or for my host. Because if you do I shall go to the American consul in Surabaya. He will tell you that I cannot be deported without reason, and I shall never give you such a reason."

With this I rose, bade him a cold good day, and walked out of his office.

In a small room directly outside there occurred an incident to which at the time I paid little attention. In this anteroom was a Balinese young man who was working as a clerk. He could hardly have avoided hearing the interview. He greeted me with something above and beyond the call of ordinary courtesy. In fact, a smile spread over his face and he bowed me out with marked ceremony. Later I realized that my argument with the controlleur would be repeated by him to all his countrymen, and the news spread over the whole island.

I drove back to the palace with a heavy heart. I must talk with the Rajah and his son and follow their advice. I certainly would not wish to be an embarrassment to them or cause them any trouble. Rather than do this I would return to Hollywood.

They were both waiting to hear the result of my interview. I told them everything.

The prince listened in silence.

"He could not have been more unpleasant. He hated me. But I hated him also. In fact I am beginning to hate all the Dutch."

"You mustn't feel like that," the prince told me. "It's not the Dutch we must hate but this ridiculous colonial system with its narrow prejudices and its fears. All Dutchmen are not like the controlleur of Klungkung, or even of Den Pasar. Dutchmen in Holland are a different breed altogether. These men are colonial diehards. If not, they are removed from office. If they like the natives they are considered unsuitable. Why, only a few months ago there was a controlleur of another province whose only fault was that he mixed too freely with us. This became known to the Resident who told the Governor . . ."

It is a long story: a transfer to a lonely island as far as possible from Bali—an added rank given in order to save face. There were other, subtle punishments for treating the Balinese as human beings.

The Rajah then told me that as far as he and his family were concerned they hoped I would continue to stay at the puri and not be frightened away. He doubted that the controlleur had the authority to make me move except on a trumped-up charge, and if it came to that he personally would take it up with the Governor. He pointed out, however, that the white colony would never receive me in their homes. I would be treated as a pariah. He said that even the Balinese nobles were not received as guests in Dutch houses or clubs and that, save for a few foreign artists, they had no social connections with white people on the island.

The prince, after translating all this for his father, added what I suspected was a warning of his own. "You might get very lonely without the company of other white people."

But I knew I should never be lonely as long as I had such wonderful friends.

8

MATTERS OF LANGUAGE AND CLOTHES

"You don't understand the customs nor speak the language," the controlleur of Klungkung had told me, and I had replied that I could learn.

During the next month I learned a great deal—language, customs, and—more than anything—a wholehearted acceptance of a way of life which was alien to me. It was, I do believe, my destiny. How, otherwise, could I so soon have regarded the palace as my rightful home? The life there was, in many ways, fantastic. Agung Nura, with his European training, was responsible for gently introducing me into it. He never let me see too much at once. I was gradually prepared for everything was too unusual.

The languages were comparatively simple for me, and my studies began by attending the village school for children. The daughter of the Rajah, Agung Ksiti, was at first my chief teacher. But she could not speak English. I was taught by the drawing of objects on a blackboard, with the Balinese word written beneath and also the Malay equivalent. In the evenings Nura himself taught me to read and write in "high Balinese." The low-caste dialect was quite different.

"One must be very careful," he warned me, "never to address a person of rank in anything but high Balinese. To the peasants you speak with low-caste tongue."

This last was difficult for me to remember to do, and I often found myself addressing peasants in the high language. But this didn't matter. In fact it pleased the peasants to be spoken to. And as a stranger in their midst, I think I felt it discourteous to speak to them in any other way. Nura also insisted that I learn something of the ancient Kawi speech and study the classic literature. He said that to understand the people I must know their background. I became steeped in the history of the country and in the works of the writers and philosophers. He translated for me the records and the stories which were written on lontar leaves. The folklore was amazingly similar to our own fairy tales.

Then there was the matter of clothes. From the first I had wanted to dress in Balinese clothes, but had hesitated to suggest it. Finally, much to my delight, the suggestion came from the two young princesses. They brought me sarongs, sashes, sandals, and at my own insistence a silk coatee called a kebaya. I refused to go barebreasted. The girls could not understand this. They told me that I was a woman like every other woman and surely I was not ashamed of my body! But I could not be persuaded. First the sarong and then the winding of the sash. This is a broad band of stiff corded silk some five yards long. Princess Ara started wrapping it around me at the hip, raising it slightly at every turn so that it formed a tight ascending spiral.

"It's so tight I can't breathe," I panted. "It's worse than any corset." I felt like a mummy folded in a shroud.

"You'll get used to it," the girls giggled. "It has to be tight because it must lie flat—flat—flat. No bulging at the hips. A straight line is most important. And for you it's more important than for us, because in the back you are not so straight as we are."

"But that is beautiful," Agung Ara hastened to say. "And being wound tightly it will still show. It is what our men most admire. You see, when we walk there is nothing to get excited about. When a white woman walks it is different."

This frankness surprised me, but it was the sort of natural frankness which no one could mind.

Now for the first time in the full Balinese costume, I took stock of myself. As I examined the fruits of their work in a mirror, Ara and Ksiti circled around me, their eyes alight with excitement. "Tjantik, tjantik!" they exclaimed. "So beautiful! So wonderful! What marvelous white skin, what perfect complexion!"

Never before in all my life had I been told that I was beautiful. Never before had I known the heart-warming thrill of being admired sincerely and without reservation. Never had I been the object of such flattering attention. I looked in my glass and looked again, examining myself from every angle, and I discovered with astonishment that I was indeed not unattractive. The straight sweep of the

sarong from hip to ankle, the contrasting color of the sash, the simplicity of the little kebaya above, gave me a grace and dignity I had
never achieved with Western garments. The effect of white skin
against rich Balinese textiles was striking. And I thought my hair
looked unusually nice, too. Shoulder length and red as a forest flame,
it had long been my one claim to beauty. All in all, this was a
dramatic transformation. Undeniably, it gave me more than a touch
of glamour.

"Tjantik," Ksiti cooed. "Njonja, how do you like it?"

"Girls," I said, with tears in my eyes, "I can't thank you enough. I
find it perfect. I am delighted with my Balinese personality. I shall
never go back to the style of the West."

I kept that promise well during all my years in Bali, except for
rare occasions when it was virtually compulsory to wear a frock or
high-heeled shoes or a hat. And when I did, how strange and foreign
it felt!

Ksiti looked out the doorway. "Here comes Agung Nura! Wait
till he sees you!"

My first impulse was to run and hide. But then I told myself that
since I had decided to become a real Balinese I had to face up to it.

Nura came in—then stopped dead as he saw me. His eyes opened
wide and a look of astonishment spread over his face.

The princesses jumped up and down with excitement. "See, see!"
they chorused. "See what has happened!"

Nura stood for a full minute staring. And then, "You are lovely,"
he said softly. "Absolutely lovely."

They said no more but it was enough. I knew that the garments
of Bali were meant for me.

Nura's enthusiasm for my new mode of dress was not without
reservations, however. My hair worried him. We must encourage it to
grow long, he said, so that it might be combed tightly on top of my
head in the Balinese manner. Perhaps in the village it might best be
rolled under a scarf, like a tight turban.

"And your walk," said Nura. "In a sarong you cannot take those
long strides. Ara—Ksiti—you must teach her to walk slowly with the
grace of the Balinese."

In the days that followed they tried very patiently to teach me to
glide, to use every muscle sinuously. They tried placing a basket of
fruit on my head to teach me balance. I spilled fruit everywhere. They

tried using a pot of water instead and were thoroughly splashed for their pains. They even tied my hands behind my back to force me to hold my shoulders erect. In the end they went to their brother and confessed failure. They would never be able to teach me to walk with Balinese grace. But they did cure me of a tendency to slouch.

The princesses and the other women of the court, envious of my fair skin, began trying to lighten their own complexions through applications of white powder. The glorious color of their skin, a shade of gold which is so hard to capture on canvas, came through the powder in a ghostly purple-blue. I protested constantly against this disfigurement of natural beauty and finally induced many of them to use restraint in applying the powder puff.

For some time after donning Balinese dress I remained rather self-consciously within the puri walls. I was no problem as far as the Rajah and his family were concerned, but I was certainly a sensation to his friends. News of me had spread to the villages, and beyond. The palace was getting many more visitors than usual.

There came a day when, of necessity, we must all go down to Den Pasar to shop. There were no shops in the village. Would I go in Balinese clothing? the Rajah wished to know.

"Why, of course," the princesses replied, "in what else?" The two girls felt responsible for me.

We crowded into the Rajah's limousine, Agung Nura and his attendant, his two sisters with their elderly serving maid, and I. It was a gay ride, made gayer by the exciting apprehension of what was to come. We were about to introduce to Bali something new—a white woman turned into a Balinese. A white woman who wore native clothing, who walked and talked only with the natives, and who considered herself one of them.

The chauffeur parked the limousine on the main street, and hardly had we stepped from it when incredulous cries reached our ears: "Adoe! Njonya! Look—look—a white girl dressed like a Balinese!"

We soon attracted a swelling crowd of natives. They bowed low before the prince and his sisters, but their main interest was obviously in the white woman who wore a sarong, a kebaya, and sandals, and whose sun-glinting hair hung down to her shoulders.

"Adoe! Adoe." This hushed exclamation of admiration followed us everywhere. Smiling natives trotted after us. When we entered a shop they waited close-packed outside until we emerged, and then trailed us down the street. From them I felt a warm surge of friendliness and welcome, of gratitude that a member of the white race had found their ways worth copying, and of keen pleasure at my evident delight. I felt that they really liked me, and I was sustained by their appreciation.

And then, as we eddied, flushed and happy, out of the crowded shop we came face to face with a party of European women, carefully groomed, expensively dressed. We all halted, our party on the one side and the white women on the other. The women stared at me, at first in mere curiosity and then in swiftly rising contempt.

"Disgraceful!" one woman exclaimed.

The others chimed in: "Shocking—horrible—" "A white woman in native dress—consorting on equal level—" As they swept past, the natives cleared a broad passage for them.

My courage and happiness vanished. "Quick, quick," I pleaded, "let's get out of here." In the distance I could see another group of white people approaching.

Nura eyed me sternly. "Don't let them upset you. What they think —or say—is not important. I suspect they're jealous."

The princesses added their own words of comfort. "Don't be frightened. Just ignore them. That is what we do when we are insulted publicly. Remember, you don't live with the Dutch any more."

No, I didn't live with the Dutch. But the white people who were drawing near were two Dutchmen and, I presumed, their wives. They stared at me intently. But if they made any sarcastic remarks I did not hear them. I closed my ears and then my eyes. We went on with our shopping, but the fun was gone.

As I have said, my red hair did not blend with the Balinese costume. As time went on I became increasingly conscious that it worried everyone. Something must be done, and it was the Rajah who made the final suggestion. It would be best if my hair were dyed black. He explained to me that in Bali only demons, witches, and the dreaded goddess of evil, Rangda, had red hair. With such hair the superstitious people might fear me and would never really accept me as one of them. My hair was the reason why the children had fled screaming from me when I had first entered the palace courtyard. So, somewhat reluctantly, I agreed.

The Rajah took a very personal interest in the transformation. He hovered over the skillful maids who were assigned to the work, clucking like a hen and issuing constant and often unneeded instruction. "Now—blue—black—blue—black—and be careful—it must be absolutely perfect."

The hair was finally cut with bangs across the forehead like an Egyptian's and let fall to my shoulders.

"Too bad," said the Rajah, "that we can't dye your gray-green eyes brown."

9

LEARNING THE WAYS OF THE BALINESE

Once given my new name I had to become a true Brahman, and to do this I must receive religious instruction. I went, therefore, to the home of the village high priest, who spoke excellent English. He taught me about karma, the transmigration of souls, the unreality of the world (maya), and the names of the Hindu deities; he also taught me how to pray and what to say. I recited after him verses from the Bhagavad-Gita, the Lord's song.

The studying I did was not easy, but being young and, I hope, reasonably intelligent, I was an apt pupil—or so I was told. I became deeply attached to the old high priest. The Brahman high priests are considered to be of higher caste than even the rajahs. Their homes are called geriyas. There was one priest in the north of the island at whose home I often stayed for days, having become a good friend of his family.

Brahmanism is a many-sided creed and takes in every aspect of life. No act, no matter how simple, is performed without an obeisance to the gods.

I attended temple feasts all over the island. They were very gay, quite unlike going to church in the West. And they were real feasts, with music from the gamelans and everyone laughing and talking. While the priests chant and prepare the holy water, young men and women sit around flirting. I saw women bring into the temple courtyard little tables upon which they set out sweetmeats and drinks for sale. At some religious feasts even domestic animals and pieces of household furniture were brought into the temple to be blessed!

One thinks of the East as a country of leisure, at least for the nobles. But nothing could be further from the truth. There was a siesta in the early afternoon because of the intense heat, but outside of that everyone was occupied from morning to night—the women as well as the men. We did everything but rest. I was rarely alone. I sometimes wondered if any disgrace was attached to being by oneself. And yet I loved it all.

I had thought I would paint. I had planned on this. Agung Nura, as he had promised, saw to it that my studio was prepared. My paintings were unpacked, with Nura and often the young princesses eagerly watching.

As each canvas was unrolled, the prince made exclamations of delight. He was amazed at the Balinese scenes which I had painted while on the way to Bali. He asked me if I would like to see his own paintings and promptly produced several. They were in modern Western style, and done with considerable feeling for composition. Later I was to learn much from him that strengthened my own feeling for composition—one of my strongest points as a painter.

He worked humor into his art, his rollicking spirit always bringing out the lighter side of a subject. Frequently I would find in my studio or bungalow a new sketch, usually a sardonic caricature of Dutch behavior. I recall one particularly bitter drawing of Dutch officials banqueting beneath a canopy. Each man wore the mask of an animal. The table was covered with bottles of liquor and rich and varied foods. Outside the canopy squatted peasants, thin and in rags. It was very well done, but the subject surprised me. I had much to learn about Agung Nura's political opinions.

I was too excited to begin painting at once, and anyhow I had very little free time. I did not mind this, for I could not yet hope to express on canvas all I was seeing. Everyone was so good to me and life was so interesting. I was not a guest, but a member of the family, a much-loved member.

There was a woman, Isteri Duah, whom I knew but did not know. The name means second wife, and vaguely I was aware that the Rajah had a second wife, but the two ideas had not connected in my mind. His first wife, Isteri Satu, I had come to know quite well. She was active in all affairs of state and attended certain state functions though she never sat down with the rajahs at official feasts. I found this curious as she functioned in many ways as any wife of a prominent statesman in America might do. I was told that other rajahs would not have sat down at the table with her. It would have been a breaking of convention.

But it was all right for them to sit with me because I was a foreigner. I was present at many feasts where I was the only woman. The Rajah insisted on my being present because I could amuse his guests. Agung Nura told me that his father was proud of me and liked to show me off. He always humorously introduced me as his fourth-born daughter.

The second wife, Isteri Duah, was of lower caste than the Rajah and much younger. She had no children. She was largely responsible for the running of the huge palace household, and hundreds of servants and underlings came to her for orders. In this department she was in a position of considerable authority. She must have been a very practical person and I know that everyone regarded her with a great deal of esteem, including the first wife who was deeply attached to her and depended on her in many ways. There was no jealousy. The Isteri Satu thought it entirely reasonable that the Rajah should have a second wife. Without question he was a man of high moral character. I think his morals would stand up rather well by any standards one could name. A neighboring rajah, also highly respected, had forty wives and a hundred children.

I recount these matters in what may seem to be too much detail, for it was a strange world to me as it may be to the reader. There were many amusing incidents. I was introduced and taken everywhere, to the palaces of all the rajahs—always accompanied by Agung Nura and several servants. Frequently the old Rajah himself was my escort, watching over me—afraid, I think, that I might be enticed away from him. All the rajahs seemed to like me, and many of them invited me to stay at their palaces.

There were brothers and brothers-in-law. The high-caste Balinese are often closely related. There was one palace quite as large and as beautiful as the one in which I lived. It belonged to an older brother, the Anak Agung Pongawa, a deeply religious and fine man. Most of the other palaces were less impressive.

As time went on I formed a friendship with a cousin of Agung Nura's; she had the same name as his younger sister, Anak Agung

Ksiti. She was tall for a Balinese woman, with a thin, intelligent face and a personality that interested and attracted me. Her father was dead, and although she was twenty-five—which made her middle-aged in that country—she had refused to marry. She was very wealthy in her own right, and lived a life of extraordinary independence. In a sense she was uneducated, a Balinese woman of the old type. She knew no English or any other European language. As soon as I gained fluency in Balinese and Malay we became very close.

Incidentally, the Malay language has adopted the Roman alphabet, which is of course like our own. But the written Balinese makes use of a sort of syllabic script, each syllable a character. This is rather difficult at first.

I have spoken so far only of the sweetness and innocent charm of Balinese life. There is another side. Some of their ceremonies involve blood sacrifices. There is, for instance, a kris dance which is performed by the men of the village, young and old. They are entranced, plunge swords, or rather krisses, into their breasts and other parts of their bodies, but mysteriously do not wound themselves or even bleed. Toward the end of the ritual the pemangku, the people's priest, as opposed to the Brahman priest, eats small chickens alive. I could never become used to this spectacle, though my friends accepted it without quibble. It is an observance which has been retained through a thousand years, and who can say that it is more to be deplored than the English or American sport of hunting? I myself have never cared for hunting. And I think the methods used in our stockyards brutal. The whole matter is difficult to explain.

There is a much rarer and more spectacular ceremony of blood sacrifice—strictly religious—which occurs only once in ten years. I was fortunate—or possibly unfortunate—enough to witness it. The affair takes place at a lake deep within the yawning crater of an extinct volcano high among misted peaks.

On this day Agung Nura and I left our car at the village of Kintamani and made our way on foot by a steep and slippery trail down to the lake's edge. We expected a canoe to be waiting for us, to take us across the lake where the Rajah and other important men of Bali had gone the afternoon before. Our destination was one of a group of very old villages, the last of those settled by the original inhabitants of Bali, who lived there long before the coming of the Hindus. They are touched but lightly by the life, or the Brahmanism, of the present and few people visit them. They are called Bali Aga villages, and are walled against intrusion.

"One can never truly know Bali," Nura had told me, "without going into them. The Bali Aga have been called nations within our nation. Intruders are resented."

There was no canoe for us and it started to rain. In fact it poured and I became soaked. The prince left me in order to find means of transportation, and I was discovered by a Balinese, fat and sweating, who turned out to be one of the few rajahs I did not already know. He spoke perfect English and insisted on taking me across the lake in his own boat. Happily, he also had a very large and beautifully decorated umbrella. I explained the situation, and told him who I was. He had heard all about me. When he proposed leaving one of his servants to tell the Anak Agung Nura that I had gone on, I consented to my rescue.

It seemed a perilous voyage enough. The boat leaked and had constantly to be bailed out. I think we were two hours on the water. But the whole story of that day is a long one altogether. On the far shore there was a cluster of small temples and huts and behind these could be seen the walls of the Bali Aga village. Near the huts I saw a shelter with a thatched canopy beneath which a long table was set with food and drink. As we stepped ashore several men greeted my benefactor with much bowing and scraping. But something one of the men said appeared to upset him. He excused himself and strode off into one of the little huts, leaving me to my own resources. It was still raining very hard.

With the water dripping from my hair and streaming down my face, I started toward the shelter with the thatched canopy. As I approached I noticed that there were several white men among the Balinese nobles seated at the table. To my horror I recognized the controlleur of Klungkung and the controlleur of Den Pasar. They saw me, too, and glared, their faces gleaming with dislike. I halted. The rain was preferable to joining them, so I turned and ran back to the shelterless shore line. It was there that Agung Nura found me, when he arrived finally in a canoe he had managed to procure.

He pacified me with the assurance that we would stay away from the Dutchmen, and then he and his father took me to a small stone house along the beach where I was given dry clothes and food. By then the rain had stopped and the sun was out, and the day's cere-

mony started with a great ringing of bells by the priests. Prayers were
intoned.

Now the peasants loaded boats with live geese, goats and chickens
and a single sad-eyed water buffalo, all to be drowned as a gesture of
propitiation to the gods. There were also boatloads of fruit, flowers,
and rice.

"Once every ten years it is necessary to appease the gods of the
lake," Agung Nura explained. "The animals are weighted down with
kapengs [native money] equal to their own weight. There must be
fortunes in Balinese money tossed into the water!" We got into a
canoe, the Rajah carefully lifting his red and gold ceremonial trappings so that they might not be soiled more than they already were,
and paddled out into the lake. The heavy-laden boats carrying the
sacrifices were taken out about a mile amid much praying and casting
of flowers. Suddenly at an appointed spot the animals were pushed
overboard. There were more prayers until the bobbing heads disappeared and the ruffled water was again quiet.

It was beginning to grow dark, but for the safety of our homeward
journey we must wait for the moonlight. We took advantage of this
to go to the walled village of the Bali Aga where, because of the
Rajah's exalted status, we were admitted. Finally the moon rose, the
night became brilliant. We could return home. I consoled myself that
at least there had been no human sacrifice.

10

A DAUGHTER OF THE PALACE

Another blood sacrifice with a religious significance was the favorite
sport of the Balinese and the old Rajah. Cockfighting was the Rajah's
only vice. He was basically a gentle person and yet he loved it. He
persuaded me to go with him, which was unusual as no Balinese
women ever went to cockfights. More and more I seemed to do what
he wished me to do. I saw things more and more through his eyes. As
for the cockfights, I cannot say that I did not come to enjoy them.

He taught me to be a good judge of fighting cocks—how to place a bet and with whom. We bet with the rich Chinese merchants and with the other rajahs. I still had some money of my own and insisted on using it for my gambling. The rajahs all bet large sums. My bets were much smaller, but I often won.

I recall sitting around a rectangle which was filled with offerings to the gods. At the center of each of the four sides was seated one of the local potentates. The birds fought and we bet. I suppose it is a cruel sport. The birds, with long sharp spurs attached to their feet, were often killed and always wounded, but I admit I grew not to notice the cruelty. Now I might feel differently, but I must record how I felt then. The picturesqueness appealed to me. It would have appealed to any artist. I later painted many pictures of these fights. The excitement was tremendous. And I told myself that any pleasure I could bring to the old Rajah was a small return for his abundant kindness. I was in a rather peculiar position with him. I had in a very real sense become his daughter—such a daughter as he could never have fathered. He loved it and I loved it. To some, my life at the puri might seem protected, almost cloistered. But I think I have told enough already to show that this was far from the truth. To use a slang phrase, "I got around."

One day a ship of the American navy anchored off the coast, and the Rajah announced that he would dearly love to go aboard a real battleship, especially an American one. I took it upon myself to write a letter to the captain, who responded warmly with an invitation to lunch. It was decided that the Rajah, the prince, the princesses, and I should accept. But there was a line drawn. The Isteri Satu and the Isteri Duah could not be allowed to leave the palace.

The harbor was shallow and no ship of battle size could dock at the quayside, so a launch was sent for us. We arrived in much state with suitable attendants, the family wearing their most splendid raiment, though I myself preferred to dress simply. The Rajah and his son had golden krisses tucked in their sashes. Jewels flashed. The girls had wrapped yards of yellow and gold brocade around their bodies. Their necks, arms, and ears sparkled with gold and diamonds and their black hair was heavily scented with frangipangi.

The captain himself escorted the Rajah and the Anak Agung Nura everywhere while officers in charge of the princesses and me followed

close at their heels. The old man was like a child at his first circus.
There was an airplane to examine right on the deck and also a fine
launch almost as large as the one which had been used for our own
transportation. But it was the guns which fascinated him most.

"If we only had had guns like these when we were invaded we
never would be a colony of Holland now!" he said.

This amused the captain greatly. In fact every comment the old
man made amused him, even though it had to be translated by
Agung Nura.

"Tell your father," the captain instructed Nura, "that we would
be delighted to let him have some guns now, but I am afraid it is a
bit late, and besides it might lead to international complications."

It was at lunch that the gaiety reached its height. The officers
were much intrigued by the six-inch-long fingernails of the Rajah
and the princesses, and were amazed at their skill in managing knives
and forks, not realizing that they had all had training in European
manners. The prince did not wear long nails, and naturally I did not.

The ice-cream course was the climax. The Rajah had never eaten
ice cream before. He asked for a second helping and a third and a
fourth. His son warned him that he would be ill. Even the princesses,
who rarely admonished their father, spoke in warning. And he did
feel a little squeamish later, particularly on the launch from ship
to shore.

In return for this hospitality the Rajah invited the captain and his
officers to the palace, arranging for them a feast of feasts. The puri
was decorated as it had been on the day of my arrival. All the neighboring rajahs were included among the guests with their families and
ministers. Dancers were brought from all over the island, gamelan
orchestras came from far and near. Even a cockfight was scheduled.

Because of the presence of the rajahs certain formalities had to be
observed. On arrival the women were immediately separated from
the men. Ara and Ksiti and I escorted them to the women's quarters
where the Isteri Satu and the Isteri Duah greeted them and we sat
around gossiping. I alone was included at the table with the rajahs
and our American guests. It was expected of me and for once I was
glad. I never enjoyed these feminine sessions, perhaps because I was
too modern.

The Americans had the time of their lives. If the Rajah had overeaten of the ship's ice cream, they certainly returned the compliment in regard to the suckling pigs roasted before their eyes, the turtle satays cooked on skewers, to say nothing of the beverages. Although the Rajah and his son did not touch alcoholic drinks, the palace was always well stocked with every type of wine and liquor, including arak and brum (this last a rich native wine). Our new friends sampled them all.

The party ended at daybreak. On leaving, the captain asked the Rajah what he would like to have from America as a remembrance of this wonderful day and night. Without hesitation, but with a twinkle in his eye, the Rajah said he would like an ice-cream-making device.

He was greatly touched when, some two months later, a brand-new refrigerator arrived from Washington. There were careful instructions on how to make ice cream. With the gift, on one of the shelves, there was a large card: WITH THE COMPLIMENTS OF THE CAPTAIN AND HIS OFFICERS OF THE AMERICAN BATTLESHIP.

It was most unfortunate that the palace had no electricity, so the gift was useless. I suggested selling it to the Dutch hotel at Den Pasar or to an official there, as electricity had been installed at Den Pasar. With the money we could buy the type of freezer using bottled gas.

The Rajah was horrified. "What? Sell the gift of the American navy? Never! This is the first gift I have ever received from America and I would not consider parting with it. When I die I shall leave it to my children."

He had his precious gift placed in his private living quarters and I heard that some of his finer apparel was kept on its shelves. I helped him to select return offerings for the captain and his officers.

The incident of the battleship was altogether pleasant. But about this time there was perceptible a growing rift—not between the prince and his father, who were always deeply attached, but between the modern and ancient ways of looking at things. The prince was modern in his outlook, and his father clung to the old customs. I suspect that my arrival and the interest it created had minimized their differences for a while, but now certain problems began to appear —or reappear. I don't think they were new.

By Balinese custom, or indeed any Eastern custom, it was full time

that the Anak Agung Nura took to himself a wife. The Rajah announced with seeming suddenness that the matter was settled. He
had chosen for Nura a suitable bride, Rati, a beautiful young girl,
not quite sixteen. The prince was outraged and flatly refused to have
anything to do with such a marriage.

The entire puri was in an uproar. The Rajah and his ministers
were dismayed. By every possible means they tried to induce Agung
Nura to change his mind and follow the customs of his forebears. But
his modern education prevailed and he was adamant. The Rajah
said that he himself would be put to shame before his court and all
the rajahs and nobles of Bali. I felt very sorry for both Agung Nura
and his father, but even more sorry for the bewildered little Rati
who, while not in love with the prince, was deeply embarrassed by
his refusal. It was nothing personal, Agung Nura assured her. She
was charming, she was very pretty, it was merely that he did not wish
to marry her.

Finally—I was never told under what pressure—a compromise was
arrived at. Agung Nura would marry Rati, but be a husband in name
only. There would be a formal ceremony, and that was all. It would
not be followed by a ceremony known as the bride wrapping, a
strange and primitive affair.

I had attended numerous bride-wrapping ceremonies during my stay
at the palace, always experiencing a degree of embarrassment, so I
could understand Agung Nura's objection to taking part as a star
performer.

By custom the bride was wrapped in many yards of white cloth,
giving her somewhat the appearance of a mummy, and was then
carried into the nuptial chambers. It was the task or privilege of the
bridegroom to unwind the cloth as a prelude to the consummation
of the marriage. As the two ends of the cloth were skillfully concealed,
it sometimes took hours for the bridegroom's nervous fingers to accomplish the unwinding. Then he must reappear before the wedding
guests with the cloth in his hand, proof that he had fulfilled his
obligation. As often as not he was deeply scratched by the bride's long
fingernails—especially if the marriage had been arranged against her
will.

The wait was always a lively affair, with feasting and laughter, but
it was as nothing to what followed the return of the bridegroom with
the cloth. Then the talk became frankly ribald.

Because Agung Nura was a prince and Rati would be his first wife, the bride-wrapping ceremony was called for. In the case of a later marriage to a woman of lower caste, the ritual was curtailed and there was no bride wrapping.

Prince Nura asked me to explain to his father why he felt as he did, and I agreed to try. As I anticipated, the old man's first reaction was shock at my audacity in speaking openly of a subject not to be discussed with women.

"But you cannot expect to send your son to European universities and then, on his return, have him accept the feudal customs of his ancestors," I pointed out.

"And what is wrong with those customs?"

"Nothing—for you perhaps. But for him a great deal."

Fortunately by this time I was able to speak quite fluently in Malay.

"A man and a woman should marry for love," I went on, "and should be allowed to choose their own mate."

"Love—love—what is love? And what has love to do with marriage? High-caste women should know nothing of love!"

"You mean because they are virgins?"

The old man was more shocked than ever. Ribaldry was one thing, but a serious discussion of intimate matters with a woman was quite another.

"I never heard such nonsense in all my life. What has love done for you people of the West? As far as I have heard, you are in and out of court, divorcing the mates you marry for this love of which you speak so admiringly. We do not have such things as divorced wives. Now what have you to say?"

"You would be surprised at all the noble deeds that have been inspired by love," I answered him, trying for a lighter tone.

"I have been surprised enough already," he said.

By chiding him in a playful way for his old-fashioned views I finally succeeded in bringing a smile to his face.

"Listen, fourth-born, you had better be quiet or I will wrap you up in yards of white cloth and deliver you to one of my neighbors. I know several of my brother-rajahs whom I would have no trouble in persuading to take you."

"I am quite sure," I told him, "that you have no intention of turning me over to any of them—no more than you have of selling your useless refrigerator to a Dutchman in Den Pasar."

With him restored to his usual good nature, I chose this auspicious moment to take my leave.

Gradually his sulks grew less. All he ever said to me after this was that he wished he had never been talked into sending his son abroad for a Western education. The Anak Agung Nura's behavior was incomprehensible to him and upsetting to the entire court. Agung Nura thanked me for my effort on his behalf, which was only partially successful.

The Rajah finally yielded to the prince's insistence that he should continue to lead a bachelor existence, and then the formal marriage to Rati took place. Tradition had been carried out at least in part. No doubt it was the father's secret hope that the son would change his mind when Rati was a little older. But in this he was to be disappointed. Agung Nura never consummated this marriage, nor did he ever marry again. So the old Rajah was cheated out of grandchildren from the male line of his family.

It was not long afterward that the elder daughter of a neighboring rajah secretly eloped with a rich young Chinese merchant.

Her father collapsed in rage and the Rajah, who was deeply sympathetic with him in his plight, engaged Agung Nura in heated disputes over the affair. It was unheard of that a girl of such high rank should marry a foreigner—a commoner moreover with different religion and customs—and without the consent of the family!

Agung Nura suggested to his father that the girl would never have received such consent. The young man was of excellent family from Peking. The two were deeply in love.

"I envy them," said Agung Nura. "They will be companions as well as husband and wife. She is a most intelligent girl—not one to be always confined in a puri. She will see the world."

"And what has companionship and seeing the world to do with marriage?" demanded the old man. He blamed his son for holding such radical views. "What difference does it make if the man is rich and has a fine home in the northern part of the island and another house in Peking? I can't stand this thing called education!"

Calamity after calamity descended upon the village. The highly superstitious people put all the blame on the Anak Agung Nura and the eloping princess, believing that the gods were angered at their revolt against the old customs.

Twins, considered an omen of evil, were born to a couple. A

double birth was bad enough when the children were of the same sex, but in this case they were not—a double tragedy. Elaborate and expensive offerings must be made to appease the gods, and laid at the crossroads and at all entrances and exits to the village. The mother must leave her kampong, for she was considered unclean, to take up residence with her twins in the Pura Dalem, the Temple of Death. There she stayed for forty days and nights, after which she returned for the purification ceremonies. Only then was she permitted to return home, to be received with feasting and dancing and an enormous cockfight.

In older times it was believed that twins of opposite sexes had been married in the womb; therefore they were required to marry each other on reaching maturity.

By such accidental happenings, interpreted in the light of ancient superstitions, the whole neighborhood was affected by the revolt of the two young people. What they had done opened the way to further disaster. The world of the past was tottering. Even more than the Dutch occupation, these things shook the simple Balinese. I could almost see the Rajah growing old before my eyes. There was fear stirring.

11

INTRODUCTION TO POLITICS

"You remember the village of Kintamani?"

Agung Nura had come into my studio, as he often did. Of course, I remembered. Kintamani was the place where we had been obliged to leave our car on the day of the rather gruesome ceremony of drowning the animals in the lake.

"Yes," I replied, "only too well. It's near the volcano."

"My father owns a large coffee plantation not far away. Beautiful country—lovely mountains. I was wondering if you would like to join my sister and me on a visit there?"

I told him I'd love to.

"The coffee," Nura explained, "is now ready for harvesting. It will be sold to Chinese and Arab traders, who come to buy the beans while still on the tree. Bali coffee is of a very high quality. I must be away from the puri for at least a month in order to attend to everything. I shouldn't want the traders to get the beans too cheap. Not only for my father's sake but for the villagers. In the past it was outrageous how the people were cheated."

"A whole month?" I questioned. "Perhaps your father wouldn't like the idea of my going."

"Not at first, perhaps, but don't worry. Between the two of us we can easily talk him into it. You always seem able to twist him around your little finger. If you really would like to go, it's as good as settled."

"I would hate to do anything which your father wouldn't approve of," I said.

"Come," said Nura, "we'll get it all arranged now."

We found the Rajah seated on a mat on the floor carving a piece of gold which he was fashioning into a brooch. The carving was fine and intricate. It depicted the figure of Ardjuno, god of love. The Rajah spent many hours sculpturing the traditional Balinese deities, sometimes in wood as well as metal. He was really very gifted.

We told him at once of my wish to accompany Nura and Ksiti to the plantation. . . . For a while he did not answer. It was almost as if he had not heard us. And then:

"Aren't you afraid you'll freeze to death up there?"

"I'm used to cold climates," I explained.

"Ksiti will have need of a companion while I am attending to the merchants," Agung Nura cut in. "And I shall want someone besides Ksiti to talk to in the evenings."

"Oh," said the Rajah jokingly, "so Ksiti needs a companion! And what of me? I shall miss K'tut's nightly stories about her fabulous country. I'll have no one to tell me about Paul Revere riding his horse, and Abraham Lincoln freeing the slaves, and George Washington and Thomas Paine and all the other American heroes. And there will be no one to give me my lessons in English. I was getting along so well, too. If you are gone a month I shall forget everything you've taught me."

"You could come with us," I suggested, "or at least drive up and see us sometimes. It's not so far."

The Rajah snorted. "You don't know in what a ridiculous place my son has built his house! It is miles from the highway. No motorcar can get anywhere near the place. Besides, I have my official duties here as regent of the district. No, I cannot join you."

Naturally, the Rajah gave in. He did so at last with a good deal of grace. "After all," he admitted, "I was being a selfish old man in wishing to keep my fourth-born by my side. I am sure K'tut will be all the happier after this trip to return to the puri—a far more appropriate and civilized environment for a young lady, even from the West."

In a few days we were ready and the Rajah was quite gay about it. "Now, fourth-born," he cautioned me, "do not run off with one of the Chinese merchants! Rajah Z lost a daughter that way and I wouldn't want to lose one the same way."

I was deeply touched by his saying this to me. Apparently it never occurred to him that I might run off with his son. He trusted me to preserve my status as a member of his family, in truth a daughter, and a sister to Agung Nura. It was indeed a rather strange relationship which existed between Agung Nura and me, a difficult one to explain. We were very close, and yet I did not love him in that sense in which love between a man and a woman is usually understood. It might have been different—this I admit—but I was wise enough to know that only by keeping our friendship on a platonic basis could I live at the puri as I desired.

The coffee plantation and Agung Nura's house were on the opposite side of the volcano from the lake where the ceremonial drownings had taken place. We had to make our way from Kintamani on foot as we had before, but the path was somewhat less difficult. I was surprised to find that Nura's house was built quite in the Western manner, like a luxurious chalet such as one might find in an expensive mountain resort in America.

He explained: "I did not have a road built from Kintamani because I wanted complete privacy—a retreat not only from the world but from the puri. Before you came I spent much time here. You are the first white woman to cross the threshold."

I didn't know what to say to this, so I said nothing, and he went on: "But that is not so strange. I no longer think of you as a white woman. It seems as if you have always been with us. What a happy Bali we could have if the Dutch were like you."

I laughed. "They would be horrified if they thought they resembled me!"

Though I spoke lightly, to me the Dutch were not a laughing matter. They were still trying to force me to leave the puri, threatening me with everything from deportation to that goona-goona which they said would sooner or later be used against me by jealous women in the palace. The fact that I had given no woman in the palace cause for jealousy they obviously did not believe. The whole Dutch colony hated me, looked upon me as a pariah. Scandalous tales about me and the prince were widely circulated.

The chalet was a lovely place, luxurious but without ostentation. Compared with the feudal quality of the puri, it possessed simplicity. Here the servants were not allowed to grovel. Agung Nura had profited by his Western education in more ways than one.

The main room was large, and smelled of pine wood from the fire of pine logs which always crackled in the enormous fireplace. A vast couch was set in front of the fireplace; in a corner was a record player, with a large library of records of the works of the great composers. Three walls were lined with books in several languages— philosophy, science, politics, biography, and, of course, the world's great novels. On either side of the fireplace were hung sports trophies won by Nura at his two universities, and a collection of krisses and spears. And all this in a forest of towering pines and coffee estates. It was for me the most peaceful place in the world.

Agung Nura and I had many talks before that fire. It was then that my mind was opened to political ideas to which I had never in the past paid much attention.

One evening Nura took his sister and me to a very small village within easy distance of his house to see a trance dance. The Balinese name for it is sanghyang. The performance was held in a wooded clearing which was lit by oil-filled coconut shells hung from the trees. Moonlight filtered down through the branches. The most gifted of scenic designers could not have improved on this setting. Hundreds of mountain people were there, either naked or clothed in rags, their mouths distorted by wads of tobacco or betel nut. They were the most primitive people I had yet seen; many of them appeared hardly human. Their eagerness had a strange animal-like quality about it.

The dance began with two boys sitting on the ground opposite each other, each boy holding a stick. The sticks were joined by a cord, attached to which, and hanging down, were two puppet dolls, representing gods. The boys held the cord taut, their arms rigid. Then their faces twisted curiously. They began to tremble, their bodies jerked spasmodically. But the sticks remained steady, the cord taut. "Now they are in a state of trance," Nura whispered.

Suddenly the dolls began to dance and shake and move violently from one end of the cord to the other. The spirit of the gods had entered into them. The boys were unconscious.

On the ground in front of the dolls two very young girls, splendidly robed, were seated. Now they began to moan softly, to sway back and forth. Finally they shook violently as if in ecstasy. The spirit of the gods had left the dolls and had entered into the bodies of the girls, who also were in a state of trance. The trances were induced, so Nura said, by the temple priests, and neither the girls nor the boys would awaken until the priests so wished. The young people had inhaled a rather heavy-smelling incense at the beginning of the dance.

Suddenly the girls leaped onto the shoulders of the boys, who immediately rose up and stood for a moment quite rigid. A fire of burning coconut shells had been spread over the ground behind them. The boys with the girls still standing on their shoulders turned and ran back and forth over the fire, barefooted. They swirled and leapt, the girls leaning this way and that, doing a kind of dance without support of any kind except for their feet planted firmly on the boys' shoulders. I expected them to fall any minute and be burned in the fire. But Nura told me that this was impossible while they were in a state of trance. Neither were they burned by the fire. The girls were not dancers, he said, and wholly untrained; their performance was due to their unconscious condition. It was the goddesses who were moving and swaying through the medium of the girls' bodies —so the Balinese people believed.

Whether Nura himself believed this I do not know. He had not protested at the eating of the live chickens, though he told me later that he hated the rite and was sorry there was nothing he could do about it. The sanghyang dances were different, and hypnotism a power generally recognized. It was an incredible phenomenon.

Deeper within the mountain fastness I saw a number of such dances, and other ceremonies, that I shall not attempt to describe. Life in these utterly remote spots was even more primitive. I tried to see as much of it as I could. For the most part the people here worked on the Rajah's coffee plantation, but a few had small holdings of their own. I have no words to describe how archaic their life was. They were completely without education. They simply couldn't grasp the purpose or use of schooling.

Kintamani itself was a mere collection of tiny Chinese shops, a market place, and a Dutch resthouse sprawled along the highway of the mountain overlooking the Batur volcano. This part of the countryside was under the jurisdiction of Nura's father. All the rajahs had been made regents of their districts by the Dutch, who gave them large incomes to serve in this capacity. The work they did took little of their time. The natives were accustomed to being ruled by the rajahs and more or less content. And the rajahs for their part found their lives comparatively undisturbed by the Dutch administration. It was a system which worked but hardly made for progress.

Agung Nura felt strongly about colonialism, and during those evenings when we sat before the fire at the chalet he told me what he thought—what he hoped to accomplish. He unfolded for me the history of colonialism in Indonesia and his dream of freeing his people.

"The poverty is appalling and totally unnecessary," he said. "You have already seen something of Dutch stupidity. But it goes deeper. The whole system is evil. The people work from sunup to sundown for a mere pittance, ten Dutch cents a day, which is much less than that in your money. Java is an island with tremendous natural resources—oil, rubber. Many millions of money go to Holland every year with no adequate return. Nothing is done to raise the living standards of the people. And something must be done."

"What?" I asked.

He did not know exactly. "Oh, the rajahs are not without blame —even my father is not. He shuts his eyes to the poverty outside the puri gates. And what could he do against the present system? Nothing, I suppose. He would consider it too great a risk, and so would all the others like him, who live in luxury. Yet my father is a man kind and good."

I agreed with all this.

"True, his own servants are practically slaves, but at least they are happy slaves. They are fed and clothed and cared for. They would not know what to do in any other life. Then there is the color bar. The Dutch are afraid of men like myself—of high rank—educated abroad. We return here and are treated as badly as they dare—all doors are closed to us where white men gather. We have no positions of consequence in the government, where we could do a great deal if we were allowed to. But that is exactly what the Dutch fear most. If it were known that I, a rajah's son, was thinking revolutionary thoughts I would be whisked off to prison and then to the Tanah Merah concentration camp kept by the Dutch in the swamps of New Guinea for native political prisoners. There are fourteen thousand of them there, I believe."

I told him I had heard of the place and reminded him of the little boy, Pito, who helped me find my way. He called it the country beyond the moon.

"Yes, that's it. I have no wish to go there," he said grimly.

Nura told me too of the taxes people paid out of their pitiful wages. "If they do not pay they are taken from their kampongs and set to road building—in this climate a grueling labor." He spoke of the great men who had tried to liberate the Indonesians from the Dutch yoke. (Bali itself was not taken by the Dutch until early in this century, though they held Java and the other islands long before that.) He told me the story of Prince Diponegoro, whose followers were all mounted on black steeds with gold and red trappings—the men in white capes and brandishing jeweled swords. This was a hundred years ago. Prince Diponegoro was captured, but his bravery had made him a national hero.

Nura did not believe in violence as a way to freedom, preferring negotiation. But without firearms—which the Dutch denied them—and without a leader, what could the Balinese accomplish? "We do have one man," he said. "He is still young, but he has been in exile for nine years. He is a man of very great stature, and there is none like him. His name is Sukarno."

This was the first time I had heard that name.

"Unless something happens," Nura said, "I am very much afraid that he will die in exile."

When the coffee had been harvested and sold, we returned to the puri, but I did so with a heavy heart. I found myself in a thoughtful mood. Agung Nura, to my surprise, was not the same outspoken person in the puri that he had been at the chalet. In his father's palace he kept his ideas carefully to himself—in part because he did not want to upset his father but also because there was always the possibility of a spy. So on the surface he appeared what he might so easily have been, a mere playboy like so many Eastern princelings.

Yet this was not the deepest cause of my curious discontent. I was beginning to realize that I had not taken advantage of my opportunities to see Bali as it really was. I had let myself be lulled into a passive state by pleasure and comfort, and this was certainly not what I had traveled half across the world for. Oh yes, I had seen the Bali Aga villages, I had seen the kampongs, I had been present at primitive ceremonies and dances and feasts. But always in the company of those whom the natives regarded as royalty. I knew nothing —positively nothing—of what was really going on in the country.

12

AMONG THE PEOPLE OF THE KAMPONGS

By now I knew that Bali, the country of my adoption, was my place in the world. And I decided that I must learn more about it than I could see from the perspective of the puri. I must go forth by myself and live with the natives of the kampongs. What Agung Nura had said to me had affected me deeply.

When I told the Rajah that I proposed to leave the puri and wander about over the island, he stared at me in amazement.

"Why, fourth-born, you don't have to leave the puri in order to learn how our people live. You have seen the most primitive villages— the kampongs—the ceremonies—and I can tell you all about the communal system. Every kampong is the home of what the Scottish people would call a clan—a family—brothers, sisters, children, husbands, wives. I know all about it, I can tell you."

But I persisted. "That's just it. I don't want to be told. I must see for myself, I must live among them, eat their food, do as they do."

"Oh—my son has been talking to you. He has an insane idea of freeing his people. They are not so badly off. We rajahs see to that. But how could you, a young woman from the West, accustomed to every comfort, live as they live? They don't mind, never having known anything else. Why, the dirt of the kampongs would disgust you, and the peasants are completely uneducated—you would have nothing in common with them. Oh, I know my son's views. He would give them bathrooms, schools, even to the lowliest. He has made you his ally in his one-man campaign against the occupation of his country by foreigners. But there is no way to the freedom he wants, except through a miracle."

"I believe in miracles!" I exclaimed.

After a fairly long argument, he gave way.

"You must love our people very much to take such interest," he said, smiling. "I will not stop you. Do I not always agree with you, fourth-born? But I shall console myself knowing that you will be returning to the puri more quickly than you think. You could never stand for long the life you propose."

When I told Agung Nura of my decision to go and live in the villages he was, in one way, delighted. It showed how I felt about his people. But he took it upon himself to warn me in greater detail about what I would face.

"You'll get ill living on their food—prepared as they prepare it. They have no notion of even the most elementary hygiene. You may get dysentery or possibly malaria. Never drink the kampong water without boiling. It comes straight from the streams which are used as sewers. Never sleep without being covered with a mosquito net—"

I grew a little apprehensive. Could I really do these things? I conveyed something of my fears to Nura, but he had no answer.

Before I left the puri the Rajah presented me with the golden brooch he had been carving, with my name and the words "You shall never be forgotten" etched in Sanskrit on the back. Agung Nura gave me something even more precious. This was a very old bronze coin, suspended from a golden chain, and known as the Ardjuno amulet of love. It is thought to have extraordinary magical powers, and to guard the wearer from evil.

The Balinese have great faith in the Ardjuno coin and believe it was carved by the gods.

"If you wear this coin, K'tut," Nura told me, "no one can steal our place in your heart or take you away from our shores without your consent."

There is no doubt that he really believed this. And I grew to believe it too. I wore the coin for as long as I stayed in Bali. I also wore, round my waist, the little carved box which the child Pito had given me. Possibly the two together were invincible. How can one prove that they were not?

By this time I was known to the people all over the island. News travels fast in Bali, and the peasants knew that I was friendly. And Agung Nura had introduced me to many of them at temple feasts and dances. It was therefore easy for me to stay at the kampongs. I just went in and said that I should like to stay with them for a few days. The peasants were delighted with the idea.

I was gone from the puri for more than two months and I did everything I had been warned against doing. I went to all corners of the island, living in unspeakable conditions in the very lowliest of kampongs, and everything that Nura had said about them was true, and more besides. Night after night I slept on a mat on the floor in dank huts without windows. I ate food prepared by women with filthy hands and dirt-caked nails. I drank unboiled water from their earthenware jugs, and their fermented palm wine out of dirty glasses or broken cups with dead mosquitoes floating on top. I bathed in the creek with the other women and for toilet facilities wandered into the bushes. I watched old women with betel-stained mouths chew food to a pulp and then stuff it into the mouths of children who lacked the teeth for chewing. I remained in excellent health, free from dysentery or malaria, though both diseases were rife. I never showed that I was shocked at anything or that I considered myself above any-body. And I received nothing but affection.

The tendency was, at first, to treat me as an honored guest. This I refused to be. I tried to help them by sending for medicines and cloth-ing. I loved these people very much and felt that they returned my affection.

I didn't spend every moment in the kampongs. As I entered each district I had to pay a visit to the local Rajah, or village chieftain. I had already met most of the rajahs; they were very surprised, and greatly interested, at what I was doing. I did not go fully into my reasons—merely said that I was curious to know how the peasants lived. They all urged me to visit them, but I had not left my own puri for any such purpose.

While I was an established member of the Rajah's puri, the Dutch officials had more or less let me alone. They had to be careful not to insult the rajahs, who made the running of the country easier for them.

But when I left the puri it was quite a different matter. My first summons came within a week of my departure. It was curt and to the point—just a line in Dutch.

"The controlleur wishes you to call upon him immediately."

This was the controlleur of Klungkung, the same man whom I had seen before and disliked so heartily. I had no choice but to obey the summons, and I must do so in my native dress, having nothing else to wear.

In the outer office the Balinese clerks turned smiling faces toward me. One said, "I shall announce you." And then, through the thin partition, "K'tut Tantri is here. She is dressed in a sarong."

Speaking to the clerk in Malay, which I now understood perfectly, the Dutchman boomed, "I refuse to meet any white woman in a sarong! This is koerang hormat!" The phrase means lese majesty—disrespect to the representative of the Dutch Queen.

The clerk came back and told me that the controlleur would not receive me unless I was dressed in European clothes.

"But I now have no other clothes. If he wants to see me I am here."

There was a brief and low-voiced conference in the private office, and then the clerk returned again and ushered me in. The controlleur glared at me.

"I see," he said, speaking in English, "that you have gone from bad to worse! The palace was too good for you. So now you have sunk to the level of the kampongs. As for your native dress, what you choose to wear privately is one thing, but coming to see me—at my office—the sheer effrontery of it . . ." He sputtered with anger, and concluded his harangue by using a phrase "masoek bangsa andjin" that is most offensive. It means in a rather loose translation, "You have entered the dog state."

I could hardly believe my ears.

"If you insult me again," I told him, "I shall write to the American consul. I am doing nothing wrong in staying at the kampongs!"

"If you return to the palace at once we may come to accept the situation. But if you persist in your present way of life we shall see about deporting you."

This was not an idle threat. I knew he had been waiting to make it for a long time.

"So that is what you wished to see me for. Well—you've seen me —native dress and all. Good day."

With that I walked out of his office. The native clerks grinned and one raised a thumb in a gesture of congratulations. These summonses occurred more than once, but I shall not trouble to repeat them as they ran true to pattern with only trifling variations.

I went back to the kampongs and found there, as always, politeness and kindness. In all the time I spent with the more lowly natives I never heard them shout or scream in rage. I never saw a child abused and rarely heard one cry. There was no complaining, no mention of the difference between their poverty and the way the rajahs lived. And of course the contrast was fantastic. To me it seemed unjust, but to them it was an accepted order. The palaces were in their way luxurious in the extreme. The kampongs only just sustained life in a mild climate.

Each kampong is surrounded by a wall of adobe topped with thatch. Inside this are a number of huts, each of one room and without windows. The floors are made of hard mud. The huts are used only for sleeping in, the people live in the common yard. There is little furniture except mats of woven bamboo on slightly raised platforms which are used as beds. The cooking is done outside. In one corner of the yard the women thresh the rice which is stored in a specially built hut. Rice, and vegetables cooked in coconut milk, with some ground chili peppers are the staple food. Cooking utensils are primitive. The yard invariably contains several shrines to the gods, usually with offerings displayed. In one corner is the pigsty. The pigs are bred mainly for the market. At the time I was there fruit—bananas and papayas—was a source of slight additional income, and eating the fruit an impossible extravagance. I often wondered how the men who worked so hard in the rice fields held their strength on a diet so meager and unvaried.

In every village there are several kampongs—each, as the Rajah told me, harboring the members and relatives of one family. Every male, when married, must join the village council. He must always remain in his own village. He must help his neighbors and receives help in return. No money is ever exchanged. Everything is shared. A headman rules the council, elected by common approval. He cannot refuse this honor. The sharing goes beyond an exchange of ordinary courtesies. All are involved in the various feasts which punctuate human progress, from birth through marriage and on to death.

That goona-goona of which I had been warned I now encountered for the first time. In the kampongs it was frequent, though practiced more often for good than for evil. Superstitions affected everything the people did. But I myself was in no position to criticize. Did I not wear as a charm a coin on a golden chain carved with a god and a little box hung by a cord round my waist?

Despite the filth, the discomfort, and the meager meals from which I always arose hungry, I found the kampongs the paradise for which I had left Hollywood. To me they contained a curious quality of peacefulness which I had not found in the palaces of the rajahs. It was an artistic, an uninhibited, way of life. Most of these poor peasants were artists of talent and power of expression.

I finally came to the village of Kuta on the west coast facing the Indian Ocean. The beach was magnificent and without a house or a hut. There were a few temples and numerous fishing smacks or praus moored close. What a site for a house! I revisited the beach frequently and it was here that the idea entered my head of building an exclusive hotel. It was merely an idea. What would I be doing with a hotel? A hotel took capital and I had by this time given most of my money away. If I only had the land . . . Moreover, under the Dutch no white person could own land, I was told.

I talked with the villagers in Kuta who owned the beach. They could lease me the land, I learned, for the amount they would have to pay the government in taxes. This was such a ridiculously low sum that I leased from two families practically the whole of Kuta Beach. I could manage somehow to build myself a small house here. There were a few white artists and writers in Bali. Most of them had built their own houses. Since living in the kampongs I had got to know them. My calls were always welcome and I learned that they were— as I was—at loggerheads with the Dutch officials.

Before I left the puri the Rajah made me promise to return for prayers at least once a week. I did this out of respect for him and to please him.

On one of these visits to the puri—that were, I must admit, a pleasure as well as a duty—I noticed again a building which had often excited my curiosity. It was a rather handsome house in the Western style standing in its own grounds, a short distance from the walled puri. It had once been used by a Dutch official stationed in the village, but the office had been discontinued and since then the house had remained untenanted.

I asked Agung Nura about it. I didn't see much of him these days. Though he visited me at the kampongs, his arrival was always a signal for the occupants to gather before him in suitable attitudes of adoration and little intelligent talk could be carried on.

"Who owns that house?" I asked Nura.

"That's a curious question."

"Why?"

"My father was speaking of it just today—I mean in connection with you. He is anxious to have you back here with us, as we all are, but we realize that in the puri you do not lead quite the independent life you prefer. If you lived in this house you would feel more free, wouldn't you? You could paint without interruption, and see your artist friends, and wander about to your heart's content." He realized that I found the restrictions of the palace a little irksome. Agung Nura could not believe that I liked living in the kampongs.

"You haven't answered my question. Who owns the house?"

"It is owned by our cousin, your friend, Anak Agung Ksiti."

I made an exclamation of pleasure. This was the wonderful woman of whom I was so fond.

"Do you think she would rent it to me for a while?"

The thought had come to me while Nura had been talking. What he said was in part true. I could certainly paint there, and I would be far more free than in the puri. The house on the beach could wait.

"Why don't you talk with her about it? I think it could easily be arranged."

The old Rajah thought so too.

I was staying at that time in one of the better kampongs with the family of a gamelan player who was a most talented musician. But I do not mean to suggest that he had money. The small amounts he made were spent on his musical instruments. We had a little bit more to eat—a piece of dried fish with the rice—and in the rooms were one or two pieces of bamboo furniture, lacking in most of the other kampongs. But otherwise conditions were generally the same.

I talked to Anak Agung Ksiti the next day. She was delighted that I wished to live in her house, but she refused the suggestion of my paying rent. Together we went through it. There were a number of fine rooms. Two at least could be used as guest rooms. This was it! The beginnings of my hotel. I would take some paying guests; they would restore my bank account at least a little. Not ordinary tourists, but writers, and artists, and those who would appreciate a place away from the usual paths of the tourist crowd staying at the Dutch hotel at Den Pasar and away from the Dutch official stationed there. And with my knowledge of the island and its language I would be an excellent guide to the off-the-beaten-track places. And I could paint and sell my paintings. I felt I had now absorbed enough of the Balinese life to put it all on canvas.

The Rajah too was delighted, partly—I felt sure—because I would still be under the protection of the puri.

As if by magic workers appeared who started to put the villa in tiptop shape. It was run down a bit, like any other building which has not been lived in, especially in the tropics. Furniture was brought. Much as I argued, I was not allowed to pay for anything. "K'tut's house" absorbed the attention of the entire palace. This was not exactly in accordance with my own plans for complete emancipation, but there was little I could do about it. My house provided everyone with a delightful new toy. The Rajah himself, suitably attended, came over daily to criticize what was being done.

"Of course," he warned me—it seemed to me that he was always warning me of something—"the Dutch won't like this when they know you are going to have white guests."

"Oh, not necessarily white!" I had long ago decided there would be no color bar.

"As you well know, the Dutch officials are against foreigners living in the villages. It is not only that you will take business away from their hotel at Den Pasar, but they want foreigners to remain under Dutch eyes."

"I should think they would be delighted that I am at last living in a Western style villa on my own. I am out of the kampongs—even out of the puri. That is what they wanted, isn't it?"

"Not exactly. They didn't want you in this part of Bali at all."

Despite his satisfaction in general, there was one thing about the house which did not suit the Rajah: the bathroom walls were shabby.

"They have been shamefully neglected. Oh, well, we'll attend to it. I know exactly what I shall do. Tomorrow I'll let a few of the prisoners out of jail and in no time you'll find the bathroom transformed."

"Prisoners!" I exclaimed. "What do you mean?"

"Just what I say. Some of them are most talented artists and workmen. They can retile the floor, do the walls with frescoes—"

I was shocked. "What have they done to be in jail?" Prisoners in my bathroom were not a pleasant prospect.

"They're just common prisoners—thieves mostly—a few murderers. I shall give orders that they arrive here the first thing in the morning."

I wondered if this was the Rajah's idea of a joke. If so, it was the kind of Balinese humor I had not happened upon before.

While the repairs were in progress, I was staying in the puri. The next morning I rose early and went over to the villa. The prisoners were no joke. I was standing in the garden when in marched a dozen men, as disreputable and ill-assorted a group as I had ever seen, with a uniformed prison guard at their heels.

"These are the men who will decorate your bathroom," the guard announced. "I shall leave them with you and call back for them at five o'clock tonight." And with that he stalked off.

I was dumfounded. But I showed the men to the back of the house where the bathroom was situated. Everything was in readiness as the Rajah had promised it would be. They were all most polite and smiling, but I thought it best to leave them to it and go away. I returned to the puri to look for Agung Nura, who was painting in his studio.

When I told him what happened he took the news with surprising calm. "Oh, don't worry about the prisoners. They like being let out."

"Yes, most prisoners would. But won't they run away?"

"Where would they run to? If they tried that they would be caught very quickly. My father, or rather the guards, doubtless picked them very carefully. They wouldn't be let out if they were really dangerous."

"Your father told me some of them were murderers."

"I doubt that. He was probably exaggerating a bit."

"But surely such men won't be able to paint frescoes!"

"The Balinese peasants are a race of artists, don't forget. Even the commonest man has a great deal of artistic feeling."

That day I avoided the villa. But shortly before the appointed hour of five, Agung Nura and I strolled over there and found the prisoners squatting around the garden waiting for the guard. They thanked Agung Nura for the food which had been sent over to them from the palace kitchens. Presently the guard appeared and escorted them back to the jail.

"I hope they haven't destroyed the walls of the bathroom," I said to Nura.

"Oh, you'll be surprised at what they've done."

We went to see. I was indeed surprised. In fact, I was stunned. The floor was beautifully tiled and the walls were covered from floor to ceiling with scenes which depicted the torments of the damned in hell. I thought it was funny, painted by the criminals themselves. I was amazed at the beauty of the color and the skill of the execution. I had noted such scenes—and but little better done—on the ceiling of the famous Hall of Justice in Klungkung, and sometimes carved on temple walls. But in my own bathroom it was a shock. Some of the incidents depicted were to Western eyes wholly indecent, but to the Indonesians they were merely a part of life, in this case, of death. To the common people sex was commonplace, like breathing. No mystery was ever made of it. I had learned this in the kampongs. In our sense of the word obscenity did not exist for them. Just what I should do about these frescoes I was not sure. I did not wish anything in my house to give a false impression to the strangers I had planned to have as guests.

For a moment I was merely embarrassed—and this because Nura was with me. But suddenly he began to laugh and then I joined in, dissolving the embarrassment.

At last the day came when the villa was ready and I moved in. The people in the kampongs would miss me, I knew, but I would continue to see them and to provide them with the little things they needed, such as medicines and kerosene for their tiny lamps. I was their only connection with the world outside. Most of them had never been off the island of Bali. They did not even know where Java was; as for America, it was hardly a name.

The villa had a large open veranda, and it was here that Agung Nura and I continued our talks. I told him in detail just what I planned about having paying guests.

"No color bar—no race prejudice at all. I shall accept Dutch artists as well as American, Indian, Chinese, and of course Indonesian."

He thought this delightful. "Perhaps we shall establish an art colony right here in our own village."

I think Agung Nura was often lonely for want of contact with people who were his intellectual equals.

"But you won't have enough room for all who will wish to come!

You will be forced to move to larger quarters. What about Kuta Beach, which you have already leased?"

I hadn't told him about Kuta Beach, but no news in Bali can be kept secret.

"So you know about that," I said, a trifle sheepishly. "Before I saw this villa I did think of building myself a little house there."

He looked at me. "A little house or a hotel?" he asked. Sometimes I thought that he could read my mind.

"Oh, that would be quite impossible."

"Yes, that would take money. I should be very happy to provide you—"

"No. You and your father have done much too much for me already. The means for such a project must come from elsewhere, or from myself."

"You and your independence!" he laughed. Then he told me that he was going away soon—to visit a friend at the court of the Sultan of Solo in Java.

"I wish to study the political conditions there. I've heard some disturbing rumors. It is a pity you can't come with me, but I'm afraid that wouldn't do."

"I can see that," I said.

"I shall, if possible, visit other places in Indonesia. And you, K'tut, while I am away, attend to your guests—save your pennies—dream of the hotel you would like to have on Kuta Beach."

"I suppose you will write to me and keep me informed?"

"I will write to you, no matter where I am."

He was silent for a moment or two, and then continued, "It is not only the news from Java that is disturbing, it is not only the Dutch. There are other elements—a great caldron which may someday boil over."

"I'll do the little things," I told him, "you the big."

He hardly heard me, and yet at that moment I felt extraordinarily close to him. I didn't ask him what he meant. I left him to his own thoughts, as he rose and quietly walked away.

13

A DREAM TAKES SHAPE

I was established in the villa, with two rooms for paying guests, and Agung Nura was gone, to be away for a long time. Now was the hoped-for opportunity to paint while I saved pennies for the future. But though I did paint, there were difficulties of many kinds. It is not a period I remember with pleasure.

The Dutch as usual received the news of my villa before it was an accomplished fact and promptly launched a bitter campaign against me as a questionable character—a white girl gone native. They were more bitter, I think, because they could not attack me directly, knowing that I had the protection of powerful nobles useful to them. Chauffeurs of hired cars were warned to keep tourists away from my place. The tourist trade was a Dutch monopoly. The inference was that I would take trade away from the Dutch-owned Den Pasar hotel. But my two guest rooms were hardly a menace—and besides I had made it clear that I did not wish to accommodate the ordinary run of tourists.

The situation was troublesome, also ludicrous, as the chauffeurs who had been given orders to avoid me were my friends. I had lived with their families in the kampongs. In consequence, they ignored the orders for the most part, especially if the tourists were American, English, or Australian—with the result that my villa became overrun with sightseers. The campaign had backfired. I was well known before, but now I was notorious.

And yet my guest rooms were not profitable. Knowing that I did not wish ordinary tourists, but people in the arts who would, in truth, be my guests, friends came to see me from all over the island and often remained for several days, in turn introducing their visiting friends. And from them I felt I could not take money, either for their room and board or for my services as a guide.

My life at the villa is not important to the story I have to tell here, so it is only necessary to touch on the highlights. In that time I experienced periods of great satisfaction and periods of almost unbearable depression. I sometimes felt that all I wanted was to be left alone by everyone. Often I was tempted to leave the island, but I could not bring myself to admit failure. It was the old Rajah who more than once stopped me by reminding me that it was my destiny to remain.

"You came here, fourth-born," he told me, "under compulsion, led to our island by the gods. It is not yet clear what the gods wish for you and what you must suffer to carry out their wishes. But you must stay."

There were days when no guests, paid or unpaid, found their way to the villa, and when I was beset by sightseers I closed my gates to them and returned to my painting. The number of canvases I was able to paint depicting the life of the Balinese was surprising. I never painted just pretty barebreasted Balinese girls with pots of fruit on their heads, but life in the kampongs, the island as I had seen it, the ceremonies, the trance dances, the temples, and the cockfights. I sold some of these pictures, but the money did not even begin to cover my expenses. Where were those pennies I was supposed to save?

While the Dutch hounded me, my friends told me that I was setting a fine example to all white people—proving that East and West can get along together on a basis of equality. And I did have many friends. I remember with fondness Walter Spies, a fine German painter who had lived in Bali for many years and was always close to the Balinese people. There was Le Mayeur, a gentle character, a Belgian who had married a Balinese dancer of exceptional beauty. They had a house on the beach at Sanur, a few miles from Den Pasar. Near them was an American couple, Mr. and Mrs. Mershon. Mrs. Mershon had opened a small clinic for the natives and supplied them with medicines. I remember that she was greatly interested in Balinese ritual. On Sanur Beach also there was a Dutch couple, Mr. and Mrs. Pol, both artists and charming people, not at all the official type. And then there was Carol Dake, also Dutch, a painter who continually was at odds with the Dutch officials. Finally, there was Theo Maier, a Swiss painter who lived wholly as a native, even to marrying two Balinese women and having a child by each. I frequently visited his house and enjoyed the extraordinary native dishes with which even I was not familiar. Theo loved to cook. He lived far from the white colony of Sanur in a very primitive village near the Gunung Agung mountain. We had one thing in common—dislike of the Dutch officials.

Among those who came to visit me were some distinguished tourists —writers and painters from England, China, Holland, India, and two princes from Siam. And very often sons of neighboring rajahs visited me with their wives. It was truly a cosmopolitan atmosphere. During this time I came to know a man whose friendship was to mean a great deal to me. Paradoxically, Tuan Daan was a Dutchman. But he had nothing in common with officialdom. He seemed more English than Dutch, for he had been educated at Cambridge. He was now a planter, running his father's large sugar plantations in Java. His family was very important in Holland, high in the Dutch aristocracy, and his connections far-reaching. I really don't know what I should have done without his help. The officials had to exercise caution after we became friends. Though they disliked him heartily, there was little they could do.

Tuan Daan loved the island of Bali and came there whenever he could. He first arrived at my villa with his wife and baby in an overloaded station wagon and took my two guest rooms, which were for the moment unoccupied. His wife was an English girl and very beautiful. Unfortunately she did not share her husband's feeling for Bali. His first stay was comparatively brief, as he had pressing business in Java. Intending to return, he left his family at the villa to wait for him, but his wife did not wait; when he came back she was gone.

My friendship with Daan grew with time. A man of wealth, he had done a great deal for the natives, and he knew everyone—including the friends I have mentioned.

In spite of the social success of my villa, it was heading for financial ruin. I suppose I did more entertaining than I could afford. Though my servants, all good friends, had come to me from the puri, I paid them and fed them. And the food I served was of the best.

I found myself with very little funds, but I still stayed on at the villa. I could have moved back to the puri, or returned to the kampongs, or asked help of the Rajah. But I had been obligated to him for too long. Had Nura been there he would have guessed the truth, being a good businessman, but his father was innocent in such matters. He took it for granted that I was making a huge success of my undertaking. He was quite proud of me, he said, and was a frequent visitor at the villa.

At this time I met an American couple. They wanted me to act as their guide during their stay in Bali. On one of our trips, I took them to the beautiful Kuta Beach, which impressed them greatly. And I told them of my plan to build a hotel there. The next day, to my surprise, they made me a proposition: they would supply the money to build a small hotel—to be enlarged later from the profits—if I would supply the land. Against my better judgment I agreed and signed away a half interest in the whole piece of land, which was divided by a dirt road leading from Kuta village. On one side of the road a bungalow was built for them, and on the other side one for me. And on their side, next to their bungalow, we built the hotel. But before long I could see that I had made a great mistake, the hotel would never be run as I wanted it run. Very soon we began to fall out over the question of the color bar, and other things. It became clear that my idea of a hotel where all nationalities would be welcome was but a dream.

Among the guests who came to stay at the hotel at this time was a rich American, Mr. Tenney, who owned pineapple plantations in Hawaii. I took him everywhere, and to places never seen by tourists. He was a sympathetic man; he felt as I did about the Balinese and decided he would like to live for a few months each year in Bali. He therefore asked the American couple and myself if we would sell him the lease of the land and the bungalow on my side of the road—my bungalow in fact. We agreed to this, but he continued to stay at the hotel and I in my bungalow.

Things were not going too well with my partners in the hotel business. They showed plainly their preference for the Dutch and their way of life. Having no head for money matters, I had paid little attention to the contract. I didn't even receive a copy of it. For a time things seemed to go from bad to worse, and I found myself in a very depressed frame of mind.

One day Mr. Tenney came to me and said, "I can see that you and your partners will never get along, and I am deeply concerned about you. Business and family matters necessitate my leaving for America at once, but before I go I wish to sign back the land and the bungalow to you. Not to the partnership but to you personally. I also want to give you my car."

He left Bali shortly afterward. A few weeks later my partners broke the contract.

I moved from the hotel, as there was nothing else I could do, and stayed at the bungalow on the other side of the road and wondered what was going to happen next. And the servants left the hotel with me. I pointed out to them that this was foolish, for I had no money to pay them for their services, but they wouldn't listen. To me they were not servants but good friends. Three of them I had brought to the hotel with me. I knew their families well. It always irked my American partners that I treated them as friends instead of menials.

One was a very famous dancer whose portrait appeared on all the guidebooks and literature about the Bali dancers. His name was Njoman. Then there was Maday, a well-known gamelan player and composer of no mean ability. Last and brainiest of the three was Wyjan, also a dancer. Wyjan was very handsome and of a charm quite unbelievable. I loved these three and I knew they returned my affection. They could neither read nor write but they were artists in every sense of the word.

We used to sit on the beautiful beach together watching the sunset, which was always a fantastic sight. They would tell me stories of ancient times. Like all their countrymen, they never worried about the future. But I was worrying.

One day, sitting on the beach, I asked the boys, "What are we going to do now? My money is almost gone."

"I will tell you what we will do," Wyjan replied calmly. "We will start to build another hotel—the kind of hotel of which you have dreamed. It will be right here on this beach, and built like a rajah's palace. It will be famous and everyone will help you. And when it is finished the foreign guests will surely come to you and you will make a fortune. We will call it Swara Negara—The Sound of the Sea. We will pound our own rice on the grounds. We will have Balinese maidens who will weave. We will have our own gamelan —Maday here will know about that—and Njoman will dance and bring in other dancers. Everyone who works at the hotel will be in some way an artist. We will have painters and sculptors. It will be an enchanted garden by the time we get it finished. We will build a coral temple and the village priests will prepare a feast and bless the ground. Beneath the temple we will bury offerings of gold and silver. If we follow all these customs all will be well and we shall prosper."

Wyjan was interrupted by the others with many exclamations of "beh adoh" which means approval and applause. Then Njoman and Maday added to the fairy tale: "We will have our own pigs, ducks and chickens—we will not cut down any of the coconut or palm trees, but build in between and around them. It brings bad luck to cut down trees without making offerings to the tree-gods. Besides, we can always sell the coconuts or use them ourselves. Many things can be done with coconuts. Oh—we can be self-supporting!"

I almost cried as I looked at the three earnest faces. "Lads," I told them, "it's a beautiful dream. But it would take a great deal of money to build such a place. The labor is not everything."

For a while we were silent. Then as my contribution I suggested selling the car. Cars were bringing fantastic prices at the time. Perhaps a Chinese trader or an Arab . . .

But Wyjan cut me short. "K'tut, we cannot and will not sell the car! If we have a hotel we will need it—not only to take our guests around, but for shopping. We are eighteen kilometers from the market at Den Pasar. No—we will not sell the car!"

Njoman and Maday agreed vigorously with Wyjan. "We will find a way. Let us leave it in the hands of the gods."

Still I was not persuaded. So the next morning I rose early and went to Den Pasar in search of a buyer. I did not go in the car; I thought I could get more for it if a buyer came to see it. Besides, I loved to travel in a native dokkar, a sort of miniature horse and cart. I managed to interest an Arab shopkeeper, who promised to come to the beach the following morning with a view to purchasing the car. On my return I told the boys what I had done.

"I think the Arab will almost certainly buy," I said.

Though I read disappointment in their faces, the boys had little comment to make then or later. I decided that they were philosophically accepting the inevitable. But the next morning, to my surprise, the boys did not appear at the bungalow. I called. No answer. I searched the beach. But nothing. My first thought was that they were hurt at my refusal of their advice and had gone back to their kampongs. I wondered unhappily if they had gone for good.

The Arab arrived at the appointed hour while I was having coffee on the veranda. I offered him a cup, which he drank quickly for he was impatient to be finished with his errand. Then we made our way to the makeshift garage that sat back from the sea in order to protect the car from the salt air.

Approaching the shed, I was bewildered to find it closed on four sides by bamboo poles set close and tied together with stout sisal rope intricately wound. It was like a fort. Hanging by an extra piece of rope was a large sign which read: MOTOR TIDAH BOLEH DIJUAL— meaning Motor Not for Sale or Not Allowed to be Sold.

My three boys must have worked all night with the help of someone more literate than they. Naturally, the Arab was indignant. He took himself off in a towering rage at having been brought so far for nothing.

I sat down on the ground, hardly knowing whether to laugh or to cry, but finally settled for laughter. I laughed as I hadn't in months. Then I returned to the bungalow where I spent a lonely day pondering the question: "What am I going to do now?" By evening I had no answer, and lacking the heart to go to the beach and watch the sunset by myself, I sat on the veranda waiting for I didn't know what.

I received my answer. Through the coconut trees a small procession approached. It was my boys returning, each with a sack slung over his shoulder. At the veranda they greeted me in unison:

"Tabe njonya besar!"

This greeting had never been used to me before. I had forbidden it. It was a greeting required of natives in addressing Dutch women. "Njonya" is a term signifying white women and "besar" means high —big—great. Tabe corresponds to our good day.

However, the three seemed very gay and obviously were teasing me.

"Where have you been?" I asked.

"To the kampongs on business."

"You have ruined my chance to sell the car! What made you do such a thing?"

Instead of answering they set down their sacks and opened them, revealing rice, eggs, coffee, chickens, and other food. The most precious they properly kept to the last for the grand climax. This was a smaller bag, filled with silver ringgits. Ringgits are big Dutch coins, each worth about two and a half guilders. Paper money followed.

I stared. I pointed. "Where did you get all that money? I hope you didn't steal it!"

"No, K'tut, we did not steal it. It is for you to build your hotel."

"But where did you get it?" I repeated.

"The people of our kampongs have borrowed money from the Chinese, using our rice fields as security," Wyjan said.

In the morning I had laughed. Now I burst into tears.

14

SOUND OF THE SEA

So the hotel was started with money from the kampongs. The coins and paper bills amounted to a little more than a thousand guilders —to the Balinese natives an enormous sum, but in American money it came to about five hundred dollars. The boys thought I was crying because of what they had done to my car, but I cried from sheer emotion at the kindness of these people who had risked everything, mortgaging their lands and their very lives, to help me.

"I shall go to your kampongs and thank them," I said.

"Thanks are not necessary," Wyjan told me. "That you are willing to accept our help is thanks enough. And someday you will help us. We will return the money. So don't cry, K'tut. This is a time for rejoicing, not for tears."

Wyjan, who could think nothing but plans for the hotel, was the organizer, the leader. I realized that we didn't have enough money even to build one more bungalow, but his ideas were grandiose beyond anything I could imagine.

"I know an architect—the cleverest builder in Bali. He lives in a kampong not too far from here. I shall take you to him."

"But, Wyjan, we haven't the money to pay for an architect!"

"Of course not. We don't pay him now. Our credit is good. We will supply the material—bamboo, coconut trees, bricks, coral. He will bring in skilled workmen, as there are many such in his kampong. Other labor we get from the village. His name is Bagus. We shall build in a royal manner, and he will feel honored to do it. When the hotel is finished, we will pay him so much every month. The Balinese are in no hurry for money, and it is our adat [custom] to help one another."

A day or so later Wyjan took me to his friend Bagus, who received us most graciously and nodded with pleasure as Wyjan unfolded his plan. "We need your clever help so badly, Bagus. In fact, without your help I am at a loss to know what we should do." Wyjan had the devil's own tact. "We are not asking you to design an ordinary hotel like the Dutch one in Den Pasar, but something which will reveal your talents in their true light."

It was not surprising that Bagus had heard of me, as he knew Anak Agung Nura well and admired him. "Any friend of his is a friend of all our people. He is a brilliant and a great prince." Then he went on to describe in even more exact detail all that the hotel would be: "Pavilions, kitchen, dining room, bathrooms, and of course a fine coral temple. No house can be higher than the temple. There must be a lotus pond and shrines—"

My astonishment grew as he continued. "I shall bring the blueprints in a couple of days," he said in conclusion, and went on to instruct Wyjan what materials to start buying.

The next morning Wyjan went off on his bicycle, refusing my offer to drive him—he said he could bargain better by himself. He was really extraordinary, a born organizer and leader. Later I was to learn that he also had the knack of controlling workmen. They never dillydallied when he was about, and yet they liked him.

In a few days Bagus appeared, not only with blueprints that would have done credit to any Western architect but with his first batch of workmen. He was ready to start. The workmen would live on the premises. They began at once to construct a primitive shed for themselves, where they would cook their meals and have a place to unroll their mats at night. I found myself caught up in activities for which I was somewhat unprepared, but I liked Bagus from the first.

We were seated on the veranda, he squatting on the floor explaining the blueprints spread out neatly around him, when there was the sound of a car approaching at high speed. It stopped suddenly. With even more suddenness a man jumped out. It was Agung Nura, whom I had not seen since a very brief visit he had paid to his father a few months before.

He looked older, as if the cares of the world sat on him more heavily than in the past. And yet his vitality and enthusiasm had never been stronger.

"K'tut—K'tut!" he shouted. At first he hardly noticed the Balinese, who had risen hastily and was bowing in the traditional manner when nobility appeared. Then he recognized his friend. "Why, Bagus —so you are taking charge. Splendid!" He turned again to me. "I heard all about your hotel. I arrived back in Bali only last night, but I must come and see for myself."

For the rest of the morning the three of us pored over the blueprints, pointing out, exclaiming, suggesting embellishments.

"Here will be the first pavilion and here is the place for the temple, though for that we must consult with the village priest. We must obtain white coral—"

And so on.

At one point Agung Nura asked, "Now, what do you need? How can I help?"

I was about to say that we needed nothing, but Bagus had other ideas. "Agung Nura, what I would like for K'tut's puri are a few carved golden doors such as adorn your own puri. There are a number of such doors to be had from the puris of the nobles. I hear they are ripping them out and selling them and with the money building Western villas which seem to suit the younger generation better. You doubtless have many friends who would let you have them at a modest price."

"How many would you need?" The prince spoke much as if Bagus had requested a drink of water.

"Oh, one for every pavilion. Say four for the present."

"I'm sure I can get you at least four. And there will be other things. I'll see what I can do."

Listening to the two men talking over my head, as if my wishes did not for the moment count, I felt that Agung was regarding me as a child who had to be kept happy.

"You must listen to the gamelan music as long as you can," he told me suddenly.

At this, he and Bagus exchanged a curious look. What did he mean? I did not know, but there came to my mind the words of the English poet: "Gather ye rosebuds while ye may—"

Later, over lunch, talk turned to larger things, to the disquieting news of the world beyond Bali where Agung Nura had been spending his time. There had been trouble aboard a Dutch battleship. The Javanese crew had tied up the white officers and sailed away, ignoring radio warnings that the ship would be bombed if it was not brought back. The situation was tense. Indonesians were being arrested right and left. "We all want freedom, but as for getting it . . . I don't know," Agung Nura said. "I am fortunate to be able to travel, but how long this fortune will last is another story. I do what I can."

When Bagus had gone, Nura told me more about his travels through Java. I was particularly pleased to hear of a visit he had made to Daan's plantation.

"Daan is not interested in politics," he explained, "so I can visit him quite openly. Besides, he is Dutch. But he is not like these other Dutch. He is a kind man, greatly loved by all those who work for him."

In a couple of weeks, Nura said, Daan intended to visit Bali in a yacht, bringing some friends, and he wanted both of us to join him on a cruise to the Spice Islands.

Agung Nura looked about him. "By the way, my father believes that you made a tremendous financial success of the villa and it is with that money that you are able to do all this. But I have reason to believe otherwise."

Then he got it out of me, the whole extraordinary story—the three boys—the money from the kampongs—Bagus' trust in me—everything. I had not meant to tell him, and had been stupid enough to think he would not guess about the financial failure of the villa. But nothing surprised him.

"It shows what the Balinese people think of you, K'tut."

"I am almost ashamed. I have done so little. And I have been absorbed in my own petty interests."

"All of us do that at times," he consoled me. "I have a feeling that someday you will be of great use to us. You still wear the Ardjuno amulet I gave you and Pito's little silver box?"

I told him I did.

The next morning Agung Nura called for me and we went together in search of the golden doors. Before nightfall we had obtained four and arranged for them to be delivered to Kuta by the owners; they were very beautiful. New doors could not have equaled them and the gold leaf alone was worth a small fortune.

We found more than doors. There were many old Balinese paintings and sculptures and some unusual musical instruments made of bamboo. In the district of Ubud the Rajah insisted on presenting me with a complete one-room pavilion called Bali Gede. This had a very large built-in four-poster bed, the posts exquisitely carved and colored and gold-leafed. There were carved panels and ceiling, and the walls were covered with parchment paintings. The floor and roof were of pink and red tiles. Months afterward, when Bagus had lovingly reassembled it and added a small archway leading to a bathroom, the first guest to occupy the Bali Gede was my own dear Rajah.

"If it weren't for the Sound of the Sea," he told me, "I wouldn't know that I'm not in my own puri."

But this takes me ahead of my story.

Life now was very full with the boys, Bagus, an increasing number of workmen, and the constant flow of materials and gifts. Agung Nura came whenever he could manage it. And in two weeks, as Nura had foretold, Tuan Daan arrived with a party of friends. Remembering Nura's story of the Dutch battleship, the arrests, and all the trouble brewing in Java, I marveled at the seemingly carefree company. Everything was very gay.

As I had no place to accommodate guests, the visitors slept aboard the yacht but dined with me, sometimes on the beach and sometimes on the veranda of my bungalow. Wyjan, whose talents were legion, managed to produce magnificent dinners. There was little money except what I made occasionally as a guide, but a Chinese shop in Den Pasar, run by a delightful family, extended me unlimited credit, and there was fruit from the kampongs and an abundance of local fish. After these dinners, which were veritable feasts, Maday would play the gamelan and Njoman would dance for Daan and his friends.

Daan took great interest in the construction of the pavilions, and it came out that he knew a good deal about building. He consulted with Bagus, presumably about technical matters, but when his visit ended and he had left Bali I learned that he had paid the architect a good part of what I owed him. I suspect he paid for other things too. This is why I came to think of the Sound of the Sea as Daan's home in Bali, and why I never accepted payment from him, his family, or his friends, however crowded the hotel might be.

So at last the hotel was completed—completed, that is to say, as much as it would ever be, because we kept having to add new pavilions in order to accommodate the swarms of guests. From the outset the place was a tremendous success, and no wonder. It might have come straight from the *Arabian Nights* with its lush gardens, its wall of white coral, and its ancient stone statues. It was a replica of a rajah's palace. There were a few concessions to Western comfort —bathrooms, deep mattresses, and later a large powerhouse to generate electricity. Foreign magazines reported it as the unique hotel of the entire Far East.

With the money I made I was able to pay back every cent I owed to the kampongs, and more besides.

For a while the Dutch let me alone, but when they lost their best tourist trade to me and the servants of the Den Pasar hotel flocked to work for me, though I tried to prevent them, the persecutions started again. Ironically, it was the presence of celebrities in my hotel which caused the most storm—and eventually saved me. The Dutch claimed that Sound of the Sea was the scene of shameful orgies, unmentionable debaucheries. Such statements brought down on their heads immediate repercussions, even from Holland itself, for statesmen and members of the titled aristocracy did not take kindly to publicity of that sort. The atmosphere became so charged that I had to be doubly careful to avoid supplying any foundation to the scandal.

Inevitably legends grew about a place as unique and successful as Sound of the Sea. The spirit of camaraderie was so marked that the guests frequently spent time in the kitchen learning from the cooks how to prepare native dishes. It was said that mine was a place where you waited on the servants instead of the servants' waiting on you. There was a joke—and it was not entirely a joke—that if I liked you and you had ten guilders in your pocket you could stay at Sound of the Sea forever. Poor artists were always welcome at my table.

But enough was enough, the Dutch thought. So far they had lost the battle but they were not through. One fine day when my hotel was full the Dutch police came down and arrested all my servants—Wyjan, Njoman, and Maday with the rest. They wanted to "interrogate" them, so they said.

I immediately cabled the American consul in Surabaya and within twenty-four hours the servants were released, but the stories with which they returned were appalling. The police had tried to make them confess that my hotel was improper.

What happened now was something far larger than K'tut Tantri and her puri, though I was involved in it. Made uneasy by the unrest in Indonesia, the Dutch decided to take steps. In a first move the Governor General ordered a cleanup of homosexuals throughout the

Dutch East Indies. This was an excuse to arrest a great many people, the innocent along with the guilty. An enormous scandal broke. Doctors, lawyers, navy officials, and even members of the Dutch administration who had not quite toed the desired political line were taken into custody. The result was hysteria, which soon spread to Bali. There were inquiries and a number of people fled the island. I was questioned along with friends and guests. However, the moral atmosphere of my hotel was above reproach and the police could discover nothing wrong, and for a while the Dutch drew back from me.

Then a series of curious incidents took place, which I did not at the time understand or even try to understand. It seemed coincidence.

I was acquainted with most of the rajahs in Bali. The younger ones especially enjoyed coming to my hotel for a gay dinner or a swim. Now I noted an increase in these visits. Then one, and another, and still another, made a point of finding me alone to ask if I would do him the honor of marrying him. The proposals were quite formal. Yes, they said, of course they already had other wives, but this, I surely knew, was the Balinese custom. Nothing could be done about it. If I would accept their offer I would never have cause for regret. I would then become a Balinese in fact, as I now was in spirit. I had received offers of marriage before during my stay in Bali, but never quite in this way. I couldn't pin down the difference exactly, but it was there. With as much courtesy as I could muster I told them, no, though I greatly appreciated the honor.

"I think it most important that you become a Balinese," one of them said. "You have made a place for yourself in all our hearts and we cannot lose you."

I realized afterward that these men were doing what they could—in fact the only thing it was within their power to do—to save me. At the time I didn't know that I was in such need of saving, and in thinking about these marriage offers I was perplexed. It was almost as if the men had discussed among themselves what they could do. They must have heard something which I had not heard.

For a time everything went smoothly with me. I was not bothered and my self-confidence was restored. Then one day a Dutch half-caste policeman arrived at my hotel with a large official envelope, long familiar to me. Some controlleur, no doubt, wished to see me. But no. This was a deportation order. If I did not leave the island within one week I would be arrested and put on the first available ship for the United States. No explanation was given.

I went at once to the controlleur in Den Pasar to ask what this meant.

"What reason—"

"The Dutch government is not called upon to supply a reason. You are an alien. And we will get you out of this island if it is the last thing we do!"

"It will indeed be the last," I replied. "I will never leave on such an order. This is a frame-up. And if you put me on a ship you will be sorrier than you have ever been in your life! I shall see to that!"

The next morning I caught the plane for Java and went at once to the American consul at Surabaya. He told me that they could not deport me unless they could prove that I ran an immoral hotel or spread communism.

"But you must get a lawyer. The matter should be taken up with the Governor General at Batavia. Get everything moving as quickly as you can." This was his final advice.

It was my idea to engage an Indonesian lawyer, but Agung Nura said that a Dutch lawyer was necessary as no Indonesian would have a chance in a Dutch court. On his urging I went to Tuan Daan, who recommended a lawyer who was one of his close associates. Soon necessary formalities were completed, the Dutch officials in Bali were notified that the case would go before the Governor General. Until a verdict was reached I could not be arrested or put off the island.

Weeks passed without a decision. From many parts of the world people who had stayed at my hotel wrote to the Governor General protesting at the treatment I was receiving. One Dutch baroness who was close to Queen Wilhelmina wrote: "If the American girl, K'tut Tantri, is put out of Bali we shall invite her to Holland, where she will have something to say." Meantime my hotel was emptied of all guests. The Dutch allowed no one to remain there, though I was permitted visitors.

"They will never permit you to be deported," my Dutch lawyer assured me. "It is no crime to get on well with the natives, to wear native clothes, even to live with native families. Only persecution and intolerance and racial prejudice are crimes."

I had more faith in what the Rajah had once told me: "It is not yet clear what the gods wish for you, but evidently you must suffer to carry out their wishes."

After weeks of tense waiting, one morning—suddenly, as always, and unheralded—Agung Nura appeared.

I was on my veranda with a number of callers. Agung Nura greeted them briefly. And then to me:

"I have something to ask you, K'tut. I have been considering it very deeply, so please listen."

"Why, of course I'll listen!"

He took me down the path to the sea's edge. I could feel the strong pressure of his hand on my arm.

"Will you marry me, K'tut Tantri?"

I was reminded of the rajahs who but a little while ago had put the same question. I said the first thing that came into my head: "Why, Nura, how could I? You have a wife already!"

"In Bali it is quite legal to have more than one wife, and you surely know the situation between Rati and me. Oh, I know there would be disadvantages—perhaps for us both. But you would be safe. You would be a Balinese. The Dutch would not dare to touch you. You belong here. You have made a place for yourself."

I did not know what to reply.

"I have spoken about it to my father and received his approval. In fact, he told me that if there were no other way out he would even marry you himself!"

This broke the strain and we both laughed a little. "I'm sure he would, Nura, I'm sure he would!"

"Well?"

I shook my head. "No, dear Nura, it's impossible. I could never accept from you such a sacrifice. The Dutch would never forgive you. You would have to give up all your dreams for your countrymen. I must fight my battles for myself. You are already in more danger than I shall ever be, no matter what happens. You are a dear friend and brother and I cannot add to that danger. I came here to Bali to obtain freedom for myself and not to take it from those I love."

It was while Anak Agung Nura was still with me that word came that his Excellency, the Governor General of the Dutch East Indies, had ordered the reversal of the deportation order.

15

TRIUMPH AND TROUBLE

So I had won my case. I could not be deported. This ought to have
meant more to me than it did. What I had been through was not
to be easily shaken off. And I believe there was another reason for my
apathy, a premonition of disaster far greater than anything I had
so far endured. The peace I had come to Bali to find was gone—
temporarily at least. I was restless and tired at the same time. There
was a great deal going on in the world, and I was not part of it.

My hotel was reopened, but it was not the same. The monsoons
had come in earnest, and if Bagus had not wired the roofs of my
pavilions to the ground, I should have seen them fly off. It was not
the season for visitors. Perhaps I had become too accustomed to the
pressure of many people and their needs. I tried to study political
economy and read books on the colonial system. From what I had
seen of this system I did not think much of it. I was waiting, but
I did not know for what.

In Europe there was a man named Hitler, and then in Europe
war broke out. It was September, 1939, that England declared war
on Germany. Hitler had marched on Poland. We heard the news
but it was far away. We were safe here, confident that nothing
could happen to us. The English in Bali and Java, I noted, were
returning to their own country. Otherwise everything was as always.
The colonial Dutch seemed to ignore the whole thing, though Holland was an ally of England. Then Hitler's armies invaded Holland.
Rotterdam was bombed. Queen Wilhelmina fled to England with her
government.

It was about this time that an old British general came to my
hotel. He was a Scotsman from the island of Skye and was returning
to England as soon as he could. Meanwhile he spent his days sitting
on the terrace overlooking the sea, and knitted. I had never seen a
man knit before, but he told me that he always knitted before he
went into action.

"Good for the nerves—and it lets you concentrate." He said I was
wrong if I thought that what had happened in Europe would not

affect Indonesia. I think I learned more from him than from the books I had been reading.

Though the Dutch could not ignore the war after Holland fell, they seemed, even yet, extraordinarily complacent. The Indonesians—at least the more educated ones in the larger islands—were much more concerned. Their political leaders were openly pro-Ally and asked the Dutch to arm and train a percentage of natives in the event of an emergency. But this request was ignored. There was a powerful pro-Nazi group among the Dutch, called the NSB. Java, it seemed, was filled with this fifth column. In Bali the Dutch life appeared unchanged.

As the weather improved, guests came to my hotel, though they were for the most part from the other islands or from Singapore. Tuan Daan came, also his father and mother, and a retired American naval captain, Captain Kilkenny, as well as military personnel of various nationalities in increasing numbers.

I was again making money, but the joy had gone out of me. Through Daan I became quite friendly with some of the Dutch, not of course the controlleurs, or the people in the KPM shipping company, or those who ran the Bali Hotel, but Dutch officers whose views, surprisingly enough, were sympathetic to my own. I should explain that the Kuta airport nearby had been taken over by the Dutch Air Force. A group of aviators placed there for advanced training and for maneuvers formed the habit of coming to my place whenever their duties permitted. They were fine young men, friendly and charming. They liked to swim from my section of the beach and to have dinner afterward.

They were a jolly lot and I enjoyed their pranks, except when as a stunt they flew their planes in formation directly over me as I sat on my terrace, so low that I expected them to crash on my head. For them everything was free—food and drinks, a car for sightseeing, and even a pavilion if they wished to remain overnight. Sometimes I wouldn't see them for days at a time, then they would reappear. Many of them were married, with homes in Java, and I visited several of them more than once.

And then there came further trouble with Dutch officialdom.

I received a telegram from the English statesman, Lord Norwich, better known as Duff Cooper, saying that he and his wife were on their way to Australia and would like to stay at my hotel for a day or two. Would I meet them at the airport? Yes, of course, I replied at once. Duff Cooper was the Resident Cabinet Minister at Singapore. His wife was the noted beauty Lady Diana Manners.

The news spread quickly. The Dutch officials informed me promptly that guests of such rank, representatives of the British crown, could not possibly stay with me, but must be entertained at the mansion of the Resident of Bali. A delegation would be at the airport to meet them.

"It's a ridiculous situation," one official said, "but it can be adjusted in a proper manner."

"Let us leave that decision to the Duff Coopers," I answered him, unable to keep the anger from my voice. "This will be simple as I shall be at the airport."

I went ahead with my preparations as if nothing was in doubt. I would prepare the most sumptuous native foods, such as Kuta had rarely seen before, and call the best dancers and the finest gamelans. The dancers were charming and talented young maidens who were almost as carefully chaperoned as the daughters of rajahs, although they had come from the kampongs. I would invite the entire village. I knew, from my years in the puri, how to entertain illustrious guests in the Balinese fashion. Wyjan, Njoman, and Maday were in their glory. Under their direction all of Kuta assisted. But actually to meet the Duff Coopers the only Europeans I invited were William and Ardene Pol from Sanur, a delightful couple and good friends of mine.

And so the great day came and I arrived at the airport. Njoman and Maday had decorated my large open car to look like a flowered float at the Pasadena Rose Bowl on New Year's Day. Wyjan had obtained a Union Jack which he attached in front. I didn't have the heart to tell them of my misgivings. The Dutch would expect to see their flag displayed, not the British flag alone. I suggested adding the Dutch flag, but the boys said, "No," and there was no time for argument. As chauffeur and footman Wyjan and Njoman sat in front dressed like princes (though bare from the waist up). The entire effect was devastating.

All the Dutch officials were present, with a number of shining black limousines which looked out of place. We had ten minutes to wait, but it seemed much longer. The Dutch were stunned speechless by my own display. Then the plane came in and out stepped our guests. The Dutch delegation immediately surrounded them.

"We shall drive you at once to Government Mansion, where we have made suitable arrangements with the Resident."

But they underestimated Duff Cooper.

"I am deeply honored," he said, "but I am on a holiday and I have made my own arrangements. Lady Diana and I are to be the guests of Miss K'tut Tantri at Kuta Beach. Please point her out to me."

"But, Excellency, her hotel is a native hotel. You would not like it—you would not be comfortable!"

"From what I have heard of her hotel I shall be extremely comfortable and will like it immensely." He smiled. "Besides, I always wanted to go native."

I was standing close by but had not as yet stepped forward. Rather unwillingly an agent of KLM, the Dutch airline, beckoned to me. "This is K'tut Tantri."

It was my hour of triumph. The Duff Coopers were cordiality itself. Nothing was lost on them, or unappreciated. Wyjan and Njoman, standing at attention, relaxed sufficiently to help them into the car.

It was no wonder that Lady Diana had made a name in the theater in addition to being a great lady. She was the most beautiful creature I had ever seen and as charming as she was lovely. She was delighted with everything. Duff Cooper was interested in the architecture of the pavilions and the garden.

The Pols arrived and we all sat in the bamboo bar waiting for the lunch gong. This turned into a very serious moment. The news Duff Cooper told us was more alarming than we had realized.

"Anything can happen," he said. "You are not safe, even here."

Our talk was cut short by word that an urgent message had come for me. Outside the bar a young man from the dancers' kampong was waiting to tell me that the manager of the Bali Hotel, and the agent for the KPM shipping company, had informed the dancers that if they danced at my hotel that night they would never again be called on to dance at Den Pasar.

Asking the Pols to assume my duties as hostess, I drove at once to the assistant resident, who was in rank above the controlleur. The man received me coldly, but listened while I told him that if he didn't see that these orders were immediately revoked I would send the whole story to the press in Britain. I said Lord Norwich would be shocked and affronted when he heard of this insult and that the Dutch would feel repercussions from the British government. I threatened to send a cable to the Dutch Governor General in Batavia. Then I returned to Kuta.

Duff Cooper, his wife, and I had a pleasant afternoon driving around the countryside. There was no news on our return. Then, just before dinner, when we and the Pols were again seated in the bar and I was almost bursting with impatience to know if the dancers were going to turn up or not, the Dutch aspirant controlleur walked in. Bowing right and left, he asked me if he might speak to me privately. We moved down to the end of the bar together.

"The dancers will come to you tonight," he said, "and the Resident wishes me to tell you that he did not know of the ultimatum given to the kampongs. It came from the management of the Bali Hotel and the KPM agent."

I asked him if he would care for a drink, but he refused, clicked his heels, and took himself off. I noticed Duff Cooper looking at him, probably aware that something had been in need of adjustment.

The party was a great success.

I tell of the Duff Coopers' visit at such length because it made a marked difference in the way the Dutch regarded me.

This was November of 1941. The news from Europe grew worse. The Dutch began to bestir themselves. With Holland fallen, the Dutch government was carrying on from England and the colonials could not afford to be disloyal.

It must have been during the last few days of November that Daan came to see me, wanting my entire hotel through Christmas and New Year's for entertaining his family and friends who were still in Java. As I was charged with arranging suitable festivities, this gave me something to take my mind off the clouds that were gathering. I often recalled what Duff Cooper had said—"you are not safe, even here." Agung Nura was in Java. Exactly where he was or what he was doing I did not know. There was a curious pall of secrecy over everything.

One morning very early I was awakened by a banging on the door of my pavilion. I rose and went to the window. One of the aviators stood there.

"Let me in, K'tut, let me in! I have something to tell you!"

I hastily put on a robe and went to the door. The young man still stood there, not moving, though he had asked to be let in.

"You're an American—"

"Why, yes, you know that."

"Well, the American navy in Pearl Harbor has been sunk by the Japanese. Your country is in the war now. The colonel sent me over to tell you the news. If Tuan Daan and Captain Kilkenny are here, you had better let them know at once."

The bearer of ill tidings left then. It was about two miles to the airport, and he evidently walked—or perhaps ran—all the way. Not taking time to dress further, I went to the pavilion where Daan and Captain Kilkenny were still sound asleep. They were both rather meticulous about the ritual of dressing, but not now. I had barely reached my own bungalow when I saw first one and then the other dashing out.

"Take a car!" I shouted.

"We were going to."

That night Daan left for Java. As a reserve officer he must report at once. The Dutch colonials would fight the Japanese if not the Germans. Japan was nearer. As for Captain Kilkenny, he managed to get away the next day. In the United States even retired navy captains would now have their use. He offered to take me with him, though how he could have managed this I do not know.

One of the aviators who was constantly flying to Java and back brought me a long letter from Agung Nura advising me to close the hotel and return to his father's puri. Even if the Japanese were to reach Bali they would not disturb the rajahs, as they might have use for them later. In the puri I would be comparatively safe. All anybody seemed to consider was personal safety, and also what would happen to their money.

Though opinion varied as to when the Japanese would come to Java, I was advised by everyone to leave the islands at once. But I did not wish to leave. I had been there for many years now and Bali had become my home. If the Dutch hadn't succeeded in sending me away, surely the Japanese wouldn't? I had come to Bali for peace and freedom. Perhaps for me the ultimate freedom lay in placing myself in the front line of battle.

The airport was very near me. For three days every week now a squadron of fliers would come over from Java. These men, I knew, would have the responsibility for the defense of all the islands. My hotel was known, even to those who had never been there. It had been opened to the air force before, but now I opened it completely. I could make what was left of their lives happier. I knew that Sound of the Sea was in danger. The airport was the only thing on Bali which would interest the Japanese in the event of bombing, and the hotel was in easy range.

I designed for the Dutch airmen a flag, an orange triangle and in each corner a black D, which I told them stood for Darling, Daring Devils. This flag became famous in Bali and Java. The young aviators were delighted with the flag, and flew it not only on their planes but on their automobiles as well.

The Dutch officials soon spread the rumor that I must be a spy, and eventually the fliers were notified that my place was out of bounds. The aviators strongly protested this order. Then the high brass of the Dutch Royal Air Force came to my hotel to investigate. I gave a party for them, which I know they enjoyed immensely, and spent the evening explaining myself.

"For whom would I be spying," I asked, "and what would I be finding out that is not already a matter of common knowledge? The fliers fly to Darwin in Australia. They bring back presents for their wives with the shop labels still attached, also packets of matches with the name of the hotel at which they stayed. However secretly they go, they are seen. I know no Japanese, I am British born and an American citizen. I have lived in Bali, without leaving, for many years. I have made some money from my hotel and if I wish to spend it on your air force what better use can I find for it? I feel I am doing very little for those who perhaps may give their lives in defense of Bali. Please don't take that little from me. I assure you that your boys might be in much worse hands."

As a result of this investigation, the out-of-bounds order was revoked. Later these high officers who had dropped in on me sent me by plane from Bandung enough fresh strawberries to feed a regiment. With the strawberries was a message: "We know that our men could not be in better care than that of K'tut Tantri."

The Japanese were getting closer to Java, but the Darling, Daring

Devils continued to come to my hotel, and the orange-and-black flag did not stop waving. Few of these men are now alive, but I have never regretted that before the curtain dropped I brought them a little happiness.

16

THE CURTAIN FALLS

Singapore fell. The Dutch were shocked into activity. Singapore was closer than Pearl Harbor, too close. The Japanese would hardly stop there. The Dutch colonial empire was directly threatened. No aviators came to Sound of the Sea now. They were too busy. They were in a war—their war. Java would be next. The Japanese had planes as well as ships and well-trained troops. They might not come to Bali, an insignificant spot on the map, but they would surely bomb the airport which English, Australian, and Dutch planes were using as a base. The beaches of Sanur and Kuta were strung with barbed wire three fences deep. Pillboxes and guns appeared. The front of my hotel seemed like some strange fort. I could sit on my terrace and look at it. In the rear an air-raid shelter was in the process of being dug. This work was stopped as it was not practical—merely a sandy pit lined with boards, which would have protected no one. I think I was the only American still here.

A Dutch officer begged me to leave my hotel. "A stray bomb," he said, "just a stray—and your entire place would be demolished."

Perhaps I had become, in truth, a Balinese. The natives were not leaving. They couldn't. Besides, they had hope in an old prophecy which predicted that a yellow race would come from the north and free them from the domination of foreigners. It rankled that their offer to bear arms to help the Dutch to defend their country had been refused. Then, when rumors came of the barbarity with which the Japanese treated those they captured, the natives didn't know what to believe. Would the Japanese come as saviors or as new tyrants? No one knew.

I received another message from Agung Nura urging me to return to the safety of his father's puri. But I didn't wish to do this. I wished to remain just where I was. I suppose I was confused, though in a sense unaware of my confusion. I even started to build more pavilions. Sound of the Sea had become for me a symbol. It was like my Ardjuno coin—I held to it with a sort of superstitious fervor. I make no attempt to explain this, I merely record it. When the airport was finally bombed I still remained. Perhaps I was so deeply shocked that the shock brought immobility.

All this occupied a comparatively brief period of time. I could not then, and cannot now, be accurate as to the hours or days. My hotel was as yet undamaged.

Then Wyjan brought news that the Japanese were off the coast of Sanur, only eight miles away. "You must leave," he told me. "You must leave at once! You don't know it yet, but panic is coming, and it is worse than shooting. The Dutch are beginning to desert. Soon you will see them running."

And that was exactly what I saw. Not the officials—they had been ordered to stay, and besides they never expected the Japanese to remain—but all the Dutch businessmen and the agents from the shipping company and even the Dutch military. I watched them running for their lives as the news spread that the Japanese had landed, not on Java but on Bali itself. I watched them as they threw away their uniforms or whatever else they wore, and donned native clothing and stained their faces brown. They managed somehow to get away. The panic grew as the Dutch set fire to all the military installations, the great warehouses where the rice was stored, the oil dumps, everything.

My beloved Bali was in flames. At last I realized that I too must go. First I had to say good-by to the Rajah, though it would be difficult now to get to the puri. Wyjan offered to drive me, but I could not let him take the risk. I might have driven myself, but it was best to go on foot through back roads and over hills and creeks. It was a long walk and the country was not easily negotiated on foot. Nevertheless, I did it, stopping now and then to rest and to watch the destruction I was for the moment escaping.

The puri was unchanged. The Rajah welcomed me with tears in his eyes. "You have come home, fourth-born!"

It was hard to tell him that I had come only to say good-by.

"I was afraid of that. I have here a letter for you. It is from Nura.

He sent it in my care, knowing evidently that you would come here to receive it."

"You must go to Gilimanuk in the north," Nura's letter ran. "I have arranged with some Madurese fishermen who will secretly take you to Java. And they will know where to find me. I shall be somewhere near Banjuwangi. Do not be too long in coming, as I am not sure how long I can remain."

I told the Rajah what the letter contained. "I must go."

"You do not have to go!" he said. "You can remain here in safety. Since when must you take orders from my son? And yet you would not marry him."

There was a silence between us then, and much unsaid.

"No, I would not marry him."

The Rajah looked at me. "You are very dear to me, K'tut, but I do not understand you."

"Sometimes I do not understand myself. I must leave you now. I have much to see about. As I cannot carry my hotel on my back I must arrange that it is cared for."

The old man shook his head. "You must be exhausted."

"I am not exhausted."

"The gods have given you their strength."

There were no farewells, just my leaving. I found that one of the puri servants was to be my guide. He carried a basket of food I was glad to have before my journey was over. At the puri I had barely touched what had been set out for me. How long my return took I cannot say. It seemed to me that I had passed through a morning and a high noon and a sunset. Sound of the Sea was still there. The Japanese were still in the midst of landing at Sanur.

That same evening I had a long talk with Wyjan. He and Njoman and Maday would care for the hotel. "If the Japanese come here," I told him, "as they doubtless will—the officers will surely take over the place—be polite—serve them—cater to them. Don't risk your lives—it will be futile. I don't want this place to be destroyed or you killed. And by the way—" I handed him a paper which I had prepared—"this is to say that if anything should happen to me the hotel belongs to you. You and Njoman and Maday. There is no one else I would leave it to."

Wyjan was overcome. "Nothing can happen to you, K'tut— nothing must, now that you are leaving." He took the paper. "You will be back. The Japanese can't stay here. America and England, if not the Dutch, will get them out of here."

All the natives believed this. I myself was not so sure.

Gilimanuk was much too far to attempt on foot. I could have driven myself, but Wyjan insisted on driving me. We left just before dawn. Part of the way I slept the best sleep I had had for a long time. I awoke to the sound of a plane overhead, and across the strait I could hear dimly the rumble of guns. Bali had fallen without a shot fired in its defense.

"We are here," Wyjan said. "I shall leave the car for you and arrange with the fishermen to load it on a prau and sail it to Java later." While he attended to this the Madurese were ready for me and waiting.

"But, Wyjan," I asked him, "how will you get back to Kuta yourself?"

"There are plenty of ways. Don't worry about me."

At our parting he broke down, just as if he were a child—mine perhaps, as I told him that I felt he was. I myself was strangely upset. It was late in the afternoon that I boarded the fishing smack, which looked like any other. The Madurese assured me that I would be quite invisible, they would cover me with fish nets.

"You will lie flat on the deck," they said. "You mustn't be seen by any low-flying Japanese plane." They evidently had everything planned most carefully.

I was not afraid of attack, and lay quiet as the fish nets were thrown over me. It was a fairly calm voyage. I could hear the lapping of the waves against the side of the boat. The nets smelled strongly of fish, but I didn't mind. It was an uneventful voyage. The men seemed to fish, but whether they really did so or if it was only a pretense I never knew. I could hear the Japanese planes flying overhead. The night was very black when they helped me to the Java shore.

"I shall now go to Banjuwangi to find Anak Agung Nura," one of the men announced. "My brother will remain to guard you."

"But Banjuwangi must be some distance off—" I had visions of waiting for days on that lonely beach.

But it was still night when a coolie touched my hand. I turned, startled. It was not a coolie, but Anak Agung Nura dressed in coolie garb.

"You came, K'tut."

"Of course."

This was all our greeting. He sat down on the sand beside me.

"Look there," he said. "You can see the red smoke across the water. That is Bali burning."

"Part of it is what the Dutch themselves have done." Then I told him what he seemed to know already—how the Dutch had fled, not firing a shot in defense of the country they themselves had conquered, and told him of the destruction they themselves had seen to.

"The Japanese have not landed in Java yet," Nura said. "They surprised everyone by taking Bali first. They have a slogan: Asia for the Asians. It lulls the natives into a false security. You remember our talks in the mountain chalet? I think I said then that only a miracle could free us from the Dutch. But this is not the sort of miracle for which I had been working. It will not be Asia for the Asians, but Asia for the Japanese. Most of the Indonesians don't realize that—not yet." As I listened to Nura I watched the red smoke curling higher and higher into the sky. He pressed my hand as if to reassure me, and then—"Perhaps I was wrong in asking you to come here. You ought to have stayed at my father's."

"Perhaps you too ought to have done that," I answered him. "You might have accomplished something—organized a Balinese army—"

"With what? A few swords—some music from the gamelan? The Japanese have planes and guns and a well-trained force. I could never have saved Bali by myself. And that is not all of Bali burning."

It must come to everyone at some time to know that for them a part of life is over. I felt so as I watched the red smoke. I shall always remember that night—Agung Nura and I together on that distant beach—even the fish smell from the nets still clung to me. It was as if a curtain had been drawn over all that had gone before. No, we, neither of us, had been able to save our beloved island—from the Dutch or from these other conquerors of whom we still knew so little. For this we both shed tears. As the sun rose the redness in the sky changed to blue and Agung Nura turned my face toward the east.

TWO

1

THE JAPANESE TAKE OVER

Anak Agung Nura and I waited only for my car to arrive on the prau from Gilimanuk, as had been arranged by Wyjan. Then we were off for Surabaya, skirting the main travel routes, dodging through the back roads of East Java. We had no way of knowing whether the Nipponese were on this island yet, or even if Surabaya had been invaded. We feared that at any turning we might run into a Japanese ambush or roadblock. But nothing of this sort developed. We had no trouble.

Surabaya we found in a state of chaos. Roads leading out of the city and the trains we could see from the highway were jammed with Dutch soldiers. They were, we quickly learned, trying to reach military headquarters at Bandung, on the other end of Java. Surabaya had been bombed several times. Panic-stricken natives were fleeing by the thousands to the safety of kampongs in the interior. The Japanese had taken the key cities of Borneo and Sumatra—Balikpapan, Sabang, Medan, Palembang—we were told. They had not yet landed anywhere in Java, but the signs were clear. They would do so certainly, and soon.

Agung Nura was concerned, not about himself—the Japanese could have no particular enmity for a Balinese—but for me, as a white woman and an American. My nationality, even more than my color, might mark me for brutal treatment. The prince decided he must go to Solo in West Java to find out if there would be a hiding place for me in the Sultan's palace.

I remained, comfortable for the moment but insecure, in Surabaya's leading hotel, the Oranje. My fellow occupants for the most part were German women, safe from the oncoming invaders because Germany was an ally of Japan, and those Dutch who had not as yet, for one reason or another, been unable to escape.

The United States consulate had been closed, and the personnel evacuated. But an American military commission was stationed there. I decided, while awaiting Nura's return, to offer my services.

Understandably the offer was accepted immediately. Help was not easy to come by at this point. Here was an American woman who could speak the Malay language, drive a car, and knew her way about Surabaya.

I became the driver and interpreter for a colonel known to the natives—for his loud and contagious laughter—as the "Laughing Yankee." The colonel had already inspired the timid natives with his good-humored refusal to enter air-raid shelters during bombings. "Those yellow devils couldn't hit the broad side of Queen Wilhelmina's barn!" he exclaimed. The natives loved his spirit and followed him everywhere.

I also found myself expressing the same contempt for Japanese aerial marksmanship. "Those Nips aren't going to hit this hotel if they can help it," the colonel said wisely. "They'll be wanting to keep it in good shape for their own use." Accordingly, when the raids would start our response was to rush up to the roof of the Oranje, the colonel carrying his motion-picture camera. He recorded on film the bomb bursts and whatever aircraft could be seen.

I learned from this gallant, bravehearted American a new toughness, a fatalistic indifference to personal danger. "Tantri," he said, "don't ever be afraid. If it is your fate to be hit by a Japanese bomb, the bomb with your name on it will find you, no matter where you hide." Just a few days later an air-raid shelter was hit directly and everyone in it was killed. "See what I mean?" the colonel said. After that I didn't worry about my own safety any more.

The colonel's duties were chiefly associated with two black-painted American ships anchored at the Surabaya docks. He confided to me that they were fully loaded with food, ammunition, and quinine, ready to sail. At a secret place on one of the islands of the Pacific, their cargo would be stored until needed.

One day when the Japanese planes crossed high overhead their bombs came much closer to the ships than on any previous raid. This time the colonel forgot to laugh. "That's what you call a near miss," he said. "We don't want any more of them."

The colonel had been awaiting sailing orders from his commanding officer in Batavia. That evening, however, he was plainly upset. "I can't afford to wait any longer," he said. "Those Japs have found our measure, and they might come back at any time. I must move the ships at once." On a map he showed me a cove down the coast in the direction of Pasuruan. "The ships will sail for this little harbor at midnight," he went on. "We should get there before daylight. I want you to drive down there in the staff car and pick me up."

The plan worked perfectly. We were both back in Surabaya before nine o'clock the following morning. At 10 A.M. the air-raid sirens wailed. This time the Japanese hit with greater force and accuracy than ever before. Within minutes the Surabaya docks were in ruins.

On March 1, 1942, the dreaded news arrived. The Japanese were landing in Java, at the port of Cheribon, two hundred miles from Surabaya. All military personnel—Dutch, American, Australian, English—were ordered to leave the city immediately. Most of them were directed to take all available transportation to Australia.

The colonel urged me to fly to Darwin with him. "We have room for you on the plane," he said. "If you stay here, as an American citizen you'll be in grave danger when the Japs arrive. You've heard over the radio what they've been doing with their prisoners, especially Americans. There are no rules of fair play in the Japanese style of war."

It would have been a welcome relief to escape to remote and relatively peaceful Australia, but it was unthinkable that I should leave this troubled island. What of the prince, and all of my other adopted Indonesian friends? What of Agung Nura's dream of freeing his people from all foreign oppression? What of my promises, during those days at his coffee plantation, to do everything in my power to help bring about a free Indonesia? With the Dutch forfeiting the reins, perhaps for all time, the Japanese might be most willing to hand over the power to the Indonesians. Certainly this would win them the approval of Asians everywhere. It would also free Japanese personnel for duty elsewhere in the swiftly expanding Nipponese empire.

There was another prospect also. High Dutch officials were confident that the Japanese had overreached themselves and that the war could not last more than three months. If they were right, this was still the time for Indonesia to assert its bid for independence. I could still be of service to my adopted land. All of white Java apparently trusted this optimistic appraisal of the Dutch leaders. As a result, thousands of Dutch women and children who might have been evacuated were caught in Java—interned by the Japanese for a war which lasted three years instead of three months.

So it was good-by to the colonel and the others flying to Australia. Shortly after arriving in Surabaya I had taken a bungalow not far from the Oranje Hotel. Here I awaited Agung Nura's return, and from a fairly well-concealed observation post I watched the Japanese enter Surabaya. The Dutch, of course, had fled, leaving the unarmed, unprotected Indonesians to meet the invaders. Surprisingly to me, the occupation of the city was most orderly. The Japanese simply marched in, moved into public buildings and the abandoned mansions of the Dutch, and quietly took charge.

I learned of no acts of violence. If there were rapings or lootings or assaults, they were rare indeed. The Japanese were a highly disciplined people. The Indonesians were delighted at the good behavior of the troops and took to welcoming them as liberators from the Dutch. Everywhere they appeared the Japanese were applauded. The red-and-white Indonesian flag, outlawed as subversive by the Dutch, blossomed from every window—often, it must be admitted, in company with the Rising Sun flag of Japan. For to many Indonesians the Japanese invasion was nothing less than the fulfillment of the ancient Djojobojo prophecy that Java would be liberated by a small-statured yellow race from the north.

Agung Nura returned from Solo with the report that the situation in West Java was confused, to say the least. Then over the radio we learned, a week after the bloodless surrender of Surabaya, that organized resistance in Java had ended. The Dutch Commander in Chief of Allied Forces, Lieutenant General ter Poorten, had surrendered in the name of the Dutch and their allies. We learned later that he apparently had done so without consulting the British and American commanders, although 8,000 to 10,000 Allied military and civilian personnel were involved. The shock and surprise of Indonesians at this quick fall of the mighty Dutch could hardly have been greater than that of the Allied personnel, and of the brave air and naval forces of the Dutch.

The Japanese commander of Surabaya ordered all Europeans to come to headquarters and register. Agung Nura went with me to the commandant and asked that I be given an order exempting me from internment, and that I be granted also a traveling pass between Java and Bali. He explained that I was his adopted sister, having lived at his father's palace for many years, and that I was an artist, completely divorced from war activity.

Apparently my native clothes, my sandals, my dyed black hair and my ability to speak both Balinese and Malay impressed the commandant. "A white Balinese," he murmured. Obviously skeptical of the prince's account of our relationship, he gave me a knowing look and good-naturedly wrote out an exemption order and a traveling pass for "one Balinese by adoption, K'tut Tantri." "Japanese do not make war with artists," he said. "You must show me your paintings someday, and I will show you my collection of Japanese scrolls."

I wondered what a Japanese officer would be doing with art scrolls in his possession during time of war, and so far from home. "Do you travel with your collection?" I asked.

"Certainly. I have brought my collection of art with me," he replied. "After a long day in military life, one needs relaxation in the evenings. I brought my paintings to be enjoyed."

He smiled at me. "If you have studied history you may remember that even the English, in the war of the Crusades, brought along clumsy musical instruments, and played at the end of the day. I have always understood this, and sympathized with it. The English are a complex race."

The commandant proved to be neither arrogant nor a bully, but kind and sympathetic—unlike other Japanese officers I was soon to come to know. Indeed, he was found to be too softhearted for his post; before long he was transferred out of Surabaya.

Normal communications between Bali and Surabaya had been cut off. We knew that Bali had been occupied by the Japanese navy, and Java by the army. Their ways were different, and it soon became evident they were jealous of each other. Agung Nura decided to return to Bali alone, to look after his family and to ascertain whether I would be safe as a lone white woman in Bali, even with his father's protection.

I would remain in Surabaya, awaiting developments. At least the Japanese commandant here was not antagonistic; and the devil you know is worth two you don't. Agung Nura warned me not to push my luck, and to stay out of sight of the Japanese as much as possible.

A number of Australian and English civilians had hidden in the mountains or in the kampongs of friendly natives. One after another these places of concealment were being discovered by the Japanese, probably through informers. Sizable rewards were offered for information leading to the capture of fugitives.

Late one night an Englishman, a friend of many years, came to my house. He was in hiding, he said, and heard through the grape-vine that I had a safety pass to travel between Java and Bali. Would I consider helping him?

He explained that the English firms which he represented had left some automobiles and important documents in his care. Could I possibly get this property to Bali and into hiding in the puri of one of my rajah friends? Surely in the puri they would be safe from the inquisitive Japanese.

"I would like to help an old friend," I said. "But I have no pass to transport an automobile. The movement of cars is forbidden, and there are Japanese roadblocks and road patrols."

The Englishman said a Chinese friend of his would forge a pass identical to the one I already held, but granting permission to transport an automobile between Java and Bali. "As you know," he said, "Japanese and Chinese Kandi writing is the same. The only difficulty will be the signature of the Japanese Commander in Chief, for that is signed in the Western manner."

"And who will forge the commandant's name?" I asked.

"I will," he replied.

And a very good forgery it was. The Englishman said he spent three days practicing it, until it was perfect.

I agreed to make the journey, not only for patriotic reasons but because it would be a pleasant change from the confinement of Surabaya, would satisfy my curiosity as to what was going on outside the city, and would get me back to Bali for a quick visit to the Rajah and Agung Nura. I did not consider it too hazardous because I knew the way so well. The guards along the way would be young, uneducated Japanese soldiers, I reasoned, unlikely to question my papers.

Several times on the drive to the East Java coast I was stopped by road guards and patrols. Each time the men passed me on, with smiles and bows. Some must have thought I was a German girl, for there were salutes and cries of "Heil Hitler!"

Crossing the Bali-Java Strait in the usual manner, I drove along Bali's small back roads to the puri of a good friend of mine, the brother of the Rajah, who married a French girl. It was more prudent to hide the automobile here than at Agung Nura's puri, the first place that would be searched should I become suspect, I decided.

As an extra bit of Scotch caution I stored the car in one place, the sealed packages at another.

From the hiding places I made my way on foot over the hills to the puri that had been my home. Nura was astonished when I walked in, and more than upset when he heard my story. Both he and the Rajah begged me not to tempt fate again. I told them I had a promise to keep, and must return to Java immediately.

Back in Surabaya, I was encouraged that the entire operation had taken only four days. I was confident I could repeat the journey without difficulty before the Japanese tightened up. The Englishman agreed on a second trip but said that a third trip would tempt fate a bit too far.

The second journey to Bali was slightly more hazardous than the first. Again I hid the property and went to the Rajah's puri. The concern and relief on the faces of father and son were so evident that I promised myself not to cause them any more worry. It was on this trip that I learned that my hotel at Kuta Beach had been completely demolished, and that Wyjan, Njoman, and Maday were hiding in their kampongs.

The following morning, during a quiet chat with the Rajah and Agung Nura, I was taken completely by surprise when the old man said, in a sudden burst of words, that he thought it would be better for his son's peace of mind—and for my own safety—if I married Agung Nura.

"As my real daughter-in-law you would be an Indonesian citizen and the Japanese wouldn't dare to interfere with you," he said.

I shook my head. Carefully I avoided Nura's gaze. "Thank you for the great honor you have suggested," I said, "but I must remind you that your son is already married."

The Rajah exploded. "What has that got to do with it, fourth-born?" he exclaimed. "We have had this out before. You know the adat of Bali—you know our custom. A Balinese man may marry as many wives as he can afford to support. And you know too that Nura does not live with Rati. They have never been husband and wife in reality, and it appears that they never will. The prince has satisfied the tradition of his ancestors. Now he is free to marry anyone else he may desire."

The old man paused, and then pursued his argument. "You know of the Balinese rajah who married a French girl in Paris." I nodded. "You know that he has two previous Balinese wives, and many children. And all concerned seem to be happy with the arrangement. You love my son, do you not?"

This time I looked straight at Nura and replied, "Yes, I do love your son very much, but more as a sister than in any other way. I could not marry him so long as he is married to Rati. I know that divorce does not exist in the Balinese adat. I could not consent to an annulment that might hurt or embarrass Rati. And I believe that two people should marry only for love and for nothing else, certainly not to save one's skin. So you see it is impossible for me to entertain any idea of marrying Anak Agung Nura to save myself from the Japanese."

Agung Nura, his face a mirror of conflicting emotions, broke his silence. "Tantri," he said softly, "I want to marry you." It was the first time he had called me other than by my sisterly name of K'tut.

"I want to marry you—and not just to save you or protect you from the Japanese. I have come to love you very much. I can't imagine being without you. About Rati, some arrangement can be made, in the same way that our rajah friend arranged for his two Balinese wives before he married the French girl. Rati will probably be happy to be free of me."

We talked further, without reaching agreement. At last I told the Rajah that I would think the problem over, but first must return to Surabaya to report the success of my mission to the Englishman.

In Surabaya I learned that the Englishman's hiding place had been discovered and that he had been sent to a concentration camp near Bandung in West Java. I promptly burned the forged papers he had given me and flushed the ashes down the toilet. Had the forged documents been found on me and traced to the Englishman, he would certainly have been shot. It happened, however, that I never saw the Englishman again. He died in the concentration camp two years later.

The Japanese, meanwhile, announced throughout Java that half-castes—Indo-Dutch, as they are called—would not be interned, and those already interned would be released. They must prove, however, that they were half of native blood.

It was shocking to me and to many of my Indonesian friends to see so many Hollanders of good family and high social standing registering as half-castes. Before the Japanese invasion these same Dutch had been snobs of the highest order. They would have been outraged at the slightest suggestion that they had native blood. It was bitterly amusing to me that some of the Dutch officials—and their wives—who had made my life miserable in Bali for mixing with the natives were now confessing to being half native themselves. Even the wife of a very high Dutch official registered as an Indo-Dutch.

The Japanese had invited Dutch civilians to help them run the country after the surrender of Java. Those who promised to co-operate would, for the most part, remain in their jobs and out of prison. I was told on good authority that 80 per cent of Dutch planters and businessmen agreed to collaborate with the Japanese. Within a few weeks almost all the Dutch businessmen outside the internment camps were wearing the flag of the Rising Sun round their sleeves. But this happy collaboration lasted only about a year. The Japanese waited until they had mastered the techniques of running Dutch plantations and Dutch business, then abruptly interned the whole lot—even their best Dutch friends. Presumably there were some interesting developments within the internment camps when the Dutch who had been prisoners from the first caught up with their fellow countrymen who had bought a year of freedom by toadying to the Japanese.

While the Dutch were feeling the weight of the invader's heel, the Indonesians too began to learn more about their new rulers. Hardly a month of Japanese administration had gone by before disillusionment set in. First, the Japanese insisted that the natives bow low in greeting and take off their fezzes upon meeting a Japanese. The black fez of the Javanese is a symbol of his religion and is not removed lightly. The Japanese were quick to beat a native who failed to remove his fez or was slow about doing so.

The men from Japan began confiscating food and goods to meet their pressing war needs. As produce and supplies became costly and scarce, less and less made their way into the hands of the natives. Wherever it suited their purpose the Japanese roughly thrust Indonesians out of their jobs. Many Indonesians were thrown into prison on slight pretexts, without fair trial. If the Japanese were building a Greater East Asia, there obviously was little provision in it for an independent Indonesia.

Among the political prisoners of the Dutch who were released by the Japanese when they took Sumatra was the long-time hero of the resistance, Sukarno. With several other leading advocates of nationalism for Indonesia, Sukarno had been thrown into a Dutch jail in 1929 for advocating the overthrow of the Netherlands East Indies government. Released briefly, he was arrested again in August, 1933, and exiled to Flores island. Later he was removed to Benkulen, in western Sumatra, from which the Japanese released him in 1942. Other political internees of the Dutch who were liberated by the Japanese included two men almost as widely known as Sukarno, Dr. Mohammed Hatta and Sutan Sjahrir.

Noting the tremendous popularity of the dynamic Sukarno with the Indonesian masses, the Japanese gave him the commanding role in Java's civil affairs, and made Dr. Hatta second-in-command. As Indonesian leaders under the occupation, these two men quickly became targets of attack for the nations opposing Japan.

Agung Nura and his friends moved back and forth between Bali and the key cities of Java. They told me that Sukarno, in spite of his fiery radio speeches in support of the Japanese, was in sympathy with an underground movement that had sprung up under a Christian Indonesian, Amir Sjarifuddin. Sjarifuddin had started with Dutch financing, and his dealings with Sukarno were through Sutan Sjahrir. The whole purpose, I was told, was to prepare Indonesia for self-government—since the Japanese were obviously not disposed to grant this—the moment that it might prove possible.

So it was that Agung Nura became involved in an underground resistance movement against the Japanese. "The top of the organization is in Batavia, but we must get organized locally as well," he said. "Communications are difficult, not merely from island to island but from town to town. We must set up a courier network." In connection with that task he set out for conferences in Batavia and Bandung, after which he would stop off at Djokjakarta and Solo. I promised to stay close to the house until he returned.

Just a few days after Agung Nura's departure a Japanese in civilian clothing rang my doorbell. It was after dark. When he asked in English if he might speak with me, I immediately took him to be a member of the Japanese secret police. The Japanese administration had forbidden anyone to speak English. Agung Nura and I had been very careful to speak only Balinese, and with the servants and with strangers I spoke Malay, the language of Java.

Telling myself not to panic—and to watch what I might say—I admitted the visitor. He identified himself immediately, to my astonishment, as an American-born Japanese from San Francisco, and as still an American citizen and of pro-American sympathies. At the present time he was helping to manage a factory taken over by the Japanese. Secretly he was organizing a small resistance group, and he heard that I might be recruited. He had been told of my background and he knew all about Anak Agung Nura. He suggested that my good relationship with the Japanese commander and other high Japanese officials, my connections with Japanese military circles and social life, might prove most valuable. And he felt that as an American citizen I would be willing to do everything I could do to help the Allies.

I was amazed at his proposal, and sure that he was trying to trick me. "You have the wrong person," I said. "My sympathies are with Dai Nippon. I am one hundred per cent pro-Japanese. If you don't go away, I shall appeal to the commandant."

The visitor was not easily discouraged. The Japanese would take his word in preference to mine, he said. He showed me American papers, a birth certificate. I told him such documents could easily be forged, and thought of the Englishman lying in jail. He proposed taking me to meet a small group of underground workers—Chinese, Indonesians, Arabs, and Dutch half-castes. I knew that hundreds of persons of those nationalities were collaborating with the Japanese. Finally he left. He was laughing as he said, "I shall be back."

Worried and confused about the strange visit from the Japanese civilian, I determined to be very discreet and not leave the house until Anak Agung Nura returned. I would speak to no one other than my own servants. I cautioned them not to speak to strangers.

Several times a week I had noticed an old Chinese peddler walking up and down the street shouting in Malay, "Salongs! Salongs! Beautiful salongs, velly cheap." The word is pronounced the same in English and Malay, but uneducated Chinese cannot pronounce the letter "r." What he was selling, of course, was sarongs, which all the native women wore, including myself. I particularly noticed that he always stopped in front of my house and shouted his loudest.

One morning the peddler knocked at my door. When I opened the door he called in Malay, "Missie, please you like look at my salongs? Maybe like to buy one for babu." The babu, or servant girl, was standing right beside me. I had to invite him in to show his wares.

As he unwrapped his bundle I watched him closely. He started to haggle with the babu, then let her have two sarongs for a ridiculously low price. The babu, delighted that she had been so clever as to beat the peddler down to a tremendous bargain, rushed back to the servants' quarters to show off her prizes. It was unlike a Chinese trader to give something for nothing. The Chinese looked slyly at me out of the corner of his eyes as he rewrapped his bundle, and then stood up and said in a cultured voice, "Forgive me, Miss K'tut Tantri, for the deception. I am a friend of Anak Agung Nura. Two days ago I saw him in Solo, and he gave me a letter to deliver to you."

The letter was in Balinese. I recognized the unmistakable handwriting of Agung Nura. His message introduced the bearer as a good friend, a professor from a university in occupied China, a worker in the underground movement, a person to be trusted fully. Nura added that he would be with me soon, and he hoped that when he arrived I would have changed my mind about marrying him, even if only for my own protection, and in name only.

I thanked the professor for bringing the letter from Anak Agung Nura and told him of my strange visit from the Japanese who had called himself American-born and an Allied sympathizer. The professor smiled and assured me, "The Japanese was telling the truth. It is perhaps as well that you did not believe him, for he will trust you more now. I, myself, work under him. He is a good man, and we call him Frisco Flip."

Late the next night, after the servants were fast asleep, I heard a gentle tapping at the living-room window. Two coolies were standing there. I opened the door; it was the honorable professor and Frisco Flip. It occurred to me that I didn't know their real names. I thought it prudent not to ask. The less one knows, in circumstances such as these, the better—in case a link in the underground becomes exposed.

Frisco Flip shook my hand. "You and your Dai Nippon." He laughed. "You didn't fool me, even for a minute. I lost no sleep thinking you would inform the Japanese police. You see, I know the prince. He had told me all about you. I am pleased you acted the way you did."

2

I JOIN THE RESISTANCE

Anak Agung Nura returned from western Java full of news of the growth of the underground. Under Amir Sjarifuddin's direction— and with the covert encouragement of Sukarno and Dr. Hatta—it was becoming well organized, not only in Java but in other parts of Indonesia as well. Should there be a weakening of the Japanese grasp over the islands, men of great leadership quality and long political experience stood ready to assert Indonesian claims to self-government.

The honorable professor, still dressed as a peddler, Frisco Flip, and I held a planning conference with Agung Nura at his apartment. The professor would remain a peddler of sarongs, walking the streets, watching the movements of the Japanese. He would be the contact man for a secret radio sender, hidden in the mountains. Frisco Flip would provide the funds; I never inquired as to the source of his revenue. He was in a position to obtain important information that would be relayed, by devious means, to the Allies—information that could hasten the day when the Japanese would be thrown out of Java and the red-and-white flag of merdeka—of Indonesian freedom —could be raised over the Governor's Palace in Batavia.

Anak Agung Nura would go back to Bali to organize his many friends into a resistance group and to further the movement in the nearby islands. Bali had become of considerable importance because the Japanese were using the excellent airport near Kuta as a base for their widespread bombing operations.

My role was to become known as the girl friend of Frisco Flip, and be introduced to Japanese officials and to mix generally in Japanese circles, and to paint pictures of pretty Balinese maidens and sell them very cheaply to the Japanese. "Easel and brush—that's the perfect cover-up job for you," Frisco exulted. "After all, over the years you have established yourself in Bali and Java to some degree as a painter."

"But I have never painted those half-nude Balinese women," I objected. "I hate that kind of painting."

"Even so," my adviser chuckled, "that's the type of art that appeals to Japanese soldiers. I know. So throw away your artistic standards and paint these pretty Balinese girls, bare breasts and all."

We agreed on a password, and swore that if any of us should be caught by the Japanese, we would die rather than implicate the others. It was a strange shivery feeling to find myself part of a spy organization, with codes and all the penny-dreadful trimmings, operating in dead earnestness and at the peril of our lives. Bali days seemed very long ago.

By day, then, I painted canvases, the quickly done, calendar-type pictures which I loathed, but which were greatly admired by the Japanese. I couldn't turn them out fast enough to keep up with the demand. Often I was surprised to find some high-ranking officer among my customers. I would have thought they would have better taste in art. I wondered if I was overdoing it a bit, and decided to paint only things I liked myself. This turned out much later to have been a very wise move.

And at night I became a playgirl, an habitué of the night clubs, a friend of the Japanese and especially of Frisco Flip. For a city at war, Surabaya was surprisingly lively—in fact, almost gay—at night. The fighting had moved thousands of miles to the east. Allied aircraft were busy defending Port Moresby and striking at Rabaul and at targets in the Solomons to give Japanese-held ports much trouble.

Popular jazz bands were playing at the leading night clubs. In addition to the Japanese patrons there was still a fair sprinkling of white clientele—Germans, Swiss, Swedes, and of course the pro-Nazi NSB Dutch who were collaborating with the Japanese. I must have been classed in this last category by most of the white people who looked speculatively about the night-club rooms.

The liquor stocks left by the Dutch—their Bols, their whiskeys and fine wines—were dwindling fast under the impact of Surabaya's night life. But the beer was plentiful—good Java beer—and rather soon some excellent Japanese beer and sake wine.

An interesting addition to the after-dark attractions of Surabaya was a group of geisha girls and a theatrical troupe, recently arrived from Tokyo. They were to tour Asia, entertaining the troops. The geisha girls were bright and charming, not at all the rough type I had expected. And full of informative chatter about conditions in

Nippon and elsewhere. The members of the theatrical troupe were most gracious. It was hard to associate them in any way with a war.

Early in the occupation of Java the Japanese allowed the Dutch women in the concentration camp at Surabaya to leave the camp once a week for two hours. This was to enable them to buy provisions for themselves. As yet the Japanese were not organized to feed so many thousands of internees. Malnutrition, bordering on starvation, was becoming all too common.

These poor, hollow-eyed women, foraging for food, had nothing but hatred in their eyes when they chanced on the streets to meet other white people who had not been interned. They could only assume that we were all working for and with the hated Japanese. The evidence of our well-fed good health understandably burned into their souls.

I was surprised, then, one day to be called upon by two Dutch women I had known well in Bali. We had never been particular friends then, and no more were we now. I was delighted to see them nonetheless, and was shocked and saddened at their account of the treatment in the internment camp.

"We are hungry all the time," they said. "But this is not our concern—it is our children. We cannot get milk or eggs or the other things they should have.

"We have heard that you have been spared from the concentration camp because of your Balinese name and background. Could you please help us to raise money to feed our children and those adults in the camp who have no money, or no jewels to sell?"

Their plan to raise funds was pitifully inadequate. They proposed to knit stockings and bellybands, which all the Japanese seemed to wear, and hoped that I would sell their products. A few of the women in the camp thought also that they might sketch pictures that could be sold to the art-loving Japanese.

I gave the women what little money I had, and promised to try and raise more by selling paintings of my own. I frankly doubted that I could be of assistance in their sales scheme. The Japanese would be wise in no time. I said I would find a way to get money to them, and asked them not to come to my house any more lest we all get into trouble.

That same night I told Frisco Flip about the deplorable conditions in the camp. "I shall see to it that the children get milk and eggs, and the mothers money," he said. We agreed that I would walk my little dog past the camp, and throw a bundle of money to a Dutch friend who would be waiting at a certain lonely place along the barbed-wire fence. The money came from Frisco Flip, who got it I knew not where. I dared not tell my Dutch friend the milk and food funds for the camp came from a Japanese.

Weeks had passed since I had heard from Agung Nura and I was beginning to worry. Then a courier arrived, with an envelope from Bali. The young man's face was very familiar; I could see that he was not a Balinese. "Don't I know you from somewhere?" I asked.

The courier gazed at me intently for a moment and then his face lit up with a pixy's grin. "Good American lady," he chanted. "You like good guide. I show you the way."

Pito! It couldn't be, but it was. The nine-year-old ragged urchin I had picked up on my first midnight ride in Java years ago, now grown into a handsome young man of eighteen or nineteen. We chatted happily.

"Your father, Pito, what of him?" I asked. "Remember, you told me the Dutch had kidnaped him and sent him to the land beyond the moon to die? Did you ever find him?"

"Oh, yes, indeed. My father was liberated from Tanah Merah when the Japanese came. He has always been a freedom worker for his country. Now he is in the underground with Amir Sjarifuddin, in West Java. That is how I have become a courier."

Pito said that when Anak Agung Nura asked him to take a letter to K'tut Tantri, he did not realize that this was the American lady he had met as a child. He remembered me well by my American name; I had not then, of course, taken a Balinese name.

Pito promised to visit me each time he passed through Surabaya. But three years were to pass before I saw him again.

The letter from Agung Nura asked that Frisco Flip send money and small firearms to Bali as soon as possible. All bank accounts in Bali had been frozen while the Japanese sorted out Dutch accounts from native accounts. The need for firearms needed no explanation.

At the factory Frisco Flip had managed somehow to fashion a crate with a false bottom. He brought it to my house, packed small weapons and ammunition into the bottom part, and filled the top part with books. Our problem was to get the shipment to Bali.

"We must find some deserted spot on the Java coast, and a loyal fisherman to sail the crate to Bali," said Flip. "It will not be easy, and it will take time. We'll have to be extremely careful. The Japanese have spies and informers everywhere."

"Perhaps I could run another car over to Bali, with the crate in the back," I suggested.

Flip said this would be much too dangerous. Besides, cars were now difficult to find. The Japanese had long since seized all the available private automobiles.

Some days later I learned that the Japanese theatrical troupe and the band of geisha girls had been ordered to go to Bali to entertain navy personnel. They would travel by special train to Banjuwangi, and then by a Japanese patrol boat across the Bali-Java Strait.

Calling at the hotel to say good-by to my little friends from Tokyo, I noticed that their stage props had been nicely crated, ready for transportation. Suddenly it dawned on me; here was the way to get our shipment of firearms to Bali. I got in touch with Frisco Flip immediately, and we worked out the details. I would ask the head of the theatrical troupe if I could go along with them to Bali. If they agreed, Frisco Flip would put our crate among the stage props. Since he was a Japanese, it should not be difficult to deceive the Indonesian guard.

All went well. The head of the troupe was delighted that I would accompany them. "We need someone to speak Balinese, to interpret for us," he said. "It would be pleasant, too, to have you as a guide."

It was necessary now to get the permission of the Japanese commandant to join the troupe going to Bali. "I am homesick for the sight of my Balinese family," I told him.

"Your family?" The commandant smiled knowingly. "You mean a particular member of the family, do you not? Your Balinese 'brother,' perhaps? For this family yearning you are even willing to travel with our singsong girls! What touching consideration—for a whole family in Bali!"

Chuckling to himself, he signed a pass for me and wrote a letter of introduction to the navy commander in Bali. Gratefully, I presented him with a large painting of a Javanese dancing girl. Delight shone in his eyes.

"Don't stay away from Surabaya too long," he said. "You have many Japanese friends here. They will miss you."

I looked at his kindly face and felt almost ashamed at my deception.

Frisco Flip delivered the crate to the prop manager, and I saw it stowed with the rest of the baggage. Then Flip and I had dinner in seclusion together, laughing at our private joke that the Japanese would be transporting the firearms that might be used against them.

The long train ride to Banjuwangi was another of the ironies of my life in the early part of the war. Here was I, a white woman in Indonesian dress, sharing in the song and revelry of show girls from Tokyo whiling time away. The geisha girls were hilarious, and sang the whole distance. I sang too, partly to banish worries over what might lie ahead for me. I am thankful now that I did not know what the future held in store.

A group of Japanese officers met the train at Banjuwangi. They raised their eyebrows in surprise when they saw me and read my pass. When they heard from the head of the troupe that I was a friend of the commandant, they smirked and exchanged sly looks. There was no doubt about it in their minds; I was the girl friend of the Commander in Chief. Many of the high Japanese officers had acquired white mistresses, most of them Dutch who preferred that kind of life to the concentration camp.

The Japanese cutter took us across the strait and in to Gilimanuk just after dark. All the way I worried about how I would retrieve my crate from the show props. I might better have eased my mind. It turned out to be almost too easy.

My fellow travelers were not in the least suspicious, nor should they have been. Was not my pass signed by their own highest authority? My friends found my crate and loaded it on a dokkar. "How heavy it is," one commented. My heart skipped a beat. I replied with what I hoped was nonchalance, "My books, I am taking them to the home of a Swiss artist, a friend living a few kilometers outside of the town."

Anak Agung Nura had given instructions that the firearms be delivered to a certain hideaway. It was almost midnight when I reached the place. Anak Agung Nura was astonished at first, and then—after hearing my story—horrified that I had undertaken such a risky venture. "How could Frisco Flip have been so foolish?" he raged. "Letting you travel with geisha girls, and on a warship! You might have been taken to Japan."

"Please, Nura," I replied. "It was not at all that bad. I was safe and comfortable and we had no trouble. We could think of no other way of getting the things here."

The arms were removed, and the books replaced, with speed. "I want you to come to my father's puri and stay there," Agung Nura said. Anticipating my refusal he added hurriedly, "At least for a few days. I am worried about you. Stay at the puri until I find out whether the Japanese are suspicious."

I shook my head. "It is much better that I go to the house of the Swiss," I said. "I have said I'm going there, and if I don't I may be missed. If all is well, I'll visit you at the puri in a few days. Right now, though, it would be unwise for me to leave a trail that might lead to you and your father."

Nura yielded to my reasoning. I reached the house of the Swiss just before daybreak. The artist was away from home, somewhere in Java, his servants said. But they knew me of course. There was no question when I said I would like to stay. They helped me put the crate in a back room. Then, utterly exhausted, I went to bed for a long, restful sleep.

Good sense dictated that I remain in the house, in hiding, for the next few days. But good sense has never been one of my conspicuous features. With nightfall I was restless again. I must find out, if I could, what was going on in Bali. I had made my way in the moonlight to the restaurant of a Chinese with whom I had long been friends, and whom I knew to be discreet. The Balinese for the most part, I knew from experience, were like inquisitive children, incapable of keeping a secret. Not so the Chinese; they tended to be close-mouthed, inscrutable. My Chinese friend gave a little clucking exclamation when he saw me.

"We heard that the Japs killed you in Java. How wonderful to see you alive!"

He beckoned me into a back room, away from curious stares, and readily responded to my hurried questions. The Japanese? Already they have become hated, far more than the Dutch in all the years of their rule. Arrogant and overbearing and brutal, they were. Both in Bali and in Java they had been rounding up thousands of Indonesians—men and women alike—from the kampongs and sending them into slave labor in other countries. Large numbers had been sent to Malaya and Burma.

And there was the question of food. Everywhere the Japanese were confiscating the rice crops and shipping them to support the Japanese troops throughout Southeast Asia. The Indonesians were beginning to hunger.

Too, the Japanese closed all the best hotels to Indonesians, treated even high Indonesian officials as gross inferiors. Resistance movements were spreading, consolidating. There had been many uprisings in Java, Sumatra, Borneo, and an especially violent outburst against the Nipponese in Blitar, in Java. Well-confirmed rumors had it that thousands of Indonesian intellectuals were arrested and shot.

I wanted to stay the night, but my friend warned me that it would not do to be found in a Chinese house. Back to my Swiss friend's house I went, my thoughts now turned to my beloved hotel, and to Wyjan, Njoman, and Maday. I must find them. Nura had told me that the hotel had been completely destroyed but I wanted to see for myself. Early the next morning I found a native with a dokkar and set out for Swara Negara, my "Sound of the Sea" hostelry.

My heart leaped as we came in sight of the sea, and the lovely white sweep of Kuta Beach, and my grove of date and coconut palms along the shore. But where was the hotel? And where were the beautiful guest bungalows that had blended so perfectly with the landscape that they were almost part of it?

As the rugged little horse pulled nearer, I could see that not one brick stood upon another. The great carved-stone statues were gone. The grove looked as though it had not been disturbed. The driver, seeing my distress, turned his eyes away. He murmured, "I thought you knew."

Stumbling to the ground, I ran to the spot where my own cottage had stood. Not a piece of bamboo remained; and of the magnificent temple, not a handful of coral. I ran about frantically, looking for a brick, a stone, some evidence that there had been a building anywhere. There was none. The only sign of human habitation was a row of ketalas, or native yams, planted across the ground.

My legs gave way under me. Sinking into the grass, I burst into tears. Could wars planned and declared in far lands do this to peaceful Bali? Why should such beauty, so lovingly wrought, be so wantonly destroyed?

I made my way to the headman of the nearest kampong, one of my friends of long ago, and I got the story from him. On the night of their landing the Japanese had bombed the airport. Terrified by the rain of explosives, my boys had fled from the grove, luckily before any were killed. "Then looters came down from the hills and swarmed all over Den Pasar, looting all that the Dutch had left," my friend said. "The Japanese were in possession of your hotel. They told the looters to tear it down, every stick, every stone. Nothing must stand that the hated white people had built." He paused, and sadly assured me: "The looters were not from the kampongs of this area. None of your friends did this to you. They were strangers from far parts of the island. When the Japanese told them to help themselves, to take, take, take—they went wild."

"My paintings," I moaned. "Eight years of work. I was just getting ready to send them to the United States for an exhibition. What of them?"

The paintings, I learned, had been loaded aboard a Japanese ship, along with my collection of Balinese art. My books had been scattered no one knew where. Nothing of mine—nothing whatever —remained.

To the house of the Swiss, late in the afternoon, came two Japanese officers of the naval police. What of the crate that had been in my possession? they asked. I had been seen removing it from the props of the dancing troupe and driving away with it. This information had come to the police, I learned, from a Balinese named Pageh, the collaborating manager of the Bali Hotel.

"The crate contained books from Java, for myself and some Balinese friends," I explained.

"Where is it now, that crate?"

"In a back room. I have been too tired to unpack it. Shall I open it for you?"

"We shall open the crate ourselves."

Ripped open, the crate produced nothing but books. Books on Japan, Japanese grammar books, Japanese fairy-tale books, Japanese history books.

They looked at me curiously, "Your papers, please," the officers demanded. My pass and papers plainly surprised and confused them.

They had not expected to see an order from the commandant that all Japanese should be helpful and pass the bearer and her personal effects safely between Java and Bali. I accepted their embarrassed apologies, and assured them that I knew it was their duty to be suspicious of anyone who might bring harm to Dai Nippon. We concluded our meeting with whiskey and soda all around, and they proposed a toast to the Tenno Haika, the Emperor of Japan.

Although it ended on an amicable note, the incident unnerved me. I must get out of Bali; I must first notify Anak Agung Nura. I hired a car from a Chinese and drove to the Rajah's puri. Somewhat to my surprise I found Nura calm and almost unconcerned. "You are unduly alarmed," he said. "The firearms have been disposed of, and absolutely no traces have been left behind. There is nothing whatever that the Japanese can pin on you." He urged me to wait out my half-imagined storm for a few more days.

Hardly had I returned to the Swiss artist's house when an invitation arrived from the Japanese naval commander to attend a feast honoring the theatrical troupe. I sent my regrets with the excuse that I was unwell, suffering from a dreadful headache. My would-be host refused to take no for an answer. His aide came to fetch me.

By this time I was thoroughly frightened. I tried hard to conceal my fears and chatted with my friends as animatedly as I could. The commandant was outwardly pleasant, but something warned me to be on my guard. "You have had much experience in running a hotel, I am told," he said. "How would you like to manage this very fine Bali Hotel for me? We need someone to keep it going well for our high officers, and visitors from Tokyo."

I assured him that I must return immediately to Java. "I promised the commandant in Surabaya not to stay away long, and I must keep my word," I said. He dropped the subject, but persisted in asking many searching questions about my relationship with the Rajah and his son. Somehow I lived through the evening. I was never more glad to have a party come to an end.

The following morning the summons came again. This time the commander offered me his protection. "You may stay in my house with me," he said. "You will be perfectly safe."

Of course I knew perfectly well what he meant. I refused his offer in polite terms, and repeated that I must return to Java. His manner became very brusque.

"What has the army to offer you that the navy cannot give?" he demanded. "You need not worry about the commandant in Surabaya. I have just learned that he is to be transferred to Makassar. You will be left without a protector. The war is young yet; this situation will go on for years."

I tried to explain that the commandant at Surabaya was not a "protector" but a friend, interested in my paintings.

"Rubbish," he barked. "Anyway, you cannot leave Bali without an exit permit from the navy. I shall see that you do not get it. Furthermore, you are not to go to the Rajah or his son. You are not to see them at all, or try to get in touch with them."

He began to question me about my life in Bali and about the natives I knew. "And why did you build your hotel next to the airport?" he asked. "Surely you knew that the Japanese would not allow you to live near it in wartime?"

I was trembling so violently I could hardly reply. "How could I know that someday Bali would be involved in a war between the Western nations and Japan?" I asked. "I did not build my hotel next to the airport. The airport built near me."

"So, if you are not going to move in with me, how will you live?" he gibed. "Have you money? There are no tourists any longer to buy your paintings."

"I shall go to the market and sell baskets, and straw mats, and bananas. I have found that you do not need much money to live in Bali."

"It would be ridiculous for a European woman to sit on her haunches selling bananas," he jeered. "We won't allow it."

I had heard, and I knew from experience, that the Japanese made indecent offers to women but did not use force. I was reminded of this when he said, "You may go now. Sooner or later you will be very glad to come to me."

The servants to whom I had attached myself had little food for themselves, let alone for me. I must forage on my own. And in spite of my boast to the Japanese commander, it was next to impossible to make a living. The same plight confronted a Balinese friend of mine who had owned an art shop but had had to close it after the occupation of Bali. She proposed that we try knitting woolen obis—belly-bands for the Japanese. "They all wear them," she said. "They are offering one guilder apiece. We can make thirty cents profit on each obi. With eggs two cents each, and bananas two for a cent, vegetables and fruits costing very little, we could get along."

We bought wool in the market and made obis with a strip of red and a strip of white. Our Japanese customers, whether they realized it or not, would be wearing the colors of the flag of the Indonesian freedom movement round their waists.

As I became more proficient in knitting I added a little blue yarn and knit in the word "merdeka," meaning freedom. My friend dissuaded me from this. "Suppose a Jap should show his obi to an Indonesian who would explain the meaning of merdeka—then where would you be?"

At the same time, however, my Balinese friend was sprinkling itch powder on every obi she delivered. It was a dangerous practice, except that the Japanese apparently never did figure out the origin of the skin rash around their stomachs.

So I knitted, rode around the town on a bicycle when I could, and gathered news here and there. Unlike the Dutch, the Japanese did not interfere with my friendship with the natives—so long as I remained in the city and did not venture out to my former home in the puri. Because there was a heavy fine and punishment for speaking English, I studied Japanese. The Japanese had opened a school for the natives where they were taught Japanese. Every evening my Indonesian friends would come to my house and teach me what they had learned that day. Since I spoke and wrote Balinese and Malay fairly well and had a liking for Oriental languages, I found Japanese comparatively easy. Whenever I met a Nipponese officer I practiced on him. The officers usually took the trouble to correct me, and they were eager too to practice their fragmentary English on me.

Word reached me that the commander had become extremely angry at my avoidance of him and at my ability to live without his assistance and was about to take some strong measures. It might be that he intended to compel me to live with him or that he planned to throw me into prison. In either case, it was imperative for me to get away quickly.

One of my Chinese friends was to be married the very next morning at six. I knew that the bridegroom had won the permission of the Japanese to charter an old bus to take his bride and some twenty members of their respective families to Java for a honeymoon trip.

I was aware, too, that the Chinese had never forgotten or forgiven the rape of Nanking. I knew that at heart they hated the Japanese and were only waiting for a chance to help remove them from conquered Indonesia.

The Chinese groom was entertaining all his friends at a party at his house. I called ostensibly to congratulate him, but really to ask for help. I told him I was in grave danger from the Japanese commander and asked his assistance in getting out of Bali. "Let me join your wedding party," I pleaded.

"I want to help you," he said. "But look at this!" It was the Japanese permit for the use of the bus.

"They have all our names listed here, and our ages. They have told us they will call our names as we enter the bus, and no one else will be allowed to get on. They will probably stop us a couple of times on the drive to Gilimanuk. And they will check again when we go aboard the patrol boat to be taken across the strait."

We talked a long time, and finally hit upon a plan that was dangerous but just might work. The bridegroom agreed to smuggle me into the bus before the wedding ceremony, and to hide me under a seat and cover me up with luggage and bedrolls. I promised that should I be discovered along the way I would say that I entered the bus and hid without the knowledge of any member of the wedding party.

I crept into the bus before daybreak. Shortly after sunrise we were on our way. There were a few bad moments when the Japanese called out the names as the wedding celebrants entered the bus. But since everyone was laughing and bustling around, the inside of the bus was not examined.

It is a long way to the western tip of Bali—some 250 kilometers. Twice the Japanese road patrols stopped the bus and ordered everyone out for a check of the names on the driver's pass. Under the luggage I tried to still my trembling with the philosophy that what was to be would be and that my fate was in the hands of the Bali gods. I was not discovered.

The road was rocky and rough; the jolting and bumping of the tin can of a bus bruised me badly. Exhaust fumes accumulating under the seats made me feel faint. The intense heat and the lack of air caused me almost to suffocate. After five hours of this I was relieved indeed to have the bus stop and discharge me at a lonely stretch of beach. I thanked my Chinese friends tearfully for making good my escape and for the money they pressed on me knowing that I had no time to arrange for such necessities before my departure. The bridegroom promised that on his return to Bali he would inform Agung Nura of my delivery from under the nose of the Japanese.

The gods were surely with me, for everything went as I had planned. It was only a mile to the fishermen's shack where two Madurese acquaintances lived. They sailed me across the strait in darkness and put me ashore at a point on Java where I would certainly meet no Japanese. Even if I did, I had the pass of the Japanese commandant of Surabaya to clear my way. But happy as I was to be out of Den Pasar and the domain of the Japanese naval officer, could I have foreseen what lay ahead for me in Java I might have been wiser to stay in Bali—at any price.

3

A PRISONER OF THE JAPANESE

I came back to Surabaya from Bali bruised, weary, worn, and filthy dirty, and a nervous wreck. Sneaking into my house after dark, I phoned Frisco Flip to find the professor and come as quickly as possible. They were aghast at my story and my appearance, but joined me in a toast to the success of the journey. "Let's hope that the firearms in Bali will be put to good use by Anak Agung Nura," said Flip. "And the navy commander is the first victim!"

My colleagues informed me that my good friend, the Surabaya commandant, had indeed been transferred to Celebes, the gossip being that he was considered a bit too soft to be stationed in a key city. Since then the Japanese had tightened their controls over Surabaya considerably. It was necessary now to lie low for a while and not to see each other.

The honorable professor said he would go to Batavia and scout around, work his way down the coast, and return in a few weeks' time. Flip said I should not venture out of the house until we found out the attitude of the new commandant. He, Flip, would go about his work as usual, and only visit me if anything extremely important developed. We said good-by to the professor.

Three weeks passed without word from the professor. Flip became increasingly worried and started inquiries through the grapevine. Then one day he came to my house in great agitation.

"The professor has been arrested," he said. "The Japanese Kempetai [Gestapo] police caught him at Cheribon. He's been charged with espionage."

I stared at Flip, unwilling to believe my ears. "That wonderful old man," I sobbed.

Flip's tone was matter-of-fact. "We have no time now to be upset or sentimental," he said. "You must get out of here immediately; it will only be a matter of time—hours perhaps—before the police come looking for you."

"And what about you, Frisco Flip?" I asked. "What will you do?"

"Nothing." His face was glum. "I don't think I am under suspicion; otherwise I would have been arrested by now. After all, I am a Japanese. Remember that."

We decided that I should go to Solo and take refuge in the puri of one of Agung Nura's titled friends. There were no more train departures that night; I would have to go the first thing in the morning.

Flip said not to worry about him. He would leave on the following day, to visit a factory some miles from Surabaya. That might give him a chance to find out what the Japanese knew about him. We drank a farewell toast to President Roosevelt—and he slipped out into the darkness. I spent the evening assembling my belongings and destroying incriminating letters and papers in my possession.

I should have known that my activities on behalf of the Indonesian freedom movement would one day lead me into serious trouble with the Japanese occupation forces. Yet, like so many who ally themselves to a cause, I only visualized danger for my fellow comrades. Although rumor came persistently from a good source— the servants of a Japanese officer in the next block—of frequent house-to-house raids in the district, I still felt safe. Until that next morning, at least, when I planned to be off to Solo.

Very early, long before time to prepare to go to the railway station, a pounding on the door jolted me out of my sleep. Dazed and frightened I called out, "Who is there?"

"Open the door," shouted a man's impatient voice. "The Kempetai."

The Kempetai! My spine froze. Jumping up, I dropped my night sarong and started to pull a dress over my head. My hands trembled so violently I could hardly use them. Still fumbling with buttons, I snatched letters and papers and my American passport from the bureau drawers and stuffed them under the mattress. Then I ran to the door, on which the pounding had risen to a crescendo.

Two Japanese officers stepped quickly out of the shadows. The entrance light gleamed on their large round horn-rimmed spectacles. They marched in, holding themselves stiffly erect, and without a word of explanation began to search the living room. I scurried into the bedroom to finish dressing. I would feel more adequate to face the terror ahead in shoes and stockings.

In less than a minute one of the men entered the bedroom, brushed past me, walked directly to the bed, and pulled the letters from their ridiculous hiding place.

"Come on outside and get in the car" were the first words I heard.

"Where are we going?" I asked, my voice quivering with fear.

"For a ride. You'll find out soon enough."

Running to the bureau, I showed the officer my pass signed by the commandant. He brushed it aside. "That will do you no good now," he growled. "You are an American citizen, and now we have your passport to prove it."

"But of what am I accused?" I asked.

"You'll soon know." It was the only answer I could get.

Having filled a suitcase with my papers and documents, they marched me out into the faint daylight to a waiting staff car.

We drove away. Outwardly I tried to appear calm. Inside I was tortured with apprehensions. After an eternity of two, three, perhaps four hours the car slowed. I caught a glimpse of red-brick buildings and recognized the familiar large town of Kediri, East Java. We stopped beside a grim, gray structure—a prison, I knew, by the look and feel of it. A guard led me into a cell—a cage, really, closed on three sides, with the fourth side an iron grille looking onto a narrow hall where Japanese sentries paraded back and forth. On the floor of my cell was a filthy mat of palm and another mat rolled around a handful of straw. The only other feature to be seen was a hole in the earthen floor—the toilet, I discovered later—with a bucket of dirty water beside it. This, then, was what it meant to be a prisoner of the Japanese.

For five or six days or maybe a week—it was hard to keep count—nothing much happened. Twice a day a banana leaf of rice was handed to me through the bars; little better than a starvation diet. I must have lost ten pounds in that first week.

At daylight each morning the guard came down the corridor, down the line of tiny cells just like mine, each with its occupant. We had orders always in the daytime to kneel, with hands clasped in front of us. The guard carried a long pole, with which he prodded us like beasts if we were not already on our knees. I could hear the whack of the pole on the heads of prisoners as he passed from cell to cell. All day long, from six in the morning until nine at night, we were required to remain on our knees, never allowed to sit no matter how sharply our muscles pained.

The first feeding, a little rice and salt, came at eleven in the morning. The next meal was at night. After the evening meal we fell over on our mats, often shivering with fear and exhaustion, trying to sleep on our arms to avoid the lice in our straw. There was no such thing as a bath; no water, even, to wash our faces. No combing of hair, no fresh clothes. Worst of all, there was no privacy. The dirt, squalor, and hunger were weapons to break down our morale, but the most bitter indignity was the guard's persistent staring to humiliate us when we were compelled to use the loathsome little holes in the floor.

There had been no charge against me, or an indictment or trial or punishment. But a day came when I was called out of my cell and taken to an interrogation room around which were seated several Japanese officers. For some minutes questions were put to me, based obviously on my papers which they had seized. This telegram from the Duff Coopers, the letters from Selby-Walker, Far Eastern director for Reuter's—how did I happen to have them? If they had been guests at my hotel, then how had that happened? What other communications had I with people of some importance?

My replies gave them no satisfaction. "Of what am I accused?" I cried. "Why are you holding me here?"

"You are an American spy. You must give us your FBI number."

An American secret agent! I almost laughed. "Absolutely not," I replied. "That is ridiculous, and quite untrue." I did not elaborate to my interrogators, of course, but time and time again Frisco Flip had told me that we were on our own, with no tie whatever with American intelligence. He insisted that he had been doing his duty as an American citizen, just as the professor had performed his duty for China, an ally of the United States.

The seated Japanese showed impatience at my responses. My chief questioner scowled fiercely, and his eyes began to flicker with a terrifying yellow light.

"Take off your clothes," he ordered. I stiffened, paralyzed with shame, and a young lieutenant tore off my one garment.

"Stand on one leg," the interrogator barked. "Now raise the other with the knee bent." When I was slow to comply he slapped me. "No, not that way!" he roared. "Turn it out."

Sobbing with humiliation, I complied. Later, much later, I grew so hardened that I began to undress automatically as soon as the door of the examination room closed behind me, but on this first morning the emotional torture was worse than that of any burn or blow.

"A very dangerous spy has been arrested," my interrogator told me. "A Chinese masquerading as a sarong peddler on the streets of Surabaya. He visited you several times. You were spying with him."

I knew that it would be of no use to deny the visits of the professor. They could easily worm out of my servants the fact that he had sold his wares at my house.

"The streets of Surabaya are full of Chinese peddlers selling all sorts of goods," I said. "They would come around to my house, and several times I bought sarongs from them, for the servants and for myself. That is all they were as far as I knew—just peddlers."

At each question I was struck with a bamboo stick that raised welts on my back. I winced and shrank with each blow, but as the pain and shame increased the punishment became less effective. A sort of numbing reaction, both mental and physical, hardened me to the brutality.

Besides, I was sure the professor had told them nothing. He had cautioned me always to have the servants present when he came to the house, so they could hear us squabble over the price of his goods. Had the professor confessed, the Japanese would have confronted me with his statement. If they had real information about me they would not have made the absurd accusation about an American agent with a spy number. They were guessing in the dark.

I was returned to my cell for another day of filth and lice and waiting. Each morning I was brought back to the room, and again stripped, grilled, and subjected to beatings and indignities. Again and again I was asked about the Duff Coopers, Captain Kilkenny, the American consul, the Chinese peddler, my official spy number, Colonel R. of the American army, and so on. At last they brought in papers. "This is the full confession of the Chinese peddler," the prison officer said. "He has told us all about you."

"May I see it?" I asked.

He handed me a sheet of paper written in Chinese characters, and said, "See—here is his signature." Weeks earlier the professor and Flip and I had agreed on certain little signs in our writing so that we could detect attempts at forgery. I knew at a glance that this was not the professor's doing, this so-called confession.

The Japanese were full of tricks. Another time they came in with an official-looking document and said that American intelligence had admitted I was one of their agents and had offered to exchange me for a Japanese spy who had been arrested in America. This was such an obvious fake that I almost laughed in the face of the inquisitor.

Next my interrogator confronted me with the accusation that I had been the driver and interpreter for an American colonel. He had flown away and left me behind to spy on the Japanese and to relay information over a secret radio transmitter hidden in the hills. "The secret station sent out very accurate reports on our activities, especially in Bali," he said. "We know without a doubt that this information came straight from you. You were in a position to gather the information. You must tell us how you got it and what you did with it, or you will go through tortures that will make the punishment you already have received seem like children's games."

Other questions dealt with my mysterious departure from Bali. "The navy commander in Bali notified our new commandant of Surabaya to be on the lookout for you," the interrogator said. "He wrote that you were forbidden to leave the island, but that you escaped somehow. We want to know who made it possible for you to get away."

Here at last I could give them an answer, and could twist the truth and still sound convincing. "I left Bali without an exit visa because I was afraid of the navy commander," I said. "He wanted me to live with him. I walked to Gilimanuk and crossed the strait with some fishermen I did not know and could not recognize if I saw them again."

"Tell us more about the commander's requirement that you live with him."

I related the whole story of the naval officer's approaches. When I came to the commander's angry query, "What has the Japanese army got that the Japanese navy hasn't?" My interrogators chortled. They laughed loudly among themselves at what they plainly considered a fine joke on the navy.

The ten days or two weeks of questioning were a nightmare. At times it all seemed unreal to me. It couldn't possibly have happened. The beatings, the black bruises, the standing stark-naked before my damnable torturers, brought me back to reality. Life had now become something hardly to be endured, a succession of miseries and horrors.

My failure to confess to knowing anything about a secret radio transmitter stung my inquisitors more than anything else. They decided to try a new refinement of torture. "If you will not tell us the truth, you shall walk the streets of Kediri naked," they said. "Everyone in Kediri shall see your shame. Your Indonesian friends will have the amusement of seeing you as the Japanese see you."

Never let it be said that the Japanese were not as good as their word. They ripped off the last pitiful bit of covering I had. In my hair they attached a large sign reading in Malay: THE YANKEE MATA HARI. And with bayonets they forced me to walk down the very center of the street.

But the Japanese had not reckoned with the Indonesian mentality. Javanese are frank about the facts of life, but modest. One glimpse of what the Japanese were doing to me and they were horrified. They fled in every direction. Doors and windows were slammed shut. No one remained on the street but the Japanese—now feeling somewhat foolish—and the bruised, filthy, dazed, and unclad white woman they were trying to deprave and unnerve. My tormentors hurried me back to the prison for another severe beating, and then tossed me into my cell. But they knew that they had, somehow, lost face. This time, in spite of the violation of my modesty, I had been the winner.

The Japanese themselves were a complex people, I was to find. Sometimes the interrogators could be human. Late one night I was pulled out of my cell, questioned persistently about the Chinese peddler, and beaten with a big pole on my shoulders and around my hips until I collapsed with pain. When the interrogation was over and I still had not confessed, the interrogators' attitude changed a little. "Would you like to have a plate of bami with us?" he asked.

Any other time a plate of bami would have sounded like heaven, for I was half starved. But the thought of taking food in front of the men who had beaten me black and blue was, to say the least, repugnant. They insisted that I eat. With the first mouthful I started to vomit, and then burst into tears. One of the inquisitors astonishingly stepped forward, with compassion on his face, and started feeding me with a spoon and stroking my hair. "Kasian, kasian, djangan menangis," he said. "What a pity. Don't cry."

On another evening I was lying huddled up on my straw mat in a corner of my cell, looking more like a bedraggled animal than a human being. I was feeling at my lowest ebb and wished that death might relieve me of this interminable torture. A little Japanese cell guard called me over to the iron grille. "Are you feeling ill, Tanchan?" he asked.

I answered that I was indeed feeling half dead.

"Would you like me to sing for you?" he asked. "All the officers have gone to a feast. I can sing you a nice song."

In spite of myself I smiled at his earnestness. In my condition I had no desire to listen to songs. But he meant well.

"Sing me one of those soft Japanese lullabies that mothers croon to their children," I suggested.

"Oh, no. I want to sing you a nice American song, 'Love in the Wilderness.' You know it?"

I confessed that I had never heard of it. The little soldier stood there in front of the bars, then, and warbled what he believed to be one of the best popular selections from the Hit Parade. It was strangely touching. To my expression of thanks he responded, "When I have a chance I will sing you more American songs."

One morning another guard asked me if I would like a hot shower. "That would be a real blessing," I told him disbelievingly. He led me across the courtyard to a series of little cubicles, each with a shower, and pushed me into one of them.

"May I have a towel and soap?" I asked hopefully. His reply was rough: "Do you think this is a hotel? Be glad you have water!"

Pulling off my dress I stepped under the shower. I was about to turn on the water when I chanced to look up at the transom. Two guards were peering through, broad grins on their faces.

The men were not leering. I was beginning to understand that nakedness means nothing to the Japanese. But they knew that it tortured a white woman to be seen naked. I realized that these two were enjoying not my nudity but my humiliation. For a moment, conscious of my ugly, bruised body, I wanted to scream and snatch my dress. But the desire for a bath was stronger. I ignored the watchers, turned on the water, and glorified in my first bath in prison for as long as the guard would let me.

After three weeks of almost daily examination, the commandant for some inscrutable reason set me free. But first he took me into his office, motioned for me to sit under a picture of a Balinese temple, and invited me to broadcast to America for the Japanese. "You will have a fine house, money, a car, a radio, every luxury," he promised.

"I could not even consider it." Even after being weakened by the treatment of the Japanese I had plenty of strength to stand firm on this issue. "What would you think of a Japanese girl who would broadcast against her own people for America, and in time of war?" I asked.

"No Japanese girl would."

"And neither would an American girl broadcast for the Japanese."

He smiled slightly, and said no more about it.

Free! At first I was too numbed, too dispirited to care. A young Japanese officer took me to the railway station and found seats for both of us in a compartment of the train to Surabaya. My dress was scarcely decent, held together only by a few pins. My bare feet were dirty. On the train the Indonesians looked at me with disdain; a white girl of the Japanese.

The smug brick houses of Kediri gave way to sawah fields with their little black-thatched temples etched against patches of green or gold. With each click of the rails, with each mile that took me farther from the hell that I had known, my spirits rose. The young officer sensed my mood and smiled at me. "I like Java—I like it very much," he said impulsively. "This is my first posting away from home. I always wanted to visit strange lands and see other peoples. I am sorry that my chance to do so came only through a war."

He watched the changing scenery in silence for a few moments, and then he resumed his theme.

"We ought not to hate each other," he said. "Why should we not like each other? The Japanese people have no hatred for individual Americans.

"There is one good aspect to this war, to my way of thinking. For hundreds of years the white races have treated the Japanese as inferiors, as little more than slant-eyed monkeys. The 'yellow peril' sort of thing.

"In their hearts the educated Japanese have known that cultured people of all races are equal. Now all through Southeast Asia we have seen the whites bowing low to the Japanese. No matter how the final victory goes, my people will never again feel inferior."

I would say that his thinking was typical of that of most of the Japanese—of the reasonable Japanese. Of course, there were fanatics on both sides.

At my house he held out his hand. "We could be friends," he said.

Safe in my own doorway, I felt almost affectionate toward him. "It was a pleasant journey," I said. "I feel that we are friends." For a moment I had forgotten the beatings, the humiliation. So elastic is the human spirit that I had even forgotten the brutal Kempetai officers.

4

SOME REFINEMENTS OF TORTURE

It was a dream come true to return to the privacy, the cleanliness, the peaceful quiet, the sheer luxury of my own house in Surabaya. Never had food tasted so good as the simple fare the servants produced. I spent hours under the shower, scrubbing away the prison grime. At last I could give some attention to my hair, my nails, my clothing, my general appearance. Never once did I venture outside; I had no wish to jeopardize my new-found freedom.

In spite of everything my security was brief. On the third morning after my return a Japanese car drew up to the door and two officers ordered me to come with them to the City Hall. These were not Kempetai, I learned, but PID—Political Intelligence Division. Their reputation was less evil than that of the Kempetai. Perhaps they were taking me in because I had failed to register.

At the City Hall the European residents of Surabaya were queuing up for registration. Lines of them stretched out into the street. They watched without expression as we pushed by and proceeded to the offices of the chief of police on the top floor. The chief, a poker-faced little man with piercing eyes, glared hard at me. As I sat before a great desk the room began to fill with officers, eying me as though I were some rare bird. "Ah, so this is the Yankee spy!" they exclaimed, brushing against me and flicking me with the ashes of their cigarettes.

At this moment the air-raid siren wailed. The police commissioner jumped up and all the officers left the room, trying not to seem hurried. A moment later the commissioner returned with a guard.

"Keep your gun on her," he instructed. "If she tries to get away, shoot." Then he left, his heels clicking rapidly down the corridor.

A great hush settled on the building and the street. It seemed as though the guard and I were the only two people left in the world. Both of us realized that we were almost next door to the airport and on the top floor. We could not be in a more dangerous spot.

I don't know which of us was the more afraid. My hands were icy cold; his face was a sickly green. His finger on the trigger trembled. I was afraid the gun might fire at any moment.

Into the middle of the silence plunged a high-pitched whine and then an explosion. For what seemed more than an hour bombs exploded all round. The building quivered and bits of plaster gave way but, miraculously, each time we remained alive. This heavy raid, by the big American bombers, was much more harrowing than the attacks by Japanese aircraft at Den Pasar had been. By the time the "all clear" sounded the Japanese guard and I could have embraced each other. Inadvertently we had provided each other with the solace of human companionship in the face of death.

Once it became apparent that there would be no further bombs the building came quickly to life. As the officers trooped back one of them walked over and struck me a sharp blow on the face.

"You are happy, aren't you?" he growled. "You knew those were Yankee planes."

I protested that I was not happy. "I do not like to see innocent people killed by bombs, no matter who they are," I said. "I do not like war."

The mood of my captors had changed. I was no longer that curious, somewhat glamorous creature, the girl spy. I was the enemy; I could feel the force of their hatred.

They motioned me out of the chair and we returned to the street, cutting a way through the lines of Dutch registrants. As we neared the car I saw several acquaintances in the line. They noted the officers and the automobile, and stared at me with contempt. When one of the officers opened the door and ushered me into the back seat with a gesture of mocking courtesy, I knew what the Dutch must suspect. "You fools—don't you see I'm a prisoner of the Japanese?" I wanted to shout. I dared not say a word.

Whether the Japanese had intended to imprison me again I will never know. I believe, however, that my unfortunate appearance at the City Hall at the precise moment of an air raid completely destroyed whatever chance of release I might otherwise have had. I found my next confinement quarters to be a cell underneath the Surabaya Kempetai Headquarters. I was quickly informed that what I had suffered at the hands of the Japanese in Kediri had been as nothing compared with what I would go through in the Surabaya Kempetai.

No use to wonder what new crime the Japanese had found against me. Hope is strong. For eight days no one came to my cell. Who were in the other cells I did not know. Sometimes I could hear them shrieking or babbling to themselves.

The interlude of quiet came to an end. The guard took me out of my cell for questioning. One glance at the room—a large hook suspended from the ceiling, a table beneath it—told me that this was a torture chamber. I shuddered, and my bones felt as though they were melting away. The two officers at the table might well have come straight from the Kediri Kempetai.

They quickly told me why I had been imprisoned. They had been in touch with the Kempetai in Kediri, they said, and had learned that I had not yet confessed to associating with traitors, a group of pro-Ally Japanese. The Japanese army had a few of these, they said, but gradually they were being discovered and "removed."

At first they were reasonably gentle, trying to make me talk. "If you will tell us everything, we will give you complete immunity from punishment," they said. "Give us the name of the Japanese you associated with. Why should you shelter him?"

Again I knew that they were not sure of their ground. I insisted that of all the Japanese I had associated with not one discussed anything with me except art and literature. The grilling became sharper. Between demands, "Now will you tell us what information your Japanese friends gave you?" a questioner would cuff me in the face. Each time he hit harder. Before long I had been battered into semiconsciousness. I heard them say finally, "We have arrested your friend. Unless you give us a confession of your dealings with him we will bring him in and hang you both naked, face to face, until you are dead." Dimly I realized that they did not know about Frisco Flip. Again they were groping in the dark.

With this they stood me on the table, tied my hands behind my back, fastened my elbows together, and then—twisting my arms backward in their sockets—looped my hands over the hook that dangled from the ceiling. Inch by inch they moved the table away, demanding with each pull that I tell them what information I had received, and from whom.

The pain of my dislocated arms was so excruciating that I writhed from side to side. The veins in my temples felt as though they were about to burst. Sweat poured down my face; I could feel it dripping on my half-naked breasts where my dress was torn away. I clenched my teeth. I could see Flip's kindly face, could hear him say, "Take half my salary to buy milk for the hungry Dutch children in the concentration camp."

With a last pull the table slid from under my feet. My weight fell full on my arms. I was hanging. I screamed in unbearable agony.

"Dear God," I prayed, "close my mouth. Don't let me spit out the words that are on my lips."

Blood drooled from the corners of my mouth. My tongue moved with a volition of its own. It twisted to speak. No human being could endure such pain any longer. But as my mouth tried to form the words, blackness swallowed me. The last thing my mind registered was a newspaper in the torturer's hands. He sat with his face behind it, pretending to read. But the paper was upside down, I noticed even in my agony.

When my mind cleared I was on the floor and the examiner was pouring cold tea down my throat. Then the guards carried me back to my cell. For days I lay on a mat half paralyzed, tossing with fever, unable to feed myself. It was several weeks before I could raise my arms.

One day a woman was dragged into my cell screaming and kicking at her jailers. At that time I was so ill from the relentless cruelty that I could not even sit up. The new arrival had evidently been beaten badly too. Her face and arms were a mass of bruises.

When the guards went away she just sat and stared at me. After a while she broke her silence. "How long have you been in this place?" she asked. "What have they done to you? You look like a female Monte Cristo."

I remained silent at first. Sometimes the Japanese put prisoners in to spy for them. Studying her, however, I concluded that she had been so terribly beaten that she would hardly be willing to work for the Japanese. I told her I had been accused of being an Allied spy.

"And I was arrested for listening to the BBC radio broadcasts from England and passing the war news to the other doctors at the Surabaya hospital," she said. "I am a doctor, Polish, but I have registered as a German. I am one of the head doctors at the hospital. An Indo-Dutch doctor was jealous of my position and informed on me to the Kempetai. They mauled me, dragged me from my house, and took my two little sons away. I do not know what has become of them, and I am crazy with worry."

My cellmate was obviously in great pain and mentally distressed. I asked her if she would like some aspirin. "I would give the world for an aspirin, but how is it that you have aspirin?" she asked. I drew the box from its hiding place and handed it to her. The printing on the box and the directions were in German. She read it with a puzzled expression, then asked where I had found the pills.

"I had been ill for days, lying on my mat hardly able to move. I was alone in the cell," I told her. "A young Japanese guard became worried, especially when I was brought back half dead after each interrogation. He was a sympathetic little chap. One day he asked me if I could use some aspirin, and I told him that if he got me an aspirin I would be able to forgive his people for much.

"He managed for a while to steal one aspirin a night from the first-aid department. Then one night he told me, 'Tanchan'—my

Japanese nickname—'something dreadful has happened to me: I am to be transferred to the prison at Cheribon, and I shall never be able to get you aspirin again. But tonight I shall steal the whole box, and you must hide it and take just one a day. If it is ever discovered, you must say you brought it into the cell hidden under your sarong, otherwise I shall lose my head.' "

The Polish doctor laughed until her eyes watered. "You know what these are, these German pills?" She choked. "This is an aphrodisiac, for old men to make them feel young again. Monkey-gland pills. No wonder you are ill. Do you think the guard gave them to you on purpose?"

I was sure that he had not. He could not read German, and they certainly looked like aspirin. It was funny in a way, but I was too sick to laugh.

Still the tortures went on. Burning me with cigarette ends was not pleasure enough for my new tormentor, an officer I called the Green Ape because of his green eyeshade, which reflected a sickly green color over his face. It was his pleasure to beat me black and blue and then to play with a bluebird that flew about the room attached to his chair by a string.

Calling it to his finger, he would talk to the bird in poetic phrases. "Of what are your thoughts, little one? What strange sights favor you that are hidden from our eyes? What beauties beyond those known to mortals?" Then he would reach over and whack me almost unconscious.

Another guard, who, I learned, had been a newspaper reporter in Tokyo before the war, was intensely interested in everything American. One day he said, as he brought in the morning rice, "Tanchan, don't you think I should have an American name? Can't you think of a nice one for me? Come, Tanchan, give me a list."

"If I do, will you give me a lump of sugar and half a cup of hot water?"

"Yes," he promised. "Two lumps."

The next morning, before the officers were around, he slipped me two stolen sugar lumps and a tin of hot water. This precious sugar would give me a little energy for the day ahead.

"Have you thought of a name yet?" he asked.

I hadn't, but the lumps of sugar gave me an inspiration. "I've a good one," I said. "How would you like 'Sugar Daddy'?"

"Suga daddee, suga daddee," he tried it out. "Sounds fine, like the name of an opera star." It was not easy to understand each other. He relied chiefly on Japanese and broken English and I on Malay.

A bit dubious about his new name, the guard went to some of the other prisoners who knew English. What did Sugar Daddy mean? They explained that sugar was just as the American woman had said —something sweet. Applied to "father." He was very pleased, and thereafter answered to his new name.

We could talk on simple things, we two, but on abstract ideas our words failed us. Sugar Daddy was something of a philosopher, and used to say, "Tanchan, how can you take so much and still not hate us?" We agreed that there was no good in hating people, only a system. There were good and bad people. It would be foolish to hate them all.

Sugar Daddy did what little kindness he could when the officers were away, and everyone liked him. It distressed and embarrassed him that my dress should be so torn that it was positively indecent.

"Don't worry, Sugar Daddy," I would say. "They can't keep me here forever." But he would shake his head.

"You don't know. It might be months, maybe years."

One of the prisoners, a beautiful half-caste girl who always came back from examinations on her own feet and with a smile on her face, had three dresses—three pretty calico prints that she kept washed and fresh. Prisoners, with no serious charge against them, were allowed to have two dresses, the one they wore and a change. But Sugar Daddy had been making observations.

"Let me see what you have in your bag," he said to her. "Bring it here to the bars—everything." She obeyed reluctantly, presenting a little wicker bag but holding onto it tight.

"Um-hum, just as I thought." Sugar Daddy pulled two dresses out through the bars and looked them over carefully. "Here, Tanchan, stand up. This ought to fit you." He made me come to the bars and, sticking his hands through, held it up to me. "Yes, just about right but a little too long. Go behind the screen and try it on." I had to do it, although I knew the half-caste girl would never forgive me. The other women in the cell looked on with malicious pleasure. They all distrusted the girl with the three dresses.

Sugar Daddy paid no attention to her grumbling. Cocking his head he looked me over, pleased with the effect. "Very pretty, Tanchan. But I still think it would look better if it weren't so long."

For some reason, probably because I was an American, the girl spy, the Yankee Mata Hari, I was Sugar Daddy's favorite. He felt that I was a celebrity, and he puffed with pride when high-ranking officers came to have a look at me. Often they swung their Samurai swords at me with remarkable precision, and just when I expected the blade to slice into my skull, they held up a neatly snipped lock of my hair. It was in such demand for souvenirs that presently I looked as though I were wearing a fright wig that had been thoroughly chewed by rats. Even the guards indulged in more childish antics with me than with the other prisoners, playing tricks on me such as sticking a piece of paper to my forehead on which was written, "I am a spy of the Allies." However, they had more humor than ill will in their voices as they shouted "monkey" and other unflattering terms at me.

Some of the other women were not so well liked. The Polish doctor, for instance. She sullenly refused to co-operate with the Japanese in any way. She was a distinguished physician, fluent in German and Dutch, yet when they brought her bottles of German or Dutch medicines and asked her what they were, she shook her head stubbornly and muttered, "I don't know." Even when they told her the medicines were for her own people, she refused to identify them.

But the doctor and the rest of the women in the cell were not political prisoners, as I was. They had simply broken ordinances. They were beaten and knocked about but they did not suffer the more refined tortures reserved for political prisoners—the knives on the end of bamboo poles, the tapers for burning one's pubic hair, the pencils with which the fingers were twisted out of joint, the hangings, and worst of all the faked deaths. That last, to me, was the most grueling of all the prison experiences.

The Japanese officers came to my cell late at night, and talked to me in very quiet and serious voices. "We have decided that there is no use going on with this," they said. "We have got nowhere; you have refused to tell us the truth. We know that you are guilty of espionage. Therefore, tomorrow at daybreak you will be shot."

I listened dully, not clearly comprehending, not deeply caring. I had suffered so much that the pronouncement that I would be put out of my misery was almost welcome. If I lived I could see no hope of escape from the continual hounding of my captors. I was sick and in constant pain. I felt I could not much longer stand the beatings and hangings—I had by now been hanged by my arms three times, each time fainting before I could blurt out what the Japanese wanted to hear. I knew that if I confessed to my dealings with my friends— Agung Nura, the professor, the American-born Japanese—I would not save my own neck, and would certainly bring them to torture and death. So if one had to die, better to die alone, saying nothing. It is curious, but I know now that if one can withstand the interrogations at the beginning without confessing, one gets stubborn with hate, and torture is less and less likely to loosen the tongue. It is the beginning that is terrifying. I was now at the end. Death would mean only release from the Japanese.

The officers waited to see if the execution pronouncement would induce in me a change of heart. "We are giving you right now your last chance to tell everything," they said. "If you do give us a complete confession, we will nurse you back to health and send you back to the Rajah in Bali to live in peace until Japan and Germany have whipped America and her allies. This is your last chance to avoid the firing squad."

All I could do was to say what I had said many times before. "I don't know what you are talking about. I can't confess to something I don't know."

The Japanese officers came very early the following morning. This time I could not even stand up unassisted. They had to carry me from my cell and out into the courtyard. They bound my hands behind my back, and tied me against a banyan tree with branches that hung down to the ground like the tentacles of an octopus. They blindfolded me, and once again one of the officers spoke: "You still have time to confess. I will count to three. If you say nothing, on the third count you will be dead. You will be with your ancestors."

His voice seemed far, far away. I heard the count in Malay. "Satu." I braced myself. "Duah." Now, now it will come. "Tiga." The shattering roar of the rifle staggered me. Almost at the same moment I felt something hot and sharp hit my chest. Everything turned black, and I fell to the ground.

When consciousness returned I was back in my cell. The Polish doctor was bending over me, feeling my pulse. I vaguely realized that somehow I was still alive.

"She is dying!" I heard the Polish woman shout. "She is dying!" Turning to the guard, not Sugar Daddy but the cruel one who prodded us, she screamed, "You must do something!" She ran to her corner and, returning, threw over me her most precious possession, the blanket she had brought from home.

"She's in shock. Can't you see? Get someone, quick." Dully I heard the guard unlock the gate and drag her into the corridor. The whacks of his pole and her screams had no meaning for me. I was past caring; these things had no reality. Again I blacked out.

Several days later I awoke in an Indonesian hospital. The Indonesian doctor and nurse told me I had been unconscious and delirious, and they did not expect me to live. They said the Japanese had fired their rifles into the air, and at the same moment had hit me with a stone from a catapult. The intent had been to make me think I had been shot. It succeeded only too well.

"The Polish doctor saved you," they said. "She convinced the Japanese that unless they got you to a hospital immediately you would die in the cell. We do not know what the Japanese have done with her. All they said was that you were to be placed in a third-class ward. No favors are to be shown, but you are to be kept alive at all costs. The Kempetai, they said, is not yet through with you."

I was in the Simpang Hospital in Surabaya. My memory was almost gone and my arms were paralyzed. But it was heaven to wake up and see friendly, smiling Javanese faces. I was terrified of most people, and would let near me only those I took, in my semidelirium, to be trustworthy. Whenever a Japanese came into the ward I became so violent, screaming and threshing about, that the doctor finally had to screen my bed from the rest of the ward. I was in the poorest part of the hospital, with the most broken-down human derelicts; but the contrast with my prison life was so great that this seemed sheer luxury.

"You are not trying hard enough to get well," the Indonesian doctor told me one day. "You must hold on, and have the will to live. Perhaps it will help you if I tell you some of the news reports that have been coming in. The Americans have been winning some great land and sea battles near New Guinea and in the Central Pacific. Over in Europe the Germans have been retreating under British fire. The Russians are holding their own. It now begins to appear that the Allies have a very good chance of winning the war."

This was the first I had heard of anything other than one incredible Japanese victory after the other. But the news at the moment did not greatly impress me. I was so weak and ill that I did not want to live.

At last the day came when the Japanese wanted to return me to the Kempetai. But the Indonesian doctor convinced them that this would be fatal. Instead, I was removed from the hospital to solitary confinement in the Surabaya jail. I took this to be a good sign. Surely the Gestapo must be through with me? Otherwise I would have been returned to the Kempetai prison. I learned later that the Japanese had theorized that solitary confinement would break my will. I would be unable to stand the loneliness, and they would get the confessions they had been unable to extract by physical torture.

5

THE PEACE OF SOLITARY
CONFINEMENT

My new cell, in the Surabaya jail, was an almost square room about six paces in each direction. The walls were high and whitewashed, and the floor was of red bricks. Between the top of the walls and the roof, along a narrow ledge, was an iron grille that provided some ventilation against the stifling heat of the day. In one wall an iron-barred door and a small window opened onto a courtyard not much larger than the cell itself. The courtyard, too, was enclosed by very high walls and a roof of iron bars. At one side a thick wooden door opened into the main prison yard. In a corner of the courtyard stood a cement tank filled with water, usually stagnant and covered with green scum and mosquitoes. The odor of the water was anything but pleasant. One hesitated to use it even for washing, but there was no alternative.

I was allowed out of the cell for ten minutes each day. These intervals in the tiny courtyard were unbelievably pleasant. One could study the blue of the sky and watch the tall castor-oil trees swaying softly in the faint breeze.

Within the cell itself there was only a woven palm mat to sleep on, a basket, and a broom. There was also the hole in the ground, and a small tank of water to swill down it in lieu of a sewage-disposal system. One accomplished this by dipping a coconut shell into the water and throwing it into the hole. The stench at times was unbearable, and at night black flying cockroaches swarmed from the hole by the hundreds. At first they terrified me. Later they became my companions. The cell walls usually had several small tjitjaks (chirping lizards) crawling back and forth, fascinating creatures to watch.

For more than two years I remained in solitary confinement, rarely seeing anyone except the Indonesian babu, who came twice a day with a plate of rice and a cup of slush called coffee. The solitude that might have proved intolerable to another prisoner was what I had longed for—time to be alone, to find peace for my tortured soul. At this point I hated the human race and was much too ill for any feeling of loneliness. It was a blessing to know that, for the time being at least, I would not be summoned to the Kempetai inquisition, would not be subject to the lewd remarks and the leering gaze of the Japanese guards. No longer would I have to listen to the screams from a torture chamber, watch a man being kicked to death, look at prisoners dying like flies in front of my very eyes. I was thankful, too, that I had been placed in solitary confinement instead of being sent to a concentration camp with Dutch women. That, indeed, would have driven me mad.

The first weeks were hard, not because of loneliness but because of the noises that set my nerves on edge. The sounds emanated largely from the jail's workshop: Whistles, sirens, grinding machinery, clanking bells. A buzz saw ripping its way through lumber where prisoners were fashioning furniture. Even the drip, drip, drip of water from the tank in the yard.

An inner voice whispered to me: Don't let the noise upset you; don't fight against it. Listen carefully. You will find that no two sounds are the same. Listen; you can hear a kind of music.

I listened and pondered. When one has time to sit and concentrate, hidden meanings come forth. In this case hidden melodies. The factory cacophony resolved itself in my ears into a kind of nature symphony. "Mankind in Despair," I called it. A prison rhapsody, lightened in theme at sundown by the chirping of the tjitjaks, the croaking of the bullfrogs, the droning of mosquitoes, the singing of birds. I had no pencil or paper with which to set down the notes, but after many years I can still reproduce in my mind the strange and plaintive songs out of solitary imprisonment.

I spent much of my time, in fact, lying on my back on the floor composing songs, dreaming up plots for operas. And when the night shadows spread softly over the cell walls, their phantom flickerings became a ballet of exquisite beauty. My dream creatures danced to lovely effects of light and shadow, darkness and moonbeams.

My first new friends, in this strange state-of-suspension existence I was now experiencing, were the birds. They came into my cell through the iron grille that ran along the top of the wall. I started leaving a bit of my rice for them each day. They would come down off the ledge and eat the food I had set out for them on the floor. Little by little they became tame, and would alight on my shoulder or lap and eat out of my hands. I noticed that when an air-raid siren sounded—and this happened with increasing frequency these days —the ledge above my cell would fill quickly with my little friends. It was as though they believed they could hide there from the noise and flame. It was amazing to observe that when the all clear sounded, they took themselves off.

The courting, preening and strutting of my tiny friends was constantly amusing. In time I learned that the males were the exhibitionists, and the aggressors. They puffed out their feathers on the top of their heads, spread and coquettishly showed their fanlike tails, and warbled their sweet songs. The females, less brilliant in coloring, at first pretended indifference. Sometimes fights would break out between two males; the fierceness of their contests was astonishing.

In my cell were gray birds, red ones, and black, and yellow; birds with blue breasts. I noticed that each type kept to its kind; there was no intermixing, no perching beside a different breed. Some form of natural "racial discrimination" operated here in a mysterious law of the animal world. In rainy weather the birds were quiet, huddled together. But when the sun shone again they all broke forth in rich and glorious song. Sometimes male and female sang a stirring duet. By day most of the birds were elsewhere, but at sundown they all came back to eat. And their best performances were at sundown.

In time I would talk to the birds, and whistle to them. They would put their little heads on one side and listen attentively. Before long some of them were imitating my whistling almost perfectly. I know that these entertainments by the birds were good medicine for any woes whether physical, mental, or spiritual.

And then there were my insect friends, the cockroaches and the ants. Some of the cockroaches were almost as big as mice. They came out from the hole in the ground at night like an invading army, flying about, crawling over the walls. At first I was horrified and disgusted, and determined to kill them. It was terrifying to have them alight on my head, or my lap. I was afraid to lie down, lest they crawl over me.

But they were too numerous to destroy, and the thought of stamping on them, or squashing them on the walls, was even more distasteful than letting them alone. I decided that instead of being afraid of them I must learn to live with them.

Could they be trained, as fleas are trained? Perhaps I could teach them—since they were scavengers looking for food—to go to a feeding place and stay away from my mat, my food plate and drinking mug. Every day I placed a little rice in the corner for the roaches. From time to time a tjitjak would die in my cell; I would place that with the rice also. In time this worked fairly well. The roaches would flock to the food, and leave my eating utensils alone.

Soon I was able to tell the males from the females. It was surprising to find that the male was smaller than the female, and that only the male had wings and could fly. The female was distinguished by a sort of bag or little sac protruding from the rear of its body. This sac contained the eggs which later they cunningly hid in secret hiding places. When they hatched, between twenty and fifty tiny roaches appeared.

My main trouble was with the ants that came and made off with the food I set aside for the roaches. Occasionally a flying cockroach would alight on its back and find itself unable to turn over. I would watch it struggle and at last weaken and lie still. While the roach was helpless, hundreds of ants would encircle it and mill around, waiting for it to die. The circle of ants would get smaller and smaller until there could be no escape for the roach. Then I would turn it over and enable it to get away. Sometimes I watched the ants build a barricade around a dead cockroach and painstakingly dissect it and store away its parts. I saw red ants and white ants, and watched them at war with one another. Ants, I am sure, are the most patient and determined of all insects. They are utterly ruthless; I usually found myself on the side of the roaches. When one has absolutely nothing to do in a cell alone, the incessant activities of insect life can be most diverting.

There was nothing whatever to read in my prison, nothing with which to write. I found myself wishing for a deck of cards, not merely to play solitaire but in order to tell my fortune. I had always considered myself psychic and able to look somewhat, at least, into the future with cards.

I stared at the white walls. What murals I would fashion there if I only had paint. I stared at the floor. Red bricks. Prisoners had tunneled under floors to escape, but one must have a pick or a crowbar or some strong tool to dislodge the bricks. They were cemented together, securely in place.

Red bricks. Paint could be made from them, if they were pounded into powder and mixed with oil, say, or turpentine. I scraped at them with my fingernails, and found them soft.

For days I scraped, until my nails were worn down to the quick. A painful process it was, but I now had half a mug of red powder. But what to mix it with, to give it the consistency of oil paint.

Water did not do the job. But there was that plate of unsugared sago that the babu brought me every morning for breakfast. Its taste was so vile that usually I emptied it into the hole in my cell. It was the consistency of starch. Why not mix the red-brick dust with it? Why not give it a try?

I mixed the sago with the brick dust and was delighted with the result, a very usable red paint. But what could I use it on? Not on the walls; the paint would not wash off, and I could risk no offenses that might bring the Kempetai back after me. The floor was no good, for red would not show on red; besides, I had no brushes. I thought of my broom, pulled out a couple of straws, and found they worked well. With one end I could draw a thin line, with the other a thicker one. I couldn't paint, but I could draw or write—if I had something to write on. A piece of white cloth, a sheet of paper, anything.

I hid my paint on a ledge just under the floor level of the toilet hole. I knew that the Japanese were much too fastidious to go poking about in such a foul-smelling place.

Every day I scraped more and more red dust. Someday, surely, I'd come into possession of a rag or bit of paper. And then it came to me. I was lying on my mat thinking of the pleasant evenings I had spent in Bali with Agung Nura, translating from the lontar leaves the ancient classics of Bali.

Lontar leaves—palm leaves, cut into long strips and dried in the sun until they were hard and stiff. The stationery of the ancients. Excitedly, I jumped up from my mat. Of course, my woven basket of palm leaves. The strips were almost two inches wide, and I could break them into sections any length I wanted. I would wash the strips and dry them in the hot sun. Each day during my ten-minute recess in the courtyard, I could dry a strip at a time without being noticed.

I worked most of the night, and by daybreak I had five good strips —more than enough for a set of playing cards. I cut the strips into fifty-two pieces with a sharp stone, then started painting hearts and diamonds—from ace to king—on the small pieces. Spades and clubs would have to wait until I could find a way to make black paint.

The next day during the recess, I searched in the courtyard for black stones, or some black soil, or for soot, or dirt from the prison-yard door. I could find no stone soft enough to pound into dust. There was no soot, and the black dust scraped from the door only made mud when mixed with liquid. And then I found a piece of arang, the coconut shell burnt black that Indonesians use for cooking. I ground the charcoal and mixed it with my breakfast sago, and had the blackest paint an artist could want. Before long I had a set of miniature playing cards that was a joy to behold.

I played bridge with myself, bidding two hands and playing all four. I invented other games. I told my fortune, and convinced myself I would come out of this dreadful ordeal alive—but that I would come near death first. I managed to persuade a friendly Javanese babu to pass the cards to some of the other cells and have the prisoners shuffle them, and then return the cards to me and I would tell their fortune. The outgrowth of that was the writing of messages on cloths —messages that could be sent from cell to cell and then washed out so that the Japanese would not know. These messages made possible the circulation of a considerable amount of news of interest to us all—war news, mainly, supplied by newly arrived prisoners. This homemade deck of cards is still in my possession, one of the few relics from the terrible years of imprisonment. It is still in good condition, the painted card signs for the most part fresh and clear—an interesting conversation piece of the war years.

Some weeks after I first entered solitary confinement a crazed woman was put in the cell next to mine. I could not see her but I could hear her beating on the bars of her cell with her tin mug and shrieking at the top of her voice in a foreign language. When the prison babu came with my plate of rice for the evening meal she informed me the woman was a Polish doctor, brought in from Kempetai headquarters. My old friend who had saved my life! She had cracked under the sadistic treatment.

"She is going raving mad," the babu said. "She won't eat, she won't obey orders. All she does is scream for her children."

Her condition became so serious, finally, that the Japanese brought her two young sons to her cell and said they could stay with her overnight. It was too late. She failed to recognize her little boys, and only stared at them with dull eyes. The Japanese hoped that the recognition would come after she was alone with her children. They were wrong. That same night, when the boys were fast asleep, she hanged herself in the cell, using the thin wire that ran crosswise for a drying line. When the little boys awoke in the morning they found their mother hanging dead. Their screams brought the Japanese to the cell.

Later I learned that the Japanese who had advised bringing the children to the cell was so upset by the tragedy that he too committed suicide. "He blamed himself and said he had only one way to atone for his error," the babu told me.

The double tragedy unnerved the Japanese prison officials more than a little. For one thing, they began to pay daily visits to my cell. They wanted to make sure I wouldn't take this way out. For another, they removed from my cell the wire on which I dried my sarong and towel. And they took greater note of other tragic developments—a Dutch woman had gone out of her mind completely and had become violently insane and an Indo-Dutch woman had opened her wrist veins with a safety pin. Apparently at last they had come to realize that the human spirit has a definite breaking point.

One Japanese officer came to me and said, "You are the only prisoner who doesn't create a din in your cell. You never beat on the bars or curse the guards, yet you have suffered more than most of them. How do you remain so calm?" The officer told me that the men were far more troublesome than the women, and went to pieces more quickly.

Now and then the Kempetai officials came to my cell to see how I was taking solitary confinement, for I was still their prisoner. One time an officer brought what he said was a confession from one of my Japanese friends. It was the same old trick. I insisted on seeing it. Frisco Flip may have given me dangerous information, but he was of the samurai code: he would die, but never confess. On examining the document I saw that it was written in Kandi.

"Where is the signature?" I asked. The Japanese pointed to a few characters at the end of the document. I knew immediately it was a forgery, for Flip had taught me to write his name in Japanese characters. "I can read a little Japanese, enough to know that that document is a forgery," I said. It was a mistake for me to be so positive, for it was hard to convince the Japanese that I could read and write Balinese and Javanese and was interested in Oriental languages, yet had no ulterior motive.

Occasionally the Kempetai officials brought visiting officials from Japan to see me; they explained my Balinese background and said I was an Allied spy of unusual cleverness and their most stubborn prisoner. I was their prime catch—a British-born American citizen where most of the other prisoners were Chinese, Indonesians, or half-caste Dutch—and many times I was forced to have my picture taken standing with the visiting Japanese.

One evening as I pressed my face to the bars, trying to see the moon that had risen behind the cell and was making lovely geometrical shadows in the courtyard, I heard the clanking of doors down the corridor. An officer was making an inspection with the matron on her evening rounds. They stood at my courtyard door. She turned the key, the bolts clanked, and the two came across to my cell. The officer looked about and, seeing me standing motionless, asked, "What do you think about, standing there?" It was a kind voice and interested, as though he really wanted to know, so I answered honestly that at the moment I was thinking about the moon, how beautiful it must be and how I wished to see it.

"Yes, it is beautiful," he said. The tone of his voice told me I had struck an emotional response. But then, curtly, he went on, "If you would confess you'd see it again and be free and safe."

I dropped my eyes and stared sullenly at my clasped hands. After all, what could I expect?

The officer went away and I lay on my mat thinking of the strangeness of the Japanese. The officer had been truly moved by even the suggestion of a beautiful moon. I had seen some common soldiers standing motionless for hours looking at it. High or low, they never failed to respond to beauty whether in a painting or a natural scene, a river or a mountain.

Arranging my arms in a position that gave me the least pain, I went to sleep. It must have been well past midnight when the clanking of the outer door awakened me. Sitting up, alert with terror, I recalled stories about the horrible experiences of women in prison. The gate closed and a figure approached. I could tell by the clinking of his sword that it was an officer.

"Don't scream," he whispered, as my mouth flew open. "I am not going to hurt you." It was the voice of the officer who had spoken to me earlier. He inserted his heavy key in my door, while I clung to it, trying to hold it closed.

"Don't be afraid. I have just come back to let you look at the moon."

He opened the iron door a little way and held out his hand. "Come into the courtyard where you can see it. I'll return in fifteen minutes and lock you up again." He led me out and stood by me a minute looking at it, glorious in its third quarter, spilling silver over the roofs. Then he went out again, locking the courtyard door.

I lay on the ground and looked directly up at the moon. If I was careful not to move my head, there were no walls or bars. It was almost like being in Bali again and lying under the palm trees looking at the light on the Indian Ocean. When the officer returned I was so drunk with remembrances of past beauty that I could scarcely bring myself to earth to say "thank you." He smiled and seemed to understand.

"Sleep well," he said gently as he locked the gate.

The very next day the examinations began again, with beatings and another hanging until my senses blacked out. New forms of torture were devised. Men with matches tried to set the hair of my body on fire. They poured castor oil into me, and once forced me to drink a pint of whiskey. They thought if I was drunk I might talk. In this they were mistaken. On an empty stomach the liquor only made me deathly sick.

For two months, on and off, they kept after me. What life remained in me fanned my determination that nothing would make me speak. What was the use now, anyway? It would be foolish to confess after having endured so much. And I was becoming immune to pain. Mercifully, my memory was leaving me. For days at a time I could not remember my name.

A month passed without further interrogation or visits to my cell by the Japanese officials. The little babu came twice a day with my food. Most of the time was relatively pleasant, and I sat on my mat all day and dreamed, making up stories about Bali and the ancient gods of the island. I listened to my bird and prison symphony. Time passed swiftly.

One day this quiet interlude was interrupted by a visit to my cell by a Japanese captain. He questioned me at great length, and then he said, "Tell me, what do you really dream about all day and night, sitting on the floor of an empty cell?"

"Nothing that you would understand," I replied.

"How do you know I wouldn't understand? Why don't you try me?"

I looked at him curiously and said, "Well, if you must know, all I dream of is a bath, bath, bath. For months I have been without a bath. The water in the courtyard is not fit for washing. It is full of water worms and dead mosquitoes, and slime, and it has a vile smell.

"It has been said that if you think of something you desire long enough, you will get it. I long for a hot bath. Sometimes my imagination runs away with me and I make believe that I am having a warm, perfumed bubble bath. I feel the soft, soapy water caressing my skin, and I soak in it and scrub until I am clean—sweet and clean and fresh. Then I come back to reality and find that I am still dirty and hardly human-looking any more. That, Mr. Officer, is what I think about more than anything else in the world."

And it was the truth. I had forgotten what a piece of soap looked like. I had, of course, nothing with which to brush my teeth. Toothpaste would have been a luxury beyond compare.

The Japanese gave me a puzzled stare and asked, "If you want a bath so badly, why don't you tell the Kempetai the truth? If you confess, they will be very easy on you. Why remain so stubborn when life could be so easy? The Japanese are winning the war. You would be wise to go along with them."

I remained silent, and he lost his temper. "You Yankee pig!" he shouted. "The Kempetai will beat you again and make that white skin of yours as black as the natives you profess to love. You will never get a bath, make sure of that. You will rot and die in the filth of your cell."

Accustomed by now to name-calling and abuse, I let the incident fade from my memory. One night a week or so later the same officer came back to my cell with the Indonesian warden. I was thoroughly frightened. The Japanese officers seldom came to the cells at night except to drag prisoners off to headquarters, where nocturnal grillings were the rule. The theory was that a prisoner half asleep, fatigued, would have less resistance than the same prisoner in the morning, fresh from a night's rest.

"Get up, you filthy spy," the officer said. "You are going back to the Kempetai for a few more questions."

Cowed by his forcefulness, I raised myself from my mat. He jerked me out of my cell and pushed me through the main prison yard and into a waiting automobile. Then he drove off, leaving the Indonesian to lock the gates. I noticed that, after leaving the Surabaya prison, he turned and drove in a direction away from the Kempetai headquarters. I thought of the Gestapo prisoners who had been found floating in the canal, and the Japanese bland insistence that they had been put to death by Indonesians. I screamed for him to stop the car. "You are not going to the Kempetai," I shouted. "It is against Japanese rules for officers to take prisoners from their cells this way. Turn back, or you will be in real trouble."

He took no notice of my shouts. If he was not going to kill me and throw me into the canal, even worse, he might be taking me to a house where prostitutes were kept, either for his pleasure or for others. I wept and pleaded for him to take me back to the prison. He remained silent. The streets were full of Japanese soldiers; I knew it would be of no use to try to jump out of the car into their clutches. We were driving now through the Darmo district of Surabaya, an area I knew well. At last we stopped outside a pretty bungalow I recognized as having belonged to a Dutch doctor. The officer dragged me out of the car and up to the entrance of the house, opened the door with a key, and shoved me inside. Closing and bolting the door, he snapped on the electric light in a pleasant living room. I stood dazed in the middle of the room, and he leaned against the door and laughed.

"Don't be frightened," he said. "You said you wanted a bath. And believe me, you need it. I did not realize just how filthy you were until I got you away from the prison.

"You seem to think I brought you here for some bad purpose. You are very wrong. I was impressed that a prisoner who could be dreaming of revenge, thinking of satisfying her hate, hoping for freedom, would long most for a bath. You shall have a bath, a good hot bath."

The officer pressed a bell on the wall and a little Indonesian serving maid came gliding into the room. She stared at me at first, then giggled nervously, "Njonya, njonya."

"Take this njonya into the bathroom and give her the hottest tubbing she can stand," the Japanese said. "Wash her hair thoroughly. And give her one of your sarongs and baju." The baju is a little coat of cotton or silk worn on top of the sarong.

"Take her dirty sarong and the towel she has wrapped round the top part of her body, and wash them and put them in the oven to dry. They must be dry in an hour."

We entered the bathroom and locked the door. She drew a bath and put in scented pine cubes. I lay in the bath, luxuriating in the suds and warmth and scent and watching the babu wash my sarong in the hand basin. Afterward she combed my newly cleaned hair, and gave me powder and lipstick to apply. I used a little powder but didn't apply lipstick.

When I entered the living room afterward the Japanese officer jumped up from his chair and exclaimed in Malay, "Adoh! Terlaloe tjantik, roepanja lain sekarang." He was remarking on my appearance and cleanliness. "Sit down; don't be afraid of me," he said. "The babu will bring some coffee and cake. We shall hear some good music while your sarong is drying. Some Shostakovich. I love Shostakovich."

If I had to listen to music, sick and weary as I was, I would have preferred something less robust. But we listened to Shostakovich to his heart's content. Between recordings I asked him how he dared kidnap a prisoner and bring her to his house.

"A big reception is on in Surabaya tonight for General Tojo," he said airily. "Everyone above me in rank is at the feast. I had to be a bit rough with you to convince the Indonesian warden—and I'm afraid I'll have to be rough in the same way when I take you back."

He recommended that, for my part, I keep my head down on reentering the prison so that my clean hair would not be noticed. It would be dark in the prison courtyard, the guards would not notice that my sarong and towel were newly washed. "I wish I could let you keep the babu's sarong and baju, but this would be impossible," he said. Obviously so, for all prisoners wore the same type of sarong, dark blue with white stripes.

The officer told me that before the war he was a private citizen. "I am a writer of sorts who imagines he can paint," he said. "My hobby is music. I was never interested in politics. I have seen the mess that politicians on all sides have gotten us into. Nor have I hated Americans.

"It is a pity that the presidents and kings of this world are not artists. If they were, there would be no wars. When the presidents, kings, emperors, dictators, and politicians are dead and buried they will not long be remembered, but the great artists of the world shall be, and their work will bring joy to future generations."

This extraordinary man added that the one reason he decided to arrange for my bath was that I was an artist—"and we should not make war on artists." "All art is universal," he continued. "The Japanese people appreciate all forms of art. After the war is over perhaps we can meet again under different circumstances. For now, we must get back to the prison before the Tojo reception is over and I am missed."

At the prison gates he pushed and shoved me again and called me unflattering names. The Indonesian guards smiled at his treatment of me, as was expected of them. I smiled too, but secretly. This night I had learned much about the Japanese—about certain types of Japanese.

6

THE SIGHT OF FREEDOM

Although the two years of life in solitary confinement were far easier for me than the months under the direct jurisdiction of the Japanese Kempetai, the earlier beatings and starvation had taken their toll. Many days and nights I lay in my cell unable to move my arms or to eat. Twice a day a Japanese doctor came to give me medicine and to try to stir my interest in life, but I grew steadily weaker and weaker. At last the doctor pronounced that I could not live longer than twenty-four hours. A few Dutch prisoners were brought into my cell and were allowed to file past to say good-by. One doctor said I was dying of a broken heart. One of the Dutch women asked permission to hypnotize me to induce an interest in living. She tried to lift me and firmly held onto my arms beseeching me not to give up. "We need you, we women in the prison need you for moral support," she said. But I asked her to leave me alone and let me die in peace. I sank into a coma, and after I had been unconscious for twenty-four hours the Japanese doctor from the jail, a very inexperienced young man, pronounced me dead. A burial number was attached to my big toe. I was to be taken away for burial at daybreak.

In the early gray dawn I opened my eyes. I was frightfully cold and could not move, could not even call out. I heard the door of my cell being unbolted. I heard voices, and then someone yelled, "Her eyes are open! She's alive!"

I was by this time sufficiently conscious to discover the tag on my toe and to realize that I had been almost on the way to my own burial. But the Japanese are a superstitious lot. My apparent return from the grave created quite a stir. In minutes I was surrounded by excited Japanese, and the doctor was feeling my pulse. Kempetai officials were sent for, since I was still technically their prisoner. They were so impressed that they ordered a mattress to be brought to my cell at once and said I must have hot milk and eggs daily.

To my tortured mind it seemed that the Japanese were determined to bury me alive. I screamed and raved and became completely unmanageable. The Kempetai officials talked of sending me to Porong, an institution for mental patients, but the doctor recommended that they wait awhile until I had recovered from the first shock. For days I lay in semiconsciousness, between life and death. The peace and quiet of my cell and the extra food that the doctor had ordered had their effect. Although I could not walk or raise my arms above the waist I was rational once again.

The mattress of straw that had been given to me as a luxury had to be removed. I showed the attendants that it was full of lice and a nesting place for the cockroaches.

From time to time Japanese officers came to see how I was getting along, and one day one of them asked me what it was like to be dead, and if there was a next world, and they asked me if I could predict who was going to win the war. I told them no one will win the war, even though one nation is forced to capitulate. Who will win the peace—that is what counts.

After several weeks had passed my captors told me that I was to be removed to a political camp hospital in the middle of Java. I was astonished at first, and then incredulous, sure they were taking me only to some Kempetai headquarters in the country. But this time they spoke the truth. I was placed on a stretcher and taken by train to the Ambarawa hospital three hundred kilometers away.

The Japanese plainly had realized by this time that they soon would lose the war. They did not want an American citizen found in a prison cell, ill and tortured and almost starved to death. Should the Allies land at Surabaya and make such a discovery, it might go badly indeed with the persons responsible. Much better if I were found in a hospital, receiving good treatment.

I was transferred to the Ambarawa hospital only six weeks before the Japanese capitulation. In those six weeks my treatment improved dramatically. I was a human being again, receiving hospital care from kindly doctors and nurses.

It must not be understood by my long narrative on my life as a prisoner of the Japanese Kempetai that I hate the Japanese, for this would not be true. Certainly I hated the Gestapo and the military police, but for every sadistic Japanese I encountered I had met two or three that were good and kind. I am convinced that, as in other races, the good Japanese people far outnumber the bad.

And then came August, 1945, and the final defeat of the Japanese all down the chain of islands they had won so easily. All we knew at the hospital was that the war was over. Shouting Indonesians stormed the hospital and also the camp at Ambarawa, disarming the Japanese. All of us behind the bars cheered and wept, and threw our arms around each other. It was a wonderful time.

The Indonesian soldiers who took the hospital by force quickly learned my story, and that I was still in a critical condition. They put me on a stretcher, placed me in a truck, and drove me to a private hospital in Surabaya. Later I was taken to the mountains to the chalet of a highly respected Indonesian doctor. I weighed only sixty-five pounds, less than half my normal weight, and was still partially paralyzed, physically and mentally. But good food—rustled up from who knows where during this period of hardship and of low commissary stocks—and tender care worked wonders. I regained health rapidly.

Japan's house of cards, based on her lying propaganda about "Asia for the Asians," had fallen about her. Indonesians, fiercely bent on revenge against the Japanese and particularly against the hated Kempetai, killed the Nipponese invaders by the hundreds, threw others into the very prisons they had operated.

Many Javanese, Sumatranese, Balinese and Chinese, and other Indonesians from the outer islands, had been tortured to death or shot, and the Indonesians were not prone at this moment to forgive.

I learned that my Chinese friend, the honorable professor, had been tortured and killed by the Gestapo. Frisco Flip had disappeared under most mysterious circumstances and was never heard from again. Some said that the ship carrying him to Makassar was bombed by the Dutch Air Force and that everyone aboard was drowned. No one really knew the truth.

And what of Anak Agung Nura? I would have no news of him until communications with Bali were restored. I was sure that this would not take long and that I myself might soon travel back to the puri that had for so many years been my home.

THREE

1

INDEPENDENCE FOR INDONESIA

It may be helpful to readers unfamiliar with Indonesian history to have a brief summary of the situation at the end of World War II. With the capitulation of the Japanese on August 15, 1945, the moment for action arrived toward which Indonesian intellectuals had so long been striving.

In the name of merdeka these people had worked, for more than forty years had suffered imprisonment, had been exiled by the Dutch. Then at the very outbreak of war the Dutch had deserted them, leaving them unarmed to the mercy of the Japanese. The Japanese in turn had driven out the Dutch, only to be chased out themselves three years later by the Allied victory. Incredibly, it had taken a world war to bring about deliverance.

The end of war found the Indonesians a bewildered and disillusioned people. But they realized that it was imperative they act at once if independence was to be assured. They were not slow to take advantage of the confusion in the Pacific, knowing that it was now or never. Should the Dutch come back as overlords, merdeka might never have another chance. So on August 17, 1945, just two days after the fall of Japan to the forces under General Douglas MacArthur, a group of dedicated Indonesians in Java forced the proclamation of independence, naming Sukarno the first president of the newborn republic, and Dr. Hatta vice-president.

The declaration of independence came about under comic-opera circumstances. Sukarno and Dr. Hatta had just returned from a conference with Japanese commanders in Dalat, near Saigon. Aware that they had lost the war and must soon surrender, the Japanese hoped to persuade the Indonesians before the war's end to declare their independence from the Netherlands in the name of the Emperor of Japan. Sukarno and Hatta were skeptical. They did not trust the Japanese, and they were resolved that when independence was declared it would not be in the name of a foreign government. Nevertheless, they listened and on their return to Batavia reported to the Indonesian leaders. These leaders, backed up by university student groups, put pressure on Sukarno to declare independence the very next day. "If we wait," they said, "this great opportunity may be snatched away from us." But Sukarno refused to act hastily. He advised waiting a few days to see how the land lay and to observe the attitude of the Allies, whose news reports had been describing him as a Japanese collaborator—and in general distorting the picture of conditions in Indonesia. In his great desire for a bloodless revolution he was adamant against all pressures.

Halfway between midnight and dawn on the 16th of August a group of very angry and determined students, all well armed, kidnaped Sukarno and Dr. Hatta from their homes and took them miles from Batavia—or Jakarta, to give it its original Javanese name—to the garrison of Rengasdengklok. For the rest of the night, and all day, the students tried to force Sukarno to change his mind. They cajoled, they threatened, they pleaded, they demanded.

I did not know Sukarno at this time, but I was acquainted with his abductors. I couldn't imagine one of them hurting him; he was much loved by all the students. It was months later, when Sukarno and I had become friends, that he told me the story of his kidnaping.

"The funniest thing that ever happened to me," he said. "There was I, flanked on all sides by angry young men brandishing guns and threatening me. I could have put them over my knee and spanked them, for I knew most of them from childhood, and their families were my friends.

"They wouldn't have harmed me, even if I had remained firm. But as I looked upon their serious, earnest faces, as they pleaded with me to declare independence immediately, I knew they were right in their demands. The future—if we were destined to have a future as a free nation—would depend upon the sincerity and the fearless spirit of these young men. They were an inspired group, and the fate of their country was in their hands. I looked at them with affection and said, 'Well, let us be getting back to Jakarta. We have much to do. Let us waste no more time talking.' "

Sukarno recalled how the faces of the students lit up with satisfaction as he capitulated. "They said to me, 'Perhaps you would like to shave now.' . . . So we returned to Jakarta and the following day, August 17, 1945, I declared the independence of Indonesia, in the name of the Indonesian people."

Those who witnessed this historic event heard President Sukarno, in his deep, emotion-charged voice, declare simply, "With the blessing of almighty Allah, the Indonesian people declare their independence." And the people wept, for the days of subjugation were over. Citizens of Indonesia would go forth with pride, no longer the slaves of any man.

The stupendous news swept over all the Indonesian islands, from Irian to Sumatra. Radios blared the developments day and night. Newspapers with bold headlines flooded the streets. The Republic of Indonesia was born.

Men raced to rip the Japanese flag from all government buildings, and from shops and houses, to the cheers of throngs of celebrants. The Japanese, absolute dictators for the years of the war, reacted sharply to the challenge of their authority; fighting between the Indonesians and the Japanese broke out from one end of Java to the other. In particular the Japanese hurled their fury at President Sukarno.

In the enormous square in front of the former palace of the Dutch Governor General, Sukarno spoke to assembled thousands. "This is our new-found freedom; I promise you we shall never give it up," he said, to thunderous applause. He urged the people to refrain from violence and to return peaceably to their homes.

Japanese tanks were milling around the square and Japanese planes were flying overhead. The Japanese had planned to arrest Sukarno and throw him into prison. Now they saw that they were too late; the millions of Indonesians were clearly behind their new president. Confused, upset by the surrender news from Tokyo, the Japanese were hesitant and fumbling in their new role. Their military command had been ordered by the Allies to maintain peace and order in Indonesia until Allied troops arrived to take control. But in the face of swelling Indonesian independence the Japanese were hopelessly ineffective. The cry of "Merdeka . . . Merdeka" was sweeping over the land.

The mortification of the Japanese at the lowering of their flag was as nothing in comparison with the reaction of the Dutch colonials in Indonesia and the Dutch reactionaries in The Hague in Holland. They were incredulous at the proclamation of Indonesian independence, and outraged beyond all reason. An atom bomb in their midst could hardly have caused greater consternation.

Dutch colonials returning from Japanese concentration camps had dreamed of going back to their elegant homes, to the old luxurious life with plenty of native servants and an inexhaustible supply of cheap labor for their plantations and offices. At first they were arrogant, presumptuous. They dismissed the independence proclamation as an Indonesian stamboel, or theatrical. Their astonishment grew when they learned otherwise. Then started the long years devoted to the sabotage of Indonesia Merdeka.

In Holland the colonial diehards, unwilling to give up the goose that had laid the golden eggs, let go of pent-up emotions. Their vindictiveness knew no limits; in slanderous radio broadcasts and newspaper reports they called Sukarno and Hatta the worst kind of collaborators, said the new Republic of Indonesia was nothing but a Japanese puppet government.

Understandably, the Dutch said nothing of their desertion of Indonesia at the onset of the Japanese attack. They said nothing of the nine years that President Sukarno and Dr. Hatta had spent as Dutch prisoners. And they said nothing of the offer that Sukarno and other Indonesian leaders had made to the Dutch when it became evident, after the Pearl Harbor attack in December, 1941, that the Japanese were on the march in Asia. Sukarno had asked the Dutch, just before the Japanese invasion, to release him and arm the Indonesians so that they might defend their homeland against the invaders. Sukarno's offer was ignored and he was left in exile in Bengkulen, where the Japanese found him when they swarmed into Indonesia.

At this time the Dutch deputy governor general, Hubertus van Mook—who had fled to Australia when the Japanese occupied Java —sent a secret and urgent message to England's Admiral Louis Mountbatten, Supreme Commander of Allied Forces in Southeast Asia. Van Mook said the Indonesian leaders were extremist rebels causing dissension throughout Java and certainly did not have the backing of the people. He said the newly born Republic was not to be taken seriously, should not be recognized by the Allies. He urged Mountbatten to help abolish the new Republic as quickly as possible.

The Allied forces had little or no intelligence in Java. Mountbatten accepted Van Mook's communiqué as being trustworthy and accurate. Mountbatten had so many pressing problems elsewhere in the Far East, things were moving so fast everywhere, that the dramatic and unforeseen action of the Indonesians bewildered him. Convinced that Sukarno was only a puppet for the Japanese, backed by a few extremist rebels, the Admiral ordered British forces to move into Java and disarm the Japanese. The British troops were instructed also to quash the rebel Republic and to return to the Dutch the properties and power they had lost more than three years before. Mountbatten and other British leaders lived to regret this decision. Too late they realized that they had been maneuvered into a false position, tricked by the Dutch.

Six weeks after the declaration of independence British troops moved into Java. They were astonished to find that the Indonesians had already disarmed the Japanese and had placed most of them in concentration camps. From the Indonesian viewpoint this was a brilliant action, for the Indonesians now had all the Japanese arms. The weapons would be needed if the infant country was to defend its freedom.

In England there was public outrage that the British people should be made to appear as suppressors of freedom in Java. It was widely remembered, too, that Dutch Lieutenant General ter Poorten had surrendered Indonesia to the Japanese in 1942, in the name of the Allies, without consulting the British High Command in Java. The memory rankled particularly because, at the time, several thousand British and American troops were in Java, willing to resist and retard the invading Japanese.

Outcries protesting the use of force by the Allies against the Indonesians poured in from all over the world. The British were accused of violating the Atlantic Charter and the Charter of the United Nations. The anti-Dutch press of the world accused the Dutch of creeping back into Java behind the British Tommy's gun. There was consternation and incredulity, meanwhile, among the Indonesians, who found it hard to believe that the British would suppress the new-found freedom and try to reinstate the Dutch. If the British were coming in to fight for the Dutch they had no moral right in Indonesia and the Indonesians, against their will, must oppose the British. In the background, the Dutch smiled and bided their time.

First the British started using Japanese soldiers to force compliance by the Indonesians. Next they made use of Nepalese Gurkha troops against the Javanese. And then, most infamous act of all, Britain's commanding general issued an ultimatum: the Indonesians must lay down their arms and surrender the following day or British planes would bomb the city of Surabaya.

The Indonesians, confident that British principles of fair play would prevail, ignored the ultimatum. Surely the British would not bomb an unarmed city, a city utterly without air-raid shelters, a city against which there had been no declaration of war. But the British did bomb Surabaya, for three days and nights. In doing so they blew up the powder keg that started bloody combat between the Indonesians and the British. For four years the battles would rage in defense of Indonesia Merdeka.

2

I CAST MY LOT
WITH THE REVOLUTION

During the first month after my deliverance from the Japanese prison hospital I lived in the shadow of death. It seemed that I was floating in space; the doctor and nurse moving about my room were as ghostly shadows. For the first two weeks I recognized no one and had no interest in living. I had not the faintest idea of what was going on in the world. The doctor allowed no visitors; all information on present conditions in Indonesia was kept from me.

In a vague way I understood that this was September, 1945, and that the war was over, and that Indonesia had declared her independence. It all meant nothing to me; I was beyond caring. The war was over. What did that mean? The war would never be over for me, and the scars left on my mind and heart would never be healed. The world was not worth the spin; man's inhumanity to man was appalling.

As I regained strength my memory cleared. It was only at night, when I lay alone in the dark, that I felt at peace. I recalled the joyful days spent in my moon garden. I remembered the beauty of the Balinese people. I remembered my life at the puri, and my life in the kampongs. I remembered with love the proud Wyjan, merry Njoman, and the sensitive and artistic Maday. And I remembered Agung Nura. What had become of him? I remembered the sweet old Rajah, who had been more of a father to me than any father I had ever known.

I remembered Frisco Flip, and the courageous old professor, and my little Pito, and many others who had woven their paths into mine in Indonesia.

The cavalcade of memories gave me great pain, but those same memories kept me alive. I learned that the will to live burns fiercely, even under the most distressing conditions. Little by little as I became stronger my interest in living returned. I must get well; I must find out what had happened to Nura, even though I realized that my tranquil days in Bali had gone forever.

Under the gentle care of the Indonesian doctor I gained strength, day by day. At last I was able to sit up in my bed. A few days later the doctor told me I was definitely in the convalescent stage, although I was still thin to the point of gauntness and as white as a ghost. I had lost sixty-five pounds in the Japanese prison, and my bones showed clearly through my flesh.

Every morning and evening the doctor came and sat by my bedside. He unfolded for me the story of the Indonesian declaration of independence. He read the daily news to me. Later he brought me a radio, that I might more readily catch up with the world. Often I wondered why he was so good to me, for I was a white woman and quite unknown to him. He knew that I was British born and that my parents were British; and at this time the Indonesians had no cause to like the British.

One day I asked the doctor the reason for his kindness and consideration. Why had he nursed me, a stranger, back to a semblance of life?

"You are not a stranger to me, K'tut Tantri," he replied. "Some day, very soon now, I shall tell you how I know all about you. It is very important to me that you get well."

The news of Indonesian freedom had filled my heart with gladness. My thoughts flew back to the days I had spent with Nura at his coffee plantation. We had not dreamed then that freedom was so near. How happy Nura must feel.

But as I thought of him and recalled his sober face, something told me that he was in trouble or in danger. I could not shake off this presentiment, although I told myself it was foolish. But was it foolish? The radio said that the Dutch had reinstated themselves in Bali. Guerrilla warfare in Bali against the Dutch was rampant. Nura was bound to be in the middle of it.

It was most disturbing to hear that the British were fighting the Indonesians and were using the Japanese against them. To me this made no sense at all. I felt shame that my people would turn a gun against any country seeking the same freedom as the people of Britain have enjoyed. Something must be wrong somewhere; I just couldn't believe it of the British. But I came to know that it was true.

One morning the doctor came to my room with a bigger smile than usual, and said, "Sudara K'tut, make yourself pretty. You have company."

Sudara in Malay is the word for a close relative—in this case, sister. "Doctor," I replied, "what company could I have? No one knows that I am here."

"News travels quickly by the Indonesian grapevine," he said. "Friends not only know that you are here, but they know that you are getting well."

My heart leaped. Could it be Nura? Or Wyjan, Njoman or Maday, perhaps? No; they could not get from their homes to Java so long as the Dutch were in control of Bali. Could it be Daan? No, again. No Dutchman could venture so far from Dutch headquarters in these times.

Make yourself pretty, the doctor had said. With what? I had no dress, no powder, no lipstick. I was propped up in bed in a pair of the doctor's pajamas. Purple pajamas at that. I hurriedly combed my hair, and inspected the result in a mirror. I muttered to myself that I looked like a dead fish, and then gazed expectantly at the door.

I was astonished when the doctor ushered in four Indonesian men in their early twenties. I gazed at them blankly for a moment, and then recognized one. Pito, grown taller, and handsomer than ever! "Pito, darling little Pito," I sobbed. "It can't be you. It can't."

He came over to my bed, bent down and rubbed my nose with his, drew in his breath. Such is the custom of the Indonesians when embracing.

Pito was dressed, as were the others, in khaki shorts and a khaki tunic on which was sewn the rank of a first lieutenant. This surprised me. He seemed young to hold that rank, and I knew he had had no formal military training. He introduced me to the other young men: Captain Bustami, First Lieutenant Affendi, Second Lieutenant Adi. I smiled at the titles, but then remembered that these young men were in the midst of a revolution. The literate would have to be the leaders of the illiterate. I have known colonels twenty-five years old, and generals in their thirties. These mere boys took themselves very seriously and acted like little old men. And very competent they were.

Pito proudly informed me that he was now in the intelligence department of Bung Tomo's guerrilla fighters for East Java—Java Timor. Bung Tomo was famous already as the guerrilla chieftain for the whole of Java. I hardly knew whether Pito's announcement startled me or amused me more. I did not laugh, but accepted the news as though it were to be expected from a man of twenty.

"We are living with Bung Tomo at his mountain hideaway outside Malang," Pito confided.

"How did you know I was here?" I asked. "This chalet is well hidden, and the good doctor has not permitted any visitors."

"I have just told you that I am in the intelligence department. In any case, the doctor sent Bung Tomo word that you were here."

"The doctor!" I exclaimed. "How would he know where the guerrillas were? How could he send such news?"

"If the doctor wouldn't know where the guerrilla headquarters were, then I don't know who would know. He is Bung Tomo's friend. He is also one of our most important guerrillas."

I sat up in amazement. The doctor! A member of Bung Tomo's ragged bamboo army of freedom fighters. What next!

"And your father?" I asked Pito.

"Oh, he is in intelligence too, but in Bandung, in West Java. He is too old to do any active fighting, but he is very valuable for intelligence work."

"Wonderful!" I laughed. "Between you and your father, the Dutch won't have a chance."

"Well, they won't be able to move very far without our knowing it," he replied. And of course, had I thought about it, I would have expected Pito and his father to be in the thick of a fight for freedom. Pito's father was a revolutionary of many years' standing.

After the pleasantries were over the doctor joined us, and his pretty wife brought native coffee—kopi tubruk—and rice cakes. We sat around talking about the revolution. One story led to another until Pito suddenly broke into the general discussion.

"Sudara K'tut," he said, very serious. "We came here to find out how you were getting along, and to see if you were getting the proper care. But we also came to ask you to consider two propositions. We hope you will find one of them agreeable."

"Two propositions, Pito?" All four young men suddenly turned shy. There was a clearing of throats, a nervous fidgeting. The doctor remained quiet, looking unconcerned as he pulled away at his pipe. The young men nudged each other.

"What are the proposals you have in mind, Pito?" I pressed. "Don't be afraid to speak up. I'm listening."

Pito looked at Captain Bustami and said brightly, "You tell Sudara K'tut, captain."

"No," Bustami replied. "You must tell her yourself."

Pito turned to the pipe-smoker. "Doctor, why don't you explain to Sudara K'tut?" he begged.

"How could the doctor tell me what you want to say, Pito?" I asked. "He is not a mind reader."

"The doctor knows what we have to say. We have no secrets from the doctor, especially on this score."

The doctor smiled. "Come, young man, speak," he said. "Tell K'tut what you came to tell her. She will understand. After all, you have been her friend over the years. It would be better if you spoke."

There was more fidgeting and coughing. At last Pito said, "All right, but I shall read the document. It will be easier that way." He drew a paper from his pocket and began to read in his soft, musical voice.

"Sudara K'tut Tantri: We, the guerrilla fighters of Java Timor, know only too well the suffering and torture that you have been subjected to by the Japanese, just as we know how the Dutch persecuted you for so many years in Bali.

"Because of the love and understanding that you have had over the years for our people we, the guerrillas of Java Timor, pledge ourselves to help you in every way possible to reach your own countrymen at Batavia. This will mean smuggling you through Dutch and British held territory, but we will see that you are delivered safely to the American consul. Then you can be evacuated to your own country where you will have the proper medicine and food, and peace away from the strife in Java. If you, Sudara K'tut, accept this proposal, we shall be sad to lose you, but we shall abide by your decision. Every Indonesian will help you on your way."

Pito halted and looked at me for my reaction. My face must have shown how deeply I was touched. Although most of Java was in the hands of the Indonesians, the area around the two largest cities, Batavia and Surabaya, was held by the British for the Dutch. I knew that any effort to get me through the British lines into either of the cities would require these young men to risk their lives. I knew, too, that they were ready to take this risk without hesitation, should I agree. I gazed at Pito's sensitive face and at the noble faces of the others. If ever I felt love it was then.

"Go on, Pito dear," I whispered. "What is the second proposal?"

Pito tightened his lips and cleared his throat. "The second proposition will seem selfish on our part, but here it is," he said. He rustled the paper nervously, then read on in a steady voice:

"It is our hope that K'tut Tantri, health permitting, will not desert us in this great hour of Indonesia's destiny. It is our hope that Sudara K'tut will find it in her heart to stay in Indonesia and help to bring our beloved country to the same state of freedom that her own people enjoy.

"In other words, we ask K'tut Tantri to join us in our struggle for self-determination. But before any decision is made we should like to point out that the road to freedom will be fraught with danger. Life will be hard and austere. There will be no luxuries; often there may be starvation. We have nothing to offer Sudara K'tut Tantri in return for such a sacrifice, except the love and esteem of seventy million Indonesians.

"No matter which proposition K'tut Tantri chooses, we swear to abide by her choice. But it is our great hope that Sudara K'tut Tantri will join the Indonesian Revolution, and become to us the Mrs. Thomas Paine of Indonesia."

The reading ended, leaving me halfway between laughter and tears. Certainly I must not laugh, but—"Mrs. Thomas Paine." What a bait! Did they know that Thomas Paine suffered great hardships, often imprisonment, and was unappreciated for his great work in the American Revolution? Did they know he was buried in a pauper's grave? The ingenuousness of their touching appeal struck a chord in my heart, a chord of the lost melody from this fantastic and fascinating land. My friends waited silently, their large black eyes fixed on me. I closed my eyes and tried to think.

Evacuation to America—my heart danced at the very thought of it! How wonderful it would be just to be safe, away from the roar of guns. I was still weak and undernourished, and far from well. I felt that I could not stand any more war.

If I remained in Java I definitely could not have the care, the medicines, the good food I required to build up my health again. The luxuries of life, once so plentiful among the white people in Java, long since had disappeared. Already food was running short. Medicines were most difficult to come by. Prices on the black market were prohibitive. The doctor had been very good to me, but I wondered how he had obtained the vitamins, liver injections, and other medicines he had given me regularly. Although he never mentioned it to me, they must have been costing him a small fortune. And the nurse had told me that he was at his wit's end trying to find more medicines. Too, I had lost everything I had worked for in Indonesia. My paradise was lost to me forever. Yes; to evacuate to America, the land of plenty—that would be sheer heaven.

Thinking of the comfort and security available to me in the States, a picture crossed my mind—a picture of Prince Diponegoro, Indonesia's great romantic hero of olden times. I saw him riding a black horse, brandishing a jeweled sword, his red-and-gold cape flying in the wind as he led his followers against the fully armed Dutch invaders. That happened more than a hundred years ago, but the story of Diponegoro's heroism lives on in the heart of every Indonesian man, woman, and child. He failed in his heroic attempt, and was captured by the Dutch and sent into exile in Celebes, where he died. His noble spirit has been the inspiration of other brave men who have tried, again and again, to free Indonesia from its Dutch masters, only to suffer imprisonment, death, or exile to the dreaded Tanah Merah. But a century had gone by since Diponegoro. The situation had changed, and merdeka was no longer impossible of attainment. It would not be easy, but with seventy million Indonesians on the march toward independence they could not lose. This time, I was sure, Allah was on their side.

The story of Prince Diponegoro had always enchanted me, but how strange that I should see him so clearly at this time! Strange visions always came to me, it seemed, when I had to make an important decision.

From Prince Diponegoro my thoughts turned to the American Revolution, and to the men of other lands—Poles, Frenchmen, Germans, and Englishmen—who had played important parts in shaping the destiny of that great democracy. I thought of the little corset-maker, Thomas Paine, who wrote in his book *The Rights of Man:* "There can be no freedom for one unless there is freedom for all."

The Atlantic Charter and the Charter of the United Nations were much in my mind, for during my convalescence the doctor had read the texts to me as part of his patient program of enlightenment. I remembered his quotation from a May 30, 1942, broadcast of Under-secretary of State Sumner Welles to the people of Asia:

"As a result of this war, we must assure sovereign equality of all peoples the world over. Our victory must bring liberation for all peoples. Imperialism is dead. The right to freedom must be recognized."

Surely the Welles pronouncement came from the heart. Certainly the Atlantic Charter, framed by Sir Winston Churchill and President Roosevelt, was not just another piece of worthless paper, to be discarded as soon as the war was won. Then England and America would have to live up to the promises of the Charter. And I was a British-born American citizen.

My decision was made.

To the lovable golden people standing before me I said, "Come what may, I shall throw in my lot with the Indonesian people. I have no choice but to stand by Indonesia in her hour of trial." To Pito, quoting his child's words to me so many years ago, I mischievously added, "Take me with you, gentle Pito, for now I shall be your eyes and your tongue. I shall help get you the right change, and I'll show you the road. Or I will die in the attempt."

To my astonishment the three young men, on hearing these words, rushed from the room, and Pito fell to his knees, hid his face in the bedclothes, and wept. I wept too. The only dry-eyed person was the doctor, who sat in a corner stoically smoking his pipe.

For the third time in my life I had made my great decision, in favor of the people of Indonesia.

3

THE BRITISH ARE SURPRISED—
AND SO AM I

Now I understood why I had been rescued from the Japanese prison
and tenderly nursed back to some semblance of health. When I asked
the doctor what he would have felt had I decided to forsake Indonesia
and make my way to America, he replied:

"Such a thought never occurred to me. All your Indonesian friends
knew you would not leave us when we most needed you. Not you,
Sudara K'tut! You know, I have a long dossier on you, going back to
the first day you came to Indonesia."

"I was not aware that you were acquainted with any of my friends,"
I said.

He laughed. "You would be surprised how many of your friends I
know. Pito, of course; and Agung Nura I have met several times. Also
the professor, and Frisco Flip, and several others. I, too, was a member
of the resistance group during the Japanese occupation. That was how
I heard of you."

"Do you know where Agung Nura is now?" I asked.

"Yes; we know that he is back home in Bali. But we have had no
intelligence from there for some time." Bali was at the time in a
state of chaos. The people were bewildered at seeing the Dutch in
charge again. "However," the doctor added, "I am sure that Agung
Nura is with one of the guerrilla groups fighting in the hills. We plan
to send Pito to Bali as quickly as possible. If Agung Nura is alive,
Pito will find him."

The doctor outlined the plans concerning me. He pointed out the
dangers that I would face in the months or years ahead, and said, "The
first thing we must do is to get you a red-and-white armband with
the inscription 'Merdeka atau Mati'—Liberty or Death. This band is
worn by the peasants active in our struggle. You must wear it at all
times. It is a means of identification. Before long you will probably
be the only white person free in Java Timor. The band may save your
life."

I protested that this seemed a bit theatrical. "Why not just a plain red-and-white band?" I asked. "The Indonesian colors ought to be sufficient. Why bother with the inscription?"

"Because this is the slogan of the revolution," he said. "Every peasant understands 'Merdeka atau Mati.' They will be greatly pleased to see that they have at least one sympathizer from a foreign land. The band will endear you to the people and protect you from being taken for a Dutch woman."

Most of the Dutch, the doctor explained, had fled to Batavia in hopes of being evacuated to Holland. As was to be expected, the Indo-Dutch were claiming to be Dutch citizens, and were not admitting to their native blood—having forgotten that during the Japanese occupation they were eager to prove themselves half-castes in order to escape the concentration camps. By ruling of the new government these people were given the choice of remaining in Indonesia as their rightful motherland, and helping to maintain its freedom, or of proclaiming themselves enemies by choosing Dutch nationality.

"You may not believe this," the doctor said, "but ninety per cent of the Eurasians chose to remain Dutch citizens and they are just as anxious to suppress our freedom as the totok Dutch—the pure Dutch —are. Maybe more so. Of course, the Dutch don't want the Eurasians. They've always looked down on the half-castes. But now it's to their advantage to have the Eurasians on their side."

The doctor then went on in a confidential tone to say that the Indonesians intended to intern all the Dutch and Indo-Dutch left in Indonesian-held territory. It was a measure of protection, for the feelings of the people were running high and might get out of control, especially if the Dutch and British used firearms against the native population.

"If that happens," the doctor concluded grimly, "no white person will be safe in Java."

"And what about me?" I asked. "I happen to have been born white."

"We shall protect you to the best of our ability. At first, however, you must be extremely cautious. You must take no chances until you become well known to our people. You must take care not to fall into Dutch hands, or into the hands of their agents. Never go anywhere with an Indonesian unless you know him well. The Dutch have spies everywhere, and especially among the Ambonese."

Over the years Christian missionaries had made some progress on the island of Ambon—as the Indonesians call Amboina. Many of the natives there were more thoroughly Westernized than those else-where in the East Indies. The Dutch had trained many Ambonese troops, and also tended to give Ambon natives the choicest civilian jobs.

The doctor said that tomorrow Pito would leave for Bali, and I would go to the Oranje Hotel in Surabaya for a week, to study the situation there. Surabaya swarmed with Dutchmen waiting im-patiently to get back to their former homes throughout Java. It would be interesting to check up on them.

"The British army is still massed at the harbor a few miles away, but it won't be long until they march into Surabaya," the doctor said. "When they do, fierce fighting will surely break out." He added that the Oranje was full of Dutch officials and army officers newly re-leased from the Japanese concentration camps. "We believe that a couple of American newspapermen also are staying at the Oranje. It would be most profitable to us to know what the Americans are think-ing about our declaration of independence, and how they regard the present situation in Java. It will be easy for you to chat with your countrymen.

"But don't ask any questions of any military or official Dutch. Above all, do not take one soul into your confidence. Be on your guard at all times. Act like any other white woman recently released from a Japanese prison camp. We don't want you to spy; that is not our purpose. But if you do accidentally hear of anything that we should know, we of course are relying on you to inform us. Do not go out of your way to find out anything. And remember we are not at war with the British—yet. We do not want to fight the British; but if we are forced to fight to maintain merdeka, we will fight to the death.

"At the end of the week I shall contact you. By that time we shall have worked out a plan for you. However, in case of an emergency—in case you wish to see me—suddenly become sick and send for the doctor. The doctor will be me. One thing more: do not wear your armband during your stay at the hotel. Hide it away carefully."

My last night at the doctor's mountain chalet was spent in the com-pany of Pito. We had much to say to each other. When morning came, and just before he was leaving, Pito asked what had become of the charm he had given to me when we first met, knowing that I had worn it constantly around my waist on a silver chain.

I told him that the Japanese had ripped it off when they questioned me at Kediri and that I had never seen it again. The Japanese also took the Ardjuno coin that Agung Nura had given to me.

"I have another charm for you," Pito stammered shyly. "This one is much stronger, and must be worn next to the skin. It will protect you from all harm in these dangerous days that are ahead of you." He pulled from his tunic pocket a long strip of white cloth stitched with designs of gods and demons and with magic words of protection in ancient Sanskrit. Handing it to me, he said, "May Allah protect you always, Sudara K'tut."

We said good-by, rubbed noses, and drew in our breath. "Selamet tinggal—live in peace," said Pito. "Selamet djalan," I replied. "Go in peace."

I found the Oranje Hotel greatly changed since the days of the Dutch and the early days of the Japanese occupation. Everything looked shoddy. Furniture and the green plants were missing from the hall and lounge. Where the orchestra had played during lunch and dinner, the stage now was bare. Gone were the fine table linen, sparkling silver, and expensive china, replaced by cheap things of Japanese make. The Indonesian staff members wore patched and shabby sarongs, and had a sullen appearance. I sat in the lounge observing the behavior of the foreigners, all of whom seemed to be drinking far too much. The arrogance of the Dutch amazed me. They had learned nothing from the war, and from their internment. They were loud and boastful of what they would do when they regained control of the city.

On my third day at the hotel I met a young Dutch officer who invited me to have a drink. He was pleased to find that I was a native of Britain, and treated me as though we were both victims of the Indonesians. "What do you think of those natives having the audacity—the gall—to declare independence?" he fumed.

It was more of an explosion than a question. I said I understood little of what was happening in Java. "I am just out of a Japanese prison myself," I explained. "I am weary of war."

My friend patted me on the shoulder and said my troubles would be over in a matter of days. "Your countrymen will be marching into Surabaya," he said.

"I understand the British ships are still massed at the harbor," I responded.

"Yes, I know. They have been waiting for Dutch reinforcements. Three days from now Indonesia will get a big surprise. I hope you are around to see the fun."

"How thrilling!" said I, leading him on. "But it would have to be something really big to surprise the Indonesians at this point."

"Well, it is something big." He pulled from his coat pocket a plan for bottling up the Indonesians in Surabaya. The British would march from the harbor in a single column as far as the Djambatan Merah, a red bridge. At that point they would separate into two columns, one entering the city from the east and the other from the west, at a point beyond where the Indonesian army was stationed.

"The Indonesians won't be able to retreat, nor will they be able to move forward," he said, chuckling. "They will have to surrender."

"It's a clever plan," I said, staring at the piece of paper, forcing my mind to memorize the details, which I could do more readily as I knew the city of Surabaya well. "A good plan. I hope it works."

"It will work all right," he said, continuing his drinking. I had hoped that he would leave the piece of paper on the table, but he was not that drunk. He returned it to his pocket.

"How in the world did you get hold of the British plans?" I asked.

He grinned knowingly. "We have our contacts. Furthermore, all Dutch officers inside the city of Surabaya are prepared for the entry of the English. We know what's up."

That same night I became "ill" and asked the djonges (room boy) to call a doctor. I gave him the telephone number. My particular doctor speedily arrived, little black bag and all. I explained to him the British occupation plan and drew a map from memory. He listened gravely until I had finished, then quickly took his leave. "You stay in bed until I return," he ordered. He said he would warn the TRI— the Indonesian military.

Since I had pledged myself to the Indonesian side I had no choice but to warn the doctor. I had no intention of allowing the Indonesians to fall into a trap that I knew had been set.

The doctor returned the next morning and said I must leave the Oranje Hotel immediately and go to the kampong home of an Indonesian friend of his. He explained that the Indonesians would raid the Oranje that very night and arrest all Dutchmen. Other foreigners would not be molested. "Some of the Dutch have firearms, and they may put up a fight. It's likely to be unsafe around the hotel tonight."

The address the doctor gave me was very near the Djambatan Merah. I stayed there three days, listening to the roar of guns and mortar shells until I felt I could stand no more. My Indonesian host told me that the hotel had been raided successfully and all the Dutch had been rounded up.

"But they put up a terrific fight in the hotel lobby. You wouldn't recognize the hotel, it's so riddled with bullets. When the fighting was over the other foreigners, afraid of more raids, left for the homes of friends. They held one American as a suspected Dutchman, but released him when his credentials proved to be all right. The shooting has chased everyone indoors. You won't find a soul on the streets of Surabaya."

I wanted to telephone the doctor, but the lines were either cut or down or the exchange deserted. Unable to endure confinement near the firing range any longer and worried, too, about the doctor, I decided to take a chance and go to the Oranje Hotel. It would be a long walk through the back streets. My host tried to discourage me, and warned me that I would not be safe from snipers.

Nevertheless, I fastened the red-and-white band around my arm and stepped boldly into the street. As my host had said, the streets were deserted. I did not meet a soul, but I did pass a few people sitting on the verandas of their homes. Some of them ignored me and some stared in amazement—smiling when they saw my armband. "Merdeka!" I saluted them. And they one and all answered, "Merdeka!"

Just before I reached the hotel I took the band from my arm and stuffed it into my pocket, as a precaution in the event Europeans were around. It was a very foolish move, I realized later.

I was surprised to find the entrance of the hotel deserted. Not even the usual dogs were in sight. I stepped into the open lobby and, before I could open my mouth, was seized by a group of young men. Each wore a red-and-white armband.

The leader of the group appeared to be a hotel chef, for he was wearing a cook's hat. He forced me into a chair, bent my head back, drew out a large carving knife from his sarong, and held the point at my throat. I was speechless with fright and indignation.

"Njonja belanda—Dutch woman!" he growled. "Where did you come from? What are you doing here?"

I stared blankly at him, too terrified to say a word. Then I remembered my armband, and pulled it from my pocket. Now it was their turn to stare.

"Where did you get that?" my assailant demanded. "Come on; tell us. From whom did you steal it?"

The knife was still at my throat, but I barely managed to croak, "I got it from Dr. S."

"Dr. S.," they said in a chorus. "How could you know about Dr. S?"

"Why don't you phone him and find out?" I asked weakly. "I am not a Dutch woman. I am an American citizen."

"American!" they exclaimed together. "You can't be American. There are no American women in Surabaya." But at the magic word "American" they took the knife away from my throat.

The ringleader ordered one of the boys to telephone the doctor. While he was gone they sat and stared at me in silence as though I were some rare animal escaped from the zoo. Presently the boy returned and said the doctor would be right over. When he arrived and heard what had happened, he called them all the uncomplimentary names he could bring to mind. "Fools," he shouted, "you might have killed her!"

"How were we to know she was an American?" one of the boys asked.

"It doesn't matter whether she is an American or not," he retorted. "Even if she were Dutch, you had no right to threaten her or to hold a knife at her throat. You only have the right to take suspicious people to the proper authorities. You cannot take the law into your own hands.

"Let this be a lesson to you, that not all white people are enemies. Even among the Dutch we still have friends. Because of their nationality they cannot take sides openly. Their countrymen would consider that treason. As for other nationalities, this is not a war. Neutral countries can choose the side their conscience tells them to choose."

After his tirade against my assailants the doctor cooled down a bit and sought to ease some of the sharpness and sting of his remarks. "I want you all to meet Sudara K'tut Tantri, from Bali," he said. "Right now she is the only white friend we have, or at least the only one openly to come to our side. From now on, see that no harm comes to her. Pass the word along to your compatriots, and to your members in the kampongs. K'tut Tantri is our ally."

There were sheepish smiles and mumbled apologies. We shook hands all around. As I left the hotel with the doctor, he turned on me furiously. "How could you be so foolish as to leave the safety of your hideout? I had intended calling for you tomorrow. You must promise never, never to take such chances again."

"I promise," I said meekly. I was still shaking at the thought of that knife at my throat.

I spent the night at the doctor's Surabaya house and heard the story of the raiding of the Hotel Oranje. We talked far into the night as the doctor unfolded his plan for me. I was to live at a secret radio station run by the guerrilla leader Bung Tomo himself, from which he broadcast twice nightly. It was called Radio Pemberontakan—the Revolutionary Radio—and was hidden in a large, rambling house not far from the official station, Radio Surabaya. "We expect the British to bomb Radio Surabaya any day now, so it wouldn't be safe for you to work there," the doctor explained. "And should Surabaya fall to the British, you would not be safe even at the secret guerrilla station. If Radio Pemberontakan should be bombed or captured, we have other secret stations spread out all over East Java, mostly in guerrilla strongholds in the mountains."

The doctor said I would broadcast twice nightly in the English language. My purpose would be to bring to the English-speaking peoples of the world the Indonesian story, from the Indonesian viewpoint.

"The English-speaking world must hear the truth of our struggle and must be brought to understand that this is not a social revolution nor a Japanese puppet government," he said. "It is the struggle of seventy million Indonesians to free themselves from all foreign domination.

"You will tell the history of our country and of our struggle over the past forty years. You will remind the English and the Americans of their famous wartime speeches that promised freedom to all peoples the world over. You can quote passages from the Atlantic Charter and the Charter of the United Nations, and report the daily happenings in Indonesia. You can tell of your own life in Indonesia."

A magazine in the English language was being started, to be called

The Voice of Free Indonesia. Through it the foreign correspondents in Batavia, and those unable to read the Indonesian language, would be fully informed about what was going on in Republican-held territory. The doctor suggested that I write for this magazine in addition to my broadcasts, and help with suggestions. "The subject matter will be left to your discretion," he said. "We don't want you to be clever, but only to tell the simple truth."

Then he warned me: "You can expect, after the Dutch have heard your broadcasts, to be maliciously slandered as they now are slandering Bung Tomo. They will ridicule your broadcasts and they'll try to riddle your reputation. They probably will depict you as an adventuress taking advantage of the situation in Indonesia. Harden your heart to all this; give it no heed. No matter what they say about you or Bung Tomo, never retaliate by slandering any individual broadcasting for the Dutch. Just give the facts. The truth will prevail."

I went to the secret station the next day and met the famous Sutomo, fondly called Bung Tomo by his followers. Bung is somewhat the equivalent of brother. It was customary for each man in Java to address another by the prefix "Bung." Even the President of Indonesia was called Bung Karno, never President Sukarno. And the President fully approved.

Right from the start Bung Tomo and I got along famously. He was a slight, handsome man, not more than twenty-six years old. His manner was charming in its simplicity and sincerity. His luminous eyes shone with an inward fire, and his gift for oratory was second only to that of President Sukarno. He was plainly a dedicated young man.

Bung Tomo formerly had been a newspaperman. He had an excellent education, was a stimulating conversationalist, and could charm the ducks off the water. He showed great genius in organizing the peasants and inspiring them to go forth and fight for freedom, even if only with machetes, bamboo spears, or bare hands.

The people worshiped Bung Tomo and followed him blindly. Next to President Sukarno, he was unquestionably the most popular man in Indonesia. The Dutch, of course, hated him with an unholy hate, and they showed their vindictiveness by spreading malicious and untrue stories about him in the press and on the air. They called him the worst sort of fanatic, and accused him of atrocities that shocked his sensitive soul.

In all the years I knew Bung Tomo I never saw him perform a brutal act. He was much too gentle. True, his broadcasts were strong and virile. He told the Dutch bluntly that they would never get back into Indonesia as overlords. He warned that if the Dutch insisted upon imposing themselves again on the people of Indonesia, the millions of peasants that he controlled would fight to the bitter end. I have no doubt—and I was in a unique position to know the truth—it was the famous broadcasts of Bung Tomo that held East Java. Neither the Dutch nor the British advanced any farther than Surabaya, only two or three miles from where they had landed. And Bung Tomo's broadcasts inspired the rest of the peasants throughout Java to rout the Dutch. No wonder they hated him—hated him enough to put a price on his head, dead or alive.

It was not long before I too became a great annoyance to the Dutch and was slandered in the same way as Bung Tomo.

4

BROADCASTING FOR THE GUERRILLAS

The situation was tense when I joined the staff of Radio Pemberontakan, the guerrilla station hidden in a back street of Surabaya, and it was only a few days later that all hell broke loose.

It started with an amazing story brought to me at the station, a story that I could not believe and refused to broadcast until I could brand it true or false. I was told that the British army, composed largely of British Indian and Gurkha troops, had been smuggling Dutch soldiers ashore at the Surabaya docks. Once on the streets of Surabaya, it was no trick for the Dutch to make their way to the locations within the unarmed and unpatrolled city where their forces could secretly be built up. The British themselves remained on their ships and on the docks, in apparent decorum.

How was the smuggling accomplished? By staining the faces of the Dutch a brown color to match the complexions of the Indians and Nepalese. How had this been discovered? Through the arrest of three soldiers believed to be Gurkhas. But the tropic heat had caused the stain to run. The Indonesians were astonished to find that one of their prisoners was a white man with a streaked face.

I insisted upon being taken to the prison where the three men were held. The Gurkhas could not speak English, but the Dutchman could. He told me the whole story, hoping that I would use my influence to gain his release. A known Dutchman in uniform would be shot by Indonesian resistance leaders the minute he strayed away from the guarded docks, the prisoner told me. Hence it had been found useful to employ disguises, such as the facial stain. Other Dutchmen had been smuggled ashore in sacks when the British unloaded food and equipment at the Surabaya docks.

I broadcast the story. So did the Gurkhas, through the medium of one of the Indian interpreters attached to our radio station. Immediately the Indonesians tightened their watch on British activities around the docks. And then, as was expected, the British marched into the lower end of the city. Terribly aroused, the Indonesian populace raged out of control, and a fierce struggle took place on the streets. The people for the most part were unarmed, incapable of combat with a well-trained British military force. Nevertheless, the people of Surabaya fought with what they had, and many a peasant went to his death with the cry of "Merdeka" on his lips.

There was one significant fact: the Indonesian regular army, the TRI, was not bottled up in Surabaya. It was prepared when the British attacked. It was not the Indonesians who were surprised, but the British and the Dutch. The TRI was able to retreat in an orderly fashion and to establish a new base a few kilometers from the Surabaya perimeter.

One disgraceful development followed another. The British tried using Japanese soldiers against the Indonesians—with some effectiveness, until a storm of protest from all over the world forced them to desist, and to change their tactics. Meanwhile more and more Dutch regular troops were landed in Java, along with battalions of British Tommies brought in from neighboring Asian countries, from Singapore, and from Burma.

The most famous of these battalions was the British West Yorkshires. On their arrival in Surabaya they quickly learned the truth—and mutinied. They laid down their firearms and said they would not fight the Indonesians.

"We have been brought here under false pretenses," their spokesman said. "We were told that we would have only to quash a rebellion of a few Indonesian extremists and Japanese puppets, bent on making mischief for the Dutch. Now we find that seventy million Indonesians are fighting to maintain their freedom. We have just fought a war to defend our own freedom. We will not fight to suppress the liberty of another country."

One of the officers of the regiment agreed that he could not force the men to fight in the absence of a declaration of war between Indonesia and Britain. "We have no right here anyway," he conceded. A few days later the regiment was called back to England. The reason for its abrupt withdrawal was hushed up, but I learned about it from a most authoritative source.

One of the tragedies of this time was the violent death of Brigadier Mallaby, shot in or near his car in the heart of Surabaya. Mallaby, commander of the British troops in the area, had just left the scene of the signing, with President Sukarno, of a temporary truce between the Indonesians and the British. Sukarno had called upon the people to refrain from violence until they heard further from him.

The British were outraged at the senseless slaying, and promptly blamed the Indonesians. The Indonesians pointed out that they had nothing to gain and much to lose from the murder of the brigadier. They attributed the killing to provocateurs, agents of the Dutch hoping to undermine the relations between British and Indonesians. Then British Lieutenant General Sir Philip Christison, Allied commander in chief for the East Indies, announced that "unless the Indonesians responsible for Brigadier Mallaby's death immediately surrender, I intend to bring the whole weight of land, air and sea forces against them until they are crushed."

It was an intemperate and irresponsible statement for a high-ranking Britisher to make, and it incensed the Indonesians. Street fighting broke out again. Surabaya became a city of lawlessness. There were horrifying atrocities on both sides. People were afraid to go into the streets, or even to open their doors. Radio Surabaya had been bombed out of existence, but as yet Radio Pemberontakan had not been discovered. We continued to send out the news. President Sukarno made a last appeal to the Prime Minister of England to withdraw all British troops from Indonesia or to prevent them from intervening on the side of the Dutch. The appeal was fruitless. No official attention was paid to Sukarno's plea.

At Radio Pemberontakan, when I was not broadcasting I was paint-ing, and drawing Indonesian banners and posters for the guerrillas. I borrowed largely on American and French history for the slogans—ex-tracts from the sayings of Jefferson, Thomas Paine, Washington, Beaumarchais, and others.

I had made a particular white banner with these words in red: ABRAHAM LINCOLN WALKS AGAIN IN INDONESIA. Referring, of course, to his freeing of the slaves. The guerrillas were exceedingly pleased with this banner. However, when the banners appeared on the streets of Surabaya I was surprised to find that the wording had been altered slightly. Now the banners read: ABE WALKS AGAIN IN INDONESIA. I was amused, but when Bung Tomo saw the new version he ordered the banners destroyed and the original wording restored. "Abe sounds like something from American comic strips," he said. "It is very dis-respectful to abbreviate the name of a man of the greatness of Abraham Lincoln." But Abe he remained to the simple people. One and all, they loved Abe Lincoln.

Bung Tomo was now living in and broadcasting from Malang, south of Surabaya in East Java. Surabaya had become unsafe for a man with such a price on his head. Arrangements had been made to trans-fer me also, if the situation became dangerous. And danger was near at hand.

Dutch planes and radio station finders had been searching every-where for Radio Pemberontakan, and the planes had been circling over our area for days. Our station was cunningly concealed. We were still undiscovered when the most shocking development of the whole Revolution occurred. It was the turning point for the Indonesians. And I nearly lost my life.

I have read many books by Americans, Dutch, English, and other nationalities on the Indonesian Revolution. Strange as it may seem, I have found none that tells the story of the bombing of Surabaya in detail. It was an atrocious deed against a defenseless city. All the authors have glossed over this revolting act of an undeclared war.

After the death of Brigadier Mallaby, a new general took charge and immediately put into effect a get-tough policy. Through thou-sands of pamphlets dropped from planes and by radio broadcasts he ordered all the Indonesian leaders, army officers, and radio officials in the Surabaya area to bring to a designated place, at a specified time, their contraband weapons. They were to drop the firearms on the ground and, with their hands over their heads, proceed to the point where the British command would be waiting to accept their formal surrender. If they did not comply by sundown of the next day, the city of Surabaya would be bombed and kept under repeated bombardment until they did comply.

This ultimatum was too childish to be taken seriously. The Indonesians accepted it naturally as some kind of monstrous joke. Surely the British would not attack an open city, a defenseless city with virtually no military aspect, a city devoid of air-raid shelters and surrounded by the kampongs of the poor.

I was shocked to hear of this ultimatum, and immediately broadcast a warning to the general that the British could make no greater mistake than to bomb Surabaya. "The Indonesians will never accept your terms, even if you bomb Surabaya to the ground and kill every man and woman and child," I blazed at him. "The ultimatum is an insult to the Indonesians and to their intelligence. If you go through with it you will add a black page indeed to British history."

The general ignored the broadcast, and the Indonesians ignored the ultimatum. The outcome was the bombing of Surabaya by the British on three consecutive days and nights. Hundreds upon hundreds were killed. The streets ran with blood, women and children lay dead in the gutters. Kampongs were in flames, and the people fled in panic to the relative safety of the rice fields. But the Indonesians did not surrender.

At Radio Pemberontakan only three of us were in the station when the shells began falling in our part of the city. Our Indonesian broadcaster had gone to the mountains only the day before to make arrangements for our removal to a new and more secure location. An Arab employee and I were in the broadcasting studio, and we were unhurt. Our Indian broadcaster had gone to the rear of the house to the toilet. Fragments of a mortar shell ripped into him, killing him almost instantly. Only my dog, Brani, lying under a table in the dining room, thumping his tail furiously and gnawing at a bone, was undisturbed. After the third day and third night of the barbarous assault, the hospital and streets were jammed with pitiful victims. Because of the sustained attack, no medical reinforcements had reached Surabaya; and there were not half enough trained nurses or doctors to attend the wounded. Sick from the terror and suffering everywhere about, and much too inexperienced to be of any use around the hospital, I decided that I might be of some help in the kampongs, among the poor people.

I shall never forget the sights in the villages. One old man sat in the corner of his hovel staring into space. "What is the matter, bapa?" I asked. "What is troubling you?" He gazed at me unseeingly for a time, then rose and led me into a small bedroom. There, laid out on the floor, were the bodies of three young men, ranging in age from about fourteen to seventeen. "My sons," said the old man. "They died for Merdeka."

These were only three of the thousands who died in the bombing of Surabaya. Back at the station I found the doctor, who had just come in from Malang. "You must leave Surabaya at once," he said. "We have arranged for you to go to the radio station at Bangkil [about sixty kilometers away]. You will leave tonight with a military escort. Bangkil will be safe for the time being, but for how long—who knows?"

I told the doctor I did not want to leave Surabaya. "I don't care a fig for my life right now," I said. "I am deeply ashamed that Englishmen should have brought so much misery to the Indonesian people."

"Don't be too distressed on that score, Sudara K'tut," the doctor said. "There are thousands of good English and good people of other countries who feel exactly as you do. Protests are coming from all over the world. It is a cruel thing to say, but the bombing of Surabaya in the long run may prove to be a good thing for the Indonesians. Until now, little attention has been given internationally to this part of the world and its troubles. Now Indonesia is very much the center of the attention of the peoples of the world, and of the United Nations."

The doctor finally agreed that I might stay in Surabaya one more day. After he had left the station I went calling on the consuls and other representatives of the foreign countries with diplomatic or commercial attachés in Surabaya—the Danes, the Swiss, the Russians, and the Swedes. I asked them to join me in a broadcast that night protesting the bombings. I urged each to tell his respective country what he thought of the British action. Everyone agreed. That night we told our story, and it had a broad effect. Stations in other lands picked up the broadcast and sent it out again to their listeners. Newspapers in distant countries picked up the text and used it for editorials. The strongest protest of all, among those I interviewed, came from a White Russian.

Yes; the bombing of Surabaya was the turning point in the Indonesian Revolution. It was also the turning point for me. Heretofore I had not worn my armband at the station. From now on I would never be seen without it. "Merdeka atau Mati." I would go forth proudly, fearlessly, with no concern for my own life. I would stay with the Indonesians, win or lose. Perhaps, as a British woman, I could make up in some small way for the incalculable harm my countrymen had wrought.

The day after the consuls' broadcast, we closed down the Surabaya facility of Radio Pemberontakan. We stored part of the equipment in an isolated house. Then, in a jeep accompanied by three TRI soldiers, I proceeded without incident to Bangkil. The next day, in Bangkil, Radio Pemberontakan once again was on the air in the English language.

Bung Tomo, heard nightly from his secret station in Malang, came to Bangkil once or twice a week to broadcast with us. It must be made clear that Radio Pemberontakan was the station of the guerrilla fighters, as distinguished from the official stations of the Republic of Indonesia—which were at Jogjakarta, the mid-Java city to which President Sukarno and other officials moved from Jakarta (Batavia) after the British had occupied that city, and at Surakarta, another inland city commonly known as Solo. Our Radio Pemberontakan had a number of transmitting stations spread throughout the mountains in East Java.

Every evening after our broadcasts we listened to the broadcasts of the Dutch-controlled stations in Jakarta and Bandung. We took special care to tune in on the unofficial stations, for it was from these stations that the worst kind of lying propaganda against Indonesia was broadcast.

One night, much to my astonishment—and to the amusement of the Indonesians listening with me—we heard a broadcast promising 50,000 guilders to any Indonesian who would bring K'tut Tantri into the Dutch military headquarters at Surabaya, or to any other Dutch-controlled place. Usually we did not bother to reply to Dutch broadcasts except when something seriously required a rebuttal. But this time we had to have our fun. I went on the air, called the Dutch station, identified myself and said I considered their offer to the Indonesians a trifle mean.

"You know that the Dutch guilder is worthless in Indonesia now," I said. "We have our own currency. But if you Dutch will donate half a million guilders to the Indonesians to continue their struggle for Merdeka, I shall most willingly walk into your headquarters under my own steam."

All the radio stations in Java picked up my broadcast, and there was much chuckling at the clumsy Dutch maneuver. We heard no more about the matter. They did not repeat the offer.

We had never a dull moment at the Bangkil station. There was always much to do. One day three young men with the familiar red-and-white armbands drew up in a jeep and asked for me, saying that they had been sent by Bung Tomo to bring me to Malang. It did not occur to me to doubt them. We had recently been talking of leaving Bangkil shortly, for the station was too accessible, too easy to find.

I packed the few things I had and joined the boys in the jeep. After we had been riding for some miles I realized that we had turned off from the road to Malang. "This is not our road," I said. "Where are you going?"

The leader of the group calmly turned toward me. "Consider yourself kidnaped," he said. "You are on your way to Tretes, in the mountains."

They went on to explain that they had a radio transmitter in their mountain retreat, under the command of an Indonesian army major. But they had no one to broadcast in the English language. They assured me that they, too, were freedom fighters, and that I had nothing to fear.

"Bung Tomo's stations have had a monopoly on your services long enough," the leader said. "Now it is our turn. You are becoming famous as a broadcaster. People all over Java tune in just to hear you."

I had heard of this major and his mountain fort, and what I had heard I did not like. He dressed all his followers in black shirts and he lived like a bandit, in considerable splendor. But he was one hundred per cent behind Merdeka. No one could accuse him of not being a real freedom fighter. He was ruthless in his methods, dangerous and fanatical. Spies, when captured, were put to death immediately, often without a chance to defend their innocence. His own followers were afraid of him.

When I was brought to his headquarters and introduced he was most agreeable, and apologized for kidnaping me. He said I would be much safer in the mountains with him than in the village of Bangkil. "And after all, it does not matter from where you broadcast." He shrugged. "It's all for the same cause."

There would be nothing gained by showing anger. I was confident that the minute I broadcast from this mountain stronghold my friends at Bangkil would guess what had happened, so I decided to make the best of it. Sometimes these young men acted like children. They enjoyed playing jokes on each other, and the Black Shirts considered this a good joke on Bung Tomo. I gathered that there also was some personal jealousy involved.

So now I was with the Black Shirts behind Tretes. They lived like Robin Hoods in the mountains, raiding rich Chinese merchants to get money and food for the men and for the villagers. A week and more went by while I wondered what my friends were thinking and whether Dr. S. had heard of my kidnaping. Then one night as I was strolling down the mountain road after my broadcast, not far from the camp but far enough to be out of view, I was startled by two young men who stepped out of the bushes.

"Sudara K'tut, don't be afraid," one said. "We are friends, from Bangkil." I recognized them at once. "We have a truck hidden down the road a little way," they said. "If you hurry we can be away from Tretes before any of the Black Shirts realize that you have not returned."

We hurried to the truck and were on our way. The next day I resumed broadcasting from Bangkil, and my rescuers amused all of Bung Tomo's boys with their tale of my rekidnaping. It was a relief to me to get away from the major. Although he was invariably charming and courteous to me, I considered him a most dangerous man and a menace to the cause. Sometime later I received a letter from him telling me that I would be back with him in Tretes before I knew it. Before this could happen he was arrested by the Indonesian minister for defense and pronounced insane.

A few weeks after my return to Bangkil Dutch planes began to circle over the town, apparently seeking the exact location of our radio station. We received instructions to dismantle the station and leave at once, and we did this under cover of night. We loaded food and our equipment into a truck and drove to the mountains to an address we had been given. From there we pushed on the next day to a place behind Modjokerto. For this trip we used horses. No trucks could proceed up the steep, rocky trail. Our new home was much like the camp of the black-shirted major, a real mountain kampong. We made ourselves as comfortable as we could and began setting up our equipment. To our distress we discovered that one of the most important parts of the transmitter had been smashed on the long trek. Without it, our Voice of Merdeka could not be heard.

Radio transmitter spare parts by now were almost impossible to find. We sat around our campfire gloomily, wondering what to do. No use to send a runner to Malang, the nearest accessible city. Radio Malang had recently had the very same trouble. "What a pity we cannot go to Surabaya," one of the young men said. "Remember? We stored a lot of equipment in that basement near our old station. In that stock is exactly what we need."

But Surabaya was out of the question. By now the British had full control, and had guarded all the entrances to the city with roadblocks and Tommies or Gurkha troops. The British had no wish to empty the city or to prevent the normal routine of living. Thus there was a constant flow of native traffic into and out of Surabaya, but every Indonesian entering or leaving was searched. The radio parts we needed would be too heavy and too large to conceal.

The next morning a courier arrived with news that the Bangkil radio station had been bombed. We had moved the equipment out just in time. We only hoped that none of the villagers had been hurt.

We were sitting on our mats having breakfast when the chieftain of this particular guerrilla camp calmly said, "Sudara K'tut, we have worked out a plan while you slept. We know how to get into Surabaya and bring back that radio equipment!"

"I knew you would come up with something," I said, with great satisfaction. "How will you do it?"

He unfolded to me his plan, and it gave me goose flesh to hear him. I had witnessed or been informed about many plans—"operations," as the guerrillas loved to call them—but none so fantastic as this one. I stared at them half in amazement, half in admiration.

It was to be known as Operation Nursie. And this was the plan: I was to become a nurse. A white uniform would be made for me, with a red band with "International Red Cross" conspicuously sewed on my sleeve. A set of papers, and a pass with my photograph attached, would claim me as—and this was sheer Indonesian corn—Molly McTavish. The Indonesians would provide an ambulance on which would be daringly printed INTERNATIONAL RED CROSS. A private hospital at Modjokerto would supply the ambulance. A guerrilla chieftain would drive the ambulance, wearing a chauffeur's uniform. Inside would be two other guerrillas, one swathed in bandages as the "patient" and the other, dressed in white, as an intern. We would drive into Surabaya right through the British roadblocks, for who would dare stop an ambulance of the International Red Cross carrying a desperately wounded man to Surabaya hospital for a blood transfusion?

"Of course, we expect to be stopped," said my informant. "That is where you come in. You, as a white woman with a very British voice, would not be suspected by a British soldier standing guard at the road-block. What with the uniform, the ambulance, and the sick man inside, we should be passed readily into the city. Inside Surabaya we will keep to the back streets and go straight to where our radio parts are hidden. The sick man and the intern will load the equipment into the ambulance and hide it under the seat. Then they will start back to camp by walking through the sawah fields, and over the mountains. You, the nurse, and I, the ambulance driver, will drive back in style."

What astonished me most about the Indonesian guerrillas was their colossal nerve and their thoroughness for detail. Time and again I was surprised that illiterate peasant men could think out the smallest details, the most strategic moves, in a realistic manner, and make them work.

I pointed out that there was at this time no International Red Cross in Java. I suggested that it might be dangerous to masquerade as such.

"Don't let that worry you," the chieftain said breezily. "British Tommies are not so bright. They wouldn't know an International Red Cross from an International Pub."

My friend was joking, of course. I knew, if he didn't, that the British forces are among the best politically informed soldiers in the world.

There was no alternative but for me to go along with their planning, foolhardy though it might be. Was I not one of them, dedicated to

Indonesia Merdeka? In just a few days I was nurse Molly McTavish, immaculate in starched white uniform and cap, secure in my identification papers stamped with a seal of the International Red Cross.

As everyone knows who has lived in Java or Bali, the Indonesians are born actors. The ambulance arrived with INTERNATIONAL RED CROSS painted brazenly on its side, complete with khaki-clad driver with a cap bearing the band of the International Red Cross. I peered inside and gasped. A man was swathed in bandages so that he was unrecognizable, and the bandages were bloody. "Don't be afraid," the sick man said. "It's only chicken blood." The intern wore a white uniform with a Red Cross emblem.

Trembling from head to foot I took my place beside the chauffeur. Then just as we were about to start one of the guerrillas handed me what he called an "egg."

"What is this?" I asked.

"It's a hand grenade, in case you run into trouble. You mustn't get captured. All you have to do is pull the pin and throw it as hard as you can."

I jumped down from the seat of the ambulance. "I did not know this was a military operation," I said angrily. "I am not going along if we take any firearms with us." I insisted on searching inside the ambulance, and was disgusted to find a Tommy gun and a couple of pistols. Obviously my companions were expecting to run into trouble.

After much arguing the men finally agreed that they would not take along any firearms, but would leave our fate in the hands of Allah. With this, we started on our adventure. I am sure that they were as nervous as I was, but they did not show it. We drove along in silence, mile after mile. When we neared the roadblock guarding this particular entrance to Surabaya, the chauffeur started the ambulance siren, hoping we might be able to drive through without stopping for inspection. But a British soldier and two Gurkhas with rifles stopped us.

The Englishman came over, and almost fell into the ambulance with surprise at seeing a white woman. "Well, fancy meeting a white woman in this God-forsaken place," he said. "What is your name, miss?"

"Molly McTavish," I replied in the strongest Scotch accent I could muster. "And what would your name be?"

He told me his name, said he hated Surabaya, and was homesick for London; and we were friends in a minute. He asked me, in cockney accents, to meet him when we were both off duty.

"I would love to, but I can't talk any longer now," I said. "The man inside the ambulance is very ill, and every minute counts. I am taking him to the Surabaya hospital for a blood transfusion. We are from the hospital at Modjokerto, and we are not equipped to give transfusions."

The cockney looked inside the ambulance. "Och, the poor man," he said. "What bloody bandages!"

"We'll be back through in about an hour," I told him. "If you're still here we can talk a little longer, perhaps, and see what we can work out on my day off."

He beamed at me, and said, "All the King's men couldn't move me out of here until you come back, Molly."

The guard waved us on our way through the empty streets of Surabaya. Not a soul was to be seen. Certainly not all the inhabitants could have fled the city, but at this hour at least they were remaining under cover. Only the poor starving dogs were around, howling the call of the dead. Whatever we had looked for, we had not expected a ghost town. We were so tense that we said never a word until we reached the deserted house where our equipment was stored. We hurried inside, then sat down and laughed hysterically.

We found the radio parts in good condition, along with a sack of American canned foods and a carton of cigarettes. Swiftly we loaded the ambulance, fearful that any minute British or Dutch soldiers might come along. The sick man unwound his bandages, and the intern discarded his uniform and donned a sarong and fez. Now they were two ordinary hungry coolies, on the prowl for food. We said our good-bys and wished them luck. It would take them two days, at least, to get back to camp.

The chieftain and I started back to camp at once. When we reached the roadblock again, sure enough, there stood our little cockney friend waiting for us. We gave him the carton of cigarettes and he was ever so pleased. We talked of England a bit, and he gave me his mother's address in London. We made tentative arrangements to meet in Surabaya at the Hotel Oranje the following Sunday—an engagement that I, of course, had no intention of keeping. "If I don't show up, you'll know we had an emergency and I couldn't get away," I said. "In that case I'll write to you."

He tried to talk to the chauffeur. "No savvy Engleesh," the chieftain said. I chuckled inwardly, for this Indonesian had been a lawyer, was educated in Holland, and could speak English much better than did the cockney.

"Molly, what a brave girl you are," the guard said as we prepared to leave. "Living alone among a lot of black men, and nursing them when they are sick. Bless you. And I'll see you on Sunday?"

"That you will," I replied.

As we drove homeward the chieftain remarked, "That was really a very sympathetic soldier. You must not stand him up next Sunday. It will be better for you to write him a note that you have been transferred to Malang. I wouldn't like to see him hurt or have him know that we have deceived him."

This did not surprise me. I had found from experience that the Indonesian men fighting for merdeka were a very sensitive lot, tenderhearted in the extreme. This man had not even been offended at having his countrymen being called "blacks." "The Englishman did not know any better," he said.

I had not fully realized the tension of our journey until weariness hit me as we reached our camp. Our return had been anxiously awaited, and we were royally welcomed, with many embraces and extravagant praise. Operation Nursie had been a great success.

That night we had a great feast: canned beans, corned beef, and pineapple chunks, and after dinner we sat around the fire while the Indonesians sang sad songs of days gone by. The following morning all evidence was destroyed. The sick man and the intern staggered into camp a day later, ravenously hungry but otherwise unharmed. With the radio transmitter repaired, once more the Voice of Free Indonesia was on the air. And all was well at the camp.

5

TRANSFER TO JOGJAKARTA

The life of an Indonesian partisan was very hard at times. There were no luxuries, and there was a general food shortage. We ate twice a day, usually the same thing—rice and ground chili pods, and half a salted duck egg for each person. Sometimes we had a soup of native leaves and vegetables boiled in coconut milk. Banana leaves served as plates, and our spoons were little scoopers fashioned from banana leaves. There was always plenty of coffee, for Java is a coffee-growing country.

Our camp was deep in the mountains between Malang and Surabaya. The nearest town was Modjokerto, twenty miles away by road. Except for Surabaya, all of East Java was still in the hands of the Indonesians. The Indonesian army from East Java was stationed a few miles from the Surabaya perimeter, and firing between the English and the Indonesians was going on constantly. Of course the guerrillas were doing their best to make life hazardous for the Dutch and the English.

In Indonesian-held territory throughout Java all was running well under the new government. This fact seemed to surprise the world, and most of all the British. They were now fully aware that they had been led by the Dutch into a false position, that the new Republic of Indonesia was not merely a rebel uprising.

President Sukarno, wishing the outside world to know that all was under control in Indonesian territory, decided to make a tour by special train to East Java. From his headquarters in Jogjakarta he invited a few foreign correspondents—all of them stationed in British- and Dutch-held Batavia, or Jakarta, as the Indonesians knew it—to join him in the inspection tour.

This was in the early days of the Revolution, not long after the bombing of Surabaya. It was unsafe for white men to move about most of Indonesia, and no Western correspondents had yet visited Jogjakarta or other Republican strongholds, or East Java. However, as members of the entourage of the President they would certainly be safe. They could see for themselves that the Indonesians were capable of running their own country.

It was decided that President Sukarno should bring the correspondents to Selecta, once a popular Dutch mountain resort and not far from Malang. Selecta had long been known for its fine resort hotel, one of the most luxurious of its type in all of Java. Now the hotel, still run by a Swiss manager, was bullet-ridden and run down. The village of Selecta itself was now a guerrilla stronghold.

To our mountain camp one day came a special courier with a letter from one of the commanders of East Java. He asked me to go immediately to Selecta to meet President Sukarno and the foreign correspondents who would be with him, so that they—the foreign correspondents—might hear from a white person the story of the Indonesian struggle for independence. And I was to be that white person.

I discarded my sarong and sandals and put on my one and only dress. To my sleeve I attached the red-and-white armband, "Merdeka atau Mati," though I knew that the band in all probability would cause raised eyebrows among the correspondents.

When I arrived at the Selecta hotel I found the meeting room filled with army personnel. Most of the guerrilla leaders of East Java were there, including Bung Tomo, who chose to remain incognito to all except President Sukarno. There were perhaps a dozen white correspondents—English, American, Australian, Canadian, French— and, understandably, no Dutchmen. There were also British Indians, Chinese, and Indonesians. The big radio networks and news services were represented—BBC, NBC, the Associated Press, Reuter's—as were magazines such as *Life, Time,* and *Newsweek,* and some of the important papers of the United States, Great Britain, and Australia.

Naturally I was extremely conspicuous in this room crowded with men—the only white woman free to travel about the interior of Java —and I was more than a little nervous. I had been aware that my broadcasts had been heard in Batavia and elsewhere and that I had been quoted by Western correspondents. I quickly learned from the newsmen that what I had thought to be a little local notoriety had actually reached global proportions. The British, apparently misunderstanding my name, had been referring to me in their dispatches as Miss Daventry.

"We have pictured you as a gun-slinging moll, a sort of camp follower of the guerrilla leaders," one correspondent said. "You don't look so dangerous, and from your voice you ought to be teaching diction in some high school."

I was amused. I have never had a gun in my hand, and I never will. I hate violence of any kind. To the questioning, I said: "I have been trying to tell the peoples of the world what the Indonesians are hoping to achieve—the liberty, the right to self-government that is justly theirs. And I try to impress the Dutch and, to a lesser degree, the British with the danger of the errors that are committed deliberately. I know that I have been damned and maliciously slandered by the Dutch. They have accused me of infamous things. The Dutch are beginning to realize they will never get back into Indonesia, so they vent their spleen on those who help the Indonesians. I have no hatred against the Dutch individually, but only against Dutch colonialism."

Some of the correspondents were sympathetic, others were antagonistic. Later I became friends with several of them.

After the interview one of the chieftains wanted to introduce me to President Sukarno. But I felt shy and embarrassed. I wanted only to get back to the camp as quickly as possible.

The following day several different radio broadcasts carried the story, and I was grieved and amazed to learn that an account of my private life was thought more important by the press than the struggle of seventy million people for freedom. Newspaper clippings which arrived later were equally upsetting, though in justice it should be said that some of the writers did try to understand my motives. An editorial from one of the leading eastern newspapers of the United States said in part:

"It is hard to think of Scottish-born K'tut Tantri leaving the land with the highest standard of living in the world and going Indonesian in an international sort of a way—at least to the extent of taking the Atlantic Charter and the UNO Charter seriously. It is hard to think of this—but it is just possible that she is way ahead of the rest of us, internationally speaking."

A week or so after the Selecta visit I was surprised to receive an official letter, delivered personally by a high-ranking Indonesian officer, inviting me to come to Jogjakarta and present myself at the Indonesian Ministry of Information. Jogjakarta—or Jogja, as we usually referred to it—had become the capital of the Republic of Indonesia, and the President and most of his Cabinet lived there. The letter said that Mr. Ali Sastroamidjojo, the minister for information, had concluded that I could better serve the cause of merdeka by broadcasting over the official radio in Djokjakarta than by remaining with the "extremist" radios of East Java. The revolutionary station, Radio Pemberontakan, could be heard only in the Indonesian islands, or perhaps as far as Singapore. Radio Djokjakarta—the Voice of Free Indonesia—could be heard around the world.

I did not want to go to Jogjakarta. I had grown to love my guerrilla friends and would have preferred staying with my own little group under the direct leadership of Bung Tomo, whom I liked and admired; with his great ardor, his integrity of purpose, his tremendous courage, and above all his humanity to his followers, he was certainly Java's most colorful figure. The superstitious looked on him as a sort of god living a charmed life. He was, in fact, a very clever young man. To confuse the Dutch, who sent hundreds of spies to hunt him down, he had at least twenty men made up to resemble him, and the man they caught was always someone else. He was the Scarlet Pimpernel of Java, a Robin Hood of the mountains. Like all the guerrillas, he had taken an oath to let his hair grow long until merdeka had been attained.

Yes, I was sad to leave Bung Tomo and East Java; but I realized that I must go.

Right from the start I loved Jogjakarta. It was not much more, really, than an overgrown village, but it was the seat of culture for all Java. The most beautiful batiks were made there, and the finest hand-tooled silverware. There was only one main street of shops, most of them owned and run by Chinese or Indians. But most of Java's artists and writers lived in Jogjakarta. It was a city of refinement, the like of which I have never seen in any other country except Bali. But then Jogja was much more sophisticated than Bali.

The surrounding country was beautiful—lovely rolling hills growing suddenly into mountains. The great Borobudur, one of the wonders of the world, was nearby. In Jogja itself was the beautiful palace of the Sultan Buwono, actually a city in itself with its own army, its own world-famous dancers. The Sultan Buwono lived there in fantastic splendor, a handsome and charming man, and an ardent revolutionary in spite of his feudal way of life and his great wealth.

I was put up at the comfortable, attractive Merdeka Hotel, in the heart of town. I found Ali Sastroamidjojo to be intelligent and sophisticated. He had lived for a time in Paris, and had traveled widely. Before the war, when Indonesia was still part of the Dutch colonial empire, he and Sukarno had campaigned through Java together, enlisting the support of village chieftains in their quest for a free Indonesia. Both he and Sukarno had been arrested by the Dutch. Later Ali was to be Prime Minister for a time, and then Indonesian ambassador to the United States, and later head of the Indonesian delegation to the United Nations. But now, in 1946, he was the minister for information.

The first thing Mr. Ali asked me to do was to write a speech in English for President Sukarno, for a radio broadcast. I demurred, for I did not consider myself competent or clever enough. I had no training in political speech-writing on this level. But Mr. Ali said, "Just try and think—if you were president, what would you say? You know the situation in Indonesia."

So prompted, I concentrated on everything I could remember written or said by the great men of the American Revolution in their fight to free themselves from the British. I could hardly go wrong in following them. After working all night, I came up with a speech that was a composite of the writings of Thomas Paine, Abraham Lincoln, Thomas Jefferson, and half a dozen other immortals! It was a good speech, if I may say so, thanks to my familiarity with the history of the American Revolution and my retentive memory.

Afterward I learned that President Sukarno spoke fluent English, and was a far better speaker and writer than I was, but this was his first broadcast in English, and I suppose he felt he should be guided by one whose mother tongue was English.

The broadcast was a great success. As I listened to the deep, emotional voice I was immensely touched. The President gave the speech a significance far beyond the words themselves. Immediately afterward he sent for me to call upon him at the palace.

As the President's Palace was only a short distance from the Merdeka Hotel, I decided to walk. I wanted the people to get accustomed to seeing me strolling alone in the streets. So I set out, dressed as usual in sarong and kebaya with red-and-white armband plainly showing. Before I had gone a hundred yards I had people following me. By the time I reached the palace I felt like the Pied Piper of Hamelin. They were intrigued at seeing a white woman in native clothing. They smiled at me and were full of good humor. I never felt safer in my life. As I turned in at the palace gates they shouted, "Merdeka!" I, of course, replied, "Tetap Merdeka." Merdeka forever, for all time!

I walked up a long driveway, to be greeted at the door by an aide who showed me into a luxurious sitting room. There was a delay of some minutes, and when the President entered I was astonished to see him in Indonesian dress—a sarong with a brief coat, and Indonesian headdress. In the hundreds of pictures I had seen of him in magazines or newspapers he was always in white duck or khaki uniform. I do not believe any white person had ever seen him wearing a sarong. Very handsome he was in it, too.

"I am sorry to have kept you waiting," he said. "I was wearing a uniform, but when I saw you coming up the drive in your lovely sarong I went and changed. I felt that if you went to the trouble to dress in native clothing, I must certainly receive you in Indonesian dress."

When his beautiful wife joined us later, she too wore native costume.

The evening passed swiftly. We talked of many things—of Bali and America, the recent war, the British attack on Indonesia, the attitude of the Dutch, and even about the Japanese occupation. When I returned to the hotel it was in the presidential limousine, in the company of two young officers. The President would not hear of me returning to the hotel on foot, since it was now dark. "We can't afford to take any chance of losing you," he said.

On this first visit President Sukarno made a point of complimenting me on the way I wore Indonesian clothes, saying that because of my small stature they were very becoming. I was reminded that he had a reputation for being very gallant to the fair sex—young or old, ugly or beautiful. Now I could believe it. He told me later that every woman has at least one good feature, and that it is only a matter of observation to discover it. Some women have beautiful hair, some a divine figure. Some women walk well, some have a genius for wearing clothes, some have bewitching eyes, and others a lovely complexion. The President evidently thought I looked well in sarong, sandals, and kebaya.

One could not help admiring President Sukarno. He was full of humor, and at times a great tease. Later, when he took me to Kediri to meet his mother, who was from Bali, it delighted him that I spoke to her in Balinese. The President loved his mother deeply and was always most humble in her presence. It was touching to see him kneel in front of her to receive her blessing, even after he had become one of the most powerful national leaders in Asia. It was this humble quality that endeared him to his people. As he once told me, he would never make a good dictator for he had not a dictator's heart.

Not long after my arrival in Jogjakarta the Indonesian minister for defense, Amir Sjarifuddin, sent for me. He also was living at the Merdeka Hotel, his rooms directly across from mine with a courtyard between. This was my first meeting with a man—one of the big four of the Revolution—whom I consider the most utterly sincere Indonesian I have known.

Even these many years later I cannot think about Bung Amir without emotion. I was very fond of him, and more closely associated with him and with the Ministry for Defense during the Revolution than I was with the Ministry of Information. With President Sukarno, Dr. Hatta and Sutan Sjahrir, he was the power behind the Revolution, a truly great man.

Bung Amir must have been born under an unlucky star. One of the important leaders of the underground during the Japanese occupation of Java, he was arrested by them, tortured and sentenced to death. Only the intervention of Sukarno saved his life. The President convinced the Japanese that if they executed a man so well loved by his people they would turn all Indonesians against them. So Sjarifuddin's sentence was reduced to life imprisonment. The capitulation of the Japanese brought about his release, and he immediately became one of the key figures in the Revolution. It was bitterly ironic, then, as well as tragic, that he was fated to be executed by his own countrymen.

Amir Sjarifuddin was a small man, about the size of Bung Tomo but a different type altogether. Where Tomo was glamorous, dashing, and mysterious, Bung Amir was just the opposite: very serious and unobtrusive, by nature quiet and extremely refined. He abhorred personal publicity. Good-natured and always smiling, he could yet be very sharp and very witty. He had been educated in law in Holland, and spoke several languages, including English and Dutch.

Above all he was a deeply religious man, having embraced the Christian religion.

At our first meeting we talked for some time of the Revolution, the Japanese occupation, and especially of the Kempetai, for we had both suffered at the hands of the Nipponese secret police. Then abruptly he asked whether I would be able to tell the difference between a Dutchman and an Australian.

"I can't imagine anyone not being able to tell the difference," I said. "The Australian accent would be enough. Why do you ask?"

"It's like this," he replied. "An officer in British uniform has been captured in the rice fields outside the Surabaya perimeter. He admits that he is an officer in an English regiment stationed in Surabaya but insists that he is an Australian. The army commandant at Modjokerto suspects that he may be a Dutch spy, for what was he doing in the sawah fields outside of Surabaya? Most of our people are unable to distinguish among the different nationalities of Europeans. They say that you white people all look alike. Now, this man may not be too safe in the Modjokerto hospital if the people get it into their heads that he is a Dutchman or a Dutch spy. If he is really an Australian, we will have to take special measures to make sure that no harm comes to him."

Bung Amir went on to say that there was another Britisher at the hospital, very seriously wounded—an English pilot shot down while flying over Modjokerto.

"I would like for you to go to Modjokerto and have a look at these two men," Sjarifuddin said. "It is a long and dangerous drive, through country held solely by the guerrillas. I will send you in a military car, and an officer will accompany you. If you are stopped, you will need him. You will have identification papers signed by me. Now, if you feel that you would rather not take on this assignment, think no more about it."

I assured Bung Amir that I would be happy to go to Modjokerto. "I am sure I shall be perfectly safe," I told him. "I have lived with the partisans in the mountains back of Modjokerto. I am well known to the people of that district. They are my friends."

An Indonesian colonel and I set out on the long drive to East Java. The roads were in a dreadful condition, and we were stopped many times by barricades. At each roadblock my papers were inspected. Because of them, and my escort of high rank, we were passed through each barrier with smiles and with cries of "Merdeka!"

At Modjokerto, while my colonel escort went to confer with the commandant, I was taken to the hospital room of the man who said he was an Australian. I found him, swathed in bandages, sitting up in bed and looking reasonably well. A young Indonesian officer sat beside him, and they had been talking.

When I walked in he stared, and exclaimed, "What do you know! A Red Cross nurse; a white woman! Am I dreaming?" I thought he was going to jump out of his bed in his obvious surprise and delight.

"Are you a Dutch girl?" he asked.

"No, I am not Dutch. I am a British-born American. And I am not a Red Cross nurse."

"Well, what is that Red Cross badge around your arm?"

I explained: "It is not a Red Cross band. It is the badge of the Revolution." I told him I had been sent by the Indonesian minister for defense to find out whether he was all right, and if there was anything that he needed.

"All right!" he exclaimed. "I have never been treated so well in my whole life! The doctors and nurses are very kind to me. My friend the lieutenant here visits me every day and brings me cigarettes. When he is not here, the cutest little English-speaking nurses come in and talk to me. I am surprised that I am treated so well, since I am supposed to be the enemy. But I am not their enemy, and I never was."

He went on to tell me the story of his regiment, the West Yorkshires. This was the first time I had heard it—how the regiment was brought to Indonesia from Burma, ostensibly to help the Dutch put down an uprising of a few extremists and Japanese puppets bent on making trouble in Java; how before long the men discovered that they had been deceived, that it was not a rebellion of a handful of extremists, but a fight for freedom on the part of seventy million Indonesians. This so disgusted the West Yorkshires, the Australian said, that they simply put down their weapons and refused to fight. High British officers came to Surabaya to look into the mutiny, and found the West Yorkshires stubbornly determined not to fire upon the Javanese. Ultimately, in the absence of a declaration of war against the Indonesians, the British High Command took new stock of its position and decided to withdraw that particular regiment as quickly and as quietly as possible.

He said that a few days before the scheduled removal, he was ordered to take a few men and go on a reconnaissance tour of Surabaya perimeter. The patrol became lost, and found itself in rice fields outside the perimeter. Trying to find their way back to the city limits, the white men were surprised by a group of natives armed with bamboo spears and machetes. A fight started, and the other members of the patrol were killed. Although badly wounded, he escaped notice by hiding in a deep ditch. Later some Indonesian soldiers of the regular army found him and took him to the Modjokerto hospital.

It was plain as could be that this was no Dutchman. He was like a jumping kangaroo the whole time he was talking, and he had a most pronounced Western Australian accent. He said he was from Perth, and gave me the address of his mother. "Please let her know that I am safe and that I will be home soon."

I assured him that I would broadcast the news that he was alive and well the very next day, and that I would also write to his mother. Then with the young Indonesian accompanying me I went down the hall to the room of the English pilot.

He was a very young man, surely no more than twenty-one years old, and very sick indeed. He was much too ill to notice attractive Indonesian nurses but was so overcome at seeing a white person that he clung to me as though I were his mother. I sat with him as long as the doctors would permit, and I promised that as soon as he was well enough to be moved I would return and take him to Jogja. He, too, asked me to get in touch with his mother.

The following day I reported to Amir Sjarifuddin the story of the Australian and of the mutiny of the West Yorkshires. He listened attentively.

"We must get those men out of Modjokerto as quickly as possible," Bung Amir said. "I would not want anything to happen to them." That same night we beamed to Australia and to England the news that the two Britishers were safe and eventually would be returned to British headquarters. I also wrote to their families.

Each day I telephoned to the hospital to check upon the condition of the British patients. At last I was able to tell Sjarifuddin that

Modjokerto's chief of medicine had declared the Australian officer well enough to leave the hospital, although technically he was a prisoner of war.

"The Australian must be removed immediately," Bung Amir said. "I have arranged for him to be brought here to stay at the home of Colonel X, which is inside the army post. Colonel X's mother and sister will look after him."

The decision demonstrated the humanity, the magnanimity of Bung Amir. He could in all justice have ordered the Australian sent to a camp for prisoners of war. Once again fierce fighting had broken out between the British and the Indonesians and a new wave of hatred for the Dutch and their allies was sweeping through East Java.

For a second time it was decided that I must go to Modjokerto, to help bring the Australian to Jogjakarta. Travel by road was more dangerous than it had ever been. On this trip Colonel X and I were accompanied by two soldiers armed with Tommy guns.

This time there were many difficulties. We were detained in every town and village through which we passed. The guerrillas, especially, were tense and trigger-happy. We managed on each occasion to convince the guards that we were on an official mission for the Defense Ministry. This was easy enough when the Indonesian army regulars stopped us; but each time that groups of partisans, armed with bamboo spears, made us halt, the outlook was ominous. They were a suspicious lot, for they knew that Dutch spies were everywhere, some of them masquerading as Indonesian officers. And of course my color at once branded me as a possible enemy. It took much talking and the full weight of Colonel X's rank to get us through. But we did get through without incident.

At Modjokerto, to our surprise, the chief physician of the hospital refused to honor the order signed by Amir Sjarifuddin for the removal of the Australian. The doctor said that the army general of the Modjokerto district, irate over the renewed heavy attacks by the British, had given orders that neither of the men was to be released under any circumstances.

"Our orders are from the General's superior, the highest military authority in Java," Colonel X pointed out. "They supersede your orders."

The doctor was adamant. "The General was very specific," he said. "I am not to release either of these enemy soldiers. Unless you have a signed order from the General himself, I cannot and will not let the Australian go."

Colonel X, his patience at an end after the daylong series of frustrations and arguments, pointed his Tommy gun at the doctor. "If this is the way it has to be, we will shoot our way out of the hospital," he said. "But we'll take the Australian with us."

The colonel's two aides also trained their guns on the doctor. This was serious.

I grabbed the colonel's arm. "Colonel X, I beg you to put your gun away," I pleaded. "This is a hospital; there are many helpless people around. Please, let's telephone Amir Sjarifuddin and tell him what the trouble is."

The colonel hesitated, then reluctantly lowered his gun and went off to telephone the minister. He returned with word that Bung Amir wanted us to go to the Surabaya front, acquaint the General with the situation, and get a release for the Australian.

Even though it was now nightfall, the colonel and I set out immediately for the Surabaya perimeter. Near the Indonesian front we had to leave our car and proceed by foot. The headlights would have given us away to the enemy; and across the rice fields there was no suitable roadway.

We cut out through the sawah terraces on what must have been some kind of trail, for the colonel had no trouble finding his way in the darkness. Guards stopped us with the order, "Siapa itoe?" Who goes there? With our identity established a soldier led us down a slope into a dugout, a room hewn out of the earth.

Inside, several men sat around a table on which was spread a large map of East Java. They had hair down to their shoulders, and several days' growth of beard. Most of them wore red-and-white scarves around their heads or necks, and their uniforms were muddied from crawling through the fields. They seemed more a band of brigands than educated officers of the Indonesian army. But I recognized the General immediately. I had met him before, through Bung Tomo.

The General was plainly dumfounded when I walked into the cavernlike room, and so were the other officers. But their faces broke out in smiles at my Indonesian dress and my proudly worn armband. They guessed my identity immediately.

The General heard us out. "I don't understand all this fuss about one Britisher, when hundreds of Indonesians lie dead because of the

British actions," he fumed. "But the story of the West Yorkshires is interesting indeed."

At first he said it would be impossible to move the prisoner safely back to Jogja, particularly through the guerrilla-held area from Modjokerto to Maduin. The people at the moment were much worked up against the British, and would be inclined to cut a white soldier to bits. But after conferring in a low voice with his staff, surprisingly he told us that he would accompany us to Modjokerto. "I shall have a talk with the soldier," he said. "If I am convinced of his sincerity, you may take him to Jogjakarta."

The doctor, understandably, was astonished at our return with the General. It was near midnight when we marched into the Aussie's room and he repeated for us the story of his brief tour of duty in Java. The General listened attentively, interrupting only once or twice. At the end he said, "Get dressed, young man. You are leaving the hospital with K'tut Tantri and Colonel X."

Over coffee in the doctor's room, the doctor chided Colonel X smilingly about the threat to shoot his way out of the hospital. The General laughed, and the colonel looked embarrassed. "I wouldn't have used my gun if you had decided to call my bluff," he said.

"That Aussie," said the General. "He is quite a pleasant young man, but very naïve for an officer. On second thought, I shall accompany you as far as Maduin. We don't want any international incidents right now."

Our drive to Jogja was uneventful. The Aussie found himself comfortable in the colonel's luxurious home, with X's pretty sister on hand to give him lessons in the Indonesian language. Amir Sjarifuddin was most pleased. And ten days later I was driving back to Modjokerto to get the English pilot.

This time my escort was an officer of army intelligence. We had no trouble until the return trip, when we were halted near Surakarta, or Solo, by a small group of soldiers under the command of an extremely zealous lieutenant who had never heard of K'tut Tantri or of her escort. However, the confusion was cleared up at army headquarters in Solo and in less than twenty minutes we were on our way again. We were worried about the pilot. He was not taking the journey well, and I think he was frightened. He was not so tough as the Australian. But after a few days in bed under the gentle care of the X family he soon began to improve.

There was a touching sequel to the story of these two men; one that shows the tender heart of the Indonesian. About a week after the pilot's arrival in Jogja, Amir Sjarifuddin called at the barracks to meet the two Britishers. They had a long talk together, after which Bung Amir said, "I shall make arrangements as soon as possible to have you both flown to Batavia and delivered to the British High Command. I am sure they will see to it that you are sent home very quickly."

The response was surprising. "It is very good of you, sir, to offer to send us back," the pilot said. "But my Aussie friend and I have decided we do not want to leave Indonesia. We believe we both can be useful to you. Between us we can train your young men for army duty and teach them to fly. We feel exactly as Miss Tantri does about your people and your country. We are ashamed that our countries have taken up arms against you. If you will permit us to stay, we are ready to help you."

The Australian nodded enthusiastic agreement. Sjarifuddin smiled, and shook his head.

"Nothing would please me more than to keep you both here to help us," said Bung Amir. "We need help badly. But technically you are prisoners of war. You are both in the British armed services. If you stayed in Indonesia and fought on our side, you would be considered deserters, guilty of treason. You could be sentenced in your absence to years in prison, and you would never be able to return to your country. When we have won our freedom and our countries are no longer enemies, we shall be happy to have you both back. But I cannot allow you to stay here now."

The Aussie said flatly, "I don't care if I am court-martialed for treason. I want to stay. I am an Australian, and my country is not fighting you. I can choose the side that I want."

"No, young man, you can't," Bung Amir replied. "You are an officer in an English regiment. Until you are demobilized you cannot join the other side, no matter how much you want to."

Sjarifuddin added that the pilot must return immediately to England for proper medical attention. The doctors said he had a piece of shrapnel still lodged near his heart and would require a delicate operation.

The two men looked downcast until the Australian suggested brightly, "All right, then, if we can't stay with you, why not make a deal with the British? They are holding two hundred Indonesian prisoners in Batavia. Make them trade us for them! At least we would know we had been of some use."

Bung Amir laughed heartily. "A smart idea, lieutenant," he said. "I shall put out feelers to the British immediately. Two hundred Indonesian prisoners for two Britishers!" We all chuckled, thinking it a wild idea.

A few days later, however, Bung Amir returned and announced that he *had* made a deal with the British. Two hundred Indonesians would be released and sent to Jogjakarta on the safe delivery of the two Britishers to Batavia.

The men were flown to Batavia. Bung Amir accompanied them and personally handed them over to the British High Command. Sjarifuddin told us that the pilot, in saying good-by to him, had boldly declared in the presence of the British officers, "Sir, I hope that your country will get its freedom very soon. Merdeka! Tetap Merdeka!"

Both soldiers speedily were sent home. Two years later when I visited Australia I met the Australian's family and was treated royally.

6

A CLOAK-AND-DAGGER AFFAIR

All the high-ranking officers of the Indonesian army were young, because the army itself was no more than a military infant, fresh from the womb of revolution. Without the chastening influence of experience most of the service chiefs tended to swagger. And yet their enthusiasm was refreshing.

One of the brightest of these young blades was a major high in the Indonesian intelligence, a young man of great charm and naughty wit. It always delighted me when he dropped in at my quarters at the Merdeka Hotel for a drink, for invariably he brought the latest news from the Surabaya front, and also the choicest gossip, spiced with his own amusing comments. Everyone mixing socially in Jogja visited the Merdeka Hotel in those days. It was the official quarters of the government and revolutionary forces.

Green bamboo blinds filtered the sunlight on my hotel balcony on a hot afternoon as the major and I sat talking of a motor accident which had just laid up Amir Sjarifuddin. The accident had occurred near Solo, about thirty miles from Jogjakarta. Fortunately the defense minister had not been seriously hurt.

Eventually the major came to the real point of his visit. Quite casually, with a disarming smile, he said, "Sjarifuddin has sent me with an urgent message for you. He would like you to help him in a matter requiring a lot of tact and nerve." Then before I had time to answer, the major in a perfectly serious tone of voice went on with a story that was the stuff of which penny-dreadful espionage thrillers are made.

"It seems that there is a plot brewing to assassinate President Sukarno and overthrow the Republic!"

I could not believe my ears. "Assassinate the President!"

"No need for panic yet," the major assured me. Efforts were being made to find out who was in the plot besides three people arrived recently from Bandung and now in Jogja. The three were known to be Dutch agents.

"Then why don't you arrest them?" I asked.

But this was too simple.

"We think the leader of the ring is a woman, a highborn princess related to the Sultan. She is very beautiful and clever, and very sly."

And then there was a friend of the princess—a man whose interest might be professional, platonic, or otherwise. The three of them had been traveling back and forth from Bandung, strewing gold around like confetti. Where did they get it? Nobody had money in Java these days except the Dutch and their agents.

"Anyhow," the major concluded, "Sjarifuddin thinks no one could help us in this as well as you. Of course," he added as though holding out a particularly luscious piece of bait, "it might be a dangerous assignment."

"I'm all ears," I replied.

"Sjarifuddin wants you to work your way into the confidence of the princess. He wants you to find out what the three of them are plotting, and who are their supporters."

"Is that all?" I asked, with heavy sarcasm. "And what would make Bung Amir think that such a clever woman would confide in me, a stranger?"

"That's just the point. Everyone in Java knows that you were arrested by the Japanese and held as an American spy. Don't you see how we can use that to our advantage and give you a chance to live up to your reputation? We shall appoint you spy extraordinary for Indonesia." He chuckled.

The wily major had a plan all prepared. The princess, his agents reported, was a very superstitious woman, extremely fond of having her fortune told by clairvoyants, palmists, and such. That was her one weakness. The major remembered how I had told the fortunes of the guerrillas in Bung Tomo's bamboo army, during the fighting in and around Surabaya. I was partly entertaining the boys, but chiefly building up morale by promising victory and glory.

"We think it will be easy to interest the princess through the medium of the cards," he said. "I will see to it that she hears indirectly of your amazing powers of foretelling the future. That will be your contact and opening gambit. When your friendship has ripened, you will insinuate that you are a secret observer for Washington and that you are merely posing as an Indonesian sympathizer. If, as we suspect, the plot is to overthrow our republic and establish a puppet government for the Dutch, the princess and her group would be eager to get recognition in the United States. We think they would be likely to make you some kind of proposition."

Just as I was about to state my objections to posing as an American agent, the major jumped up, took my hand and said, "We knew you wouldn't let us down, K'tut. Don't be afraid—we'll guard you every minute. You must never go to the princess' house, nor meet her anywhere outside. Always encourage her to come here. As for the Americans, they will never hear about it. And if they should? We will pacify them with a submarine base or something."

I didn't like any part of the scheme, but there I was caught in it. As for the major, one would have thought he had nothing more serious on his mind than a cockfight.

Only a few days later I was awakened from my afternoon siesta by the ringing of the telephone. It was the princess. Would I call on her? Or, if I preferred, she would call on me. She said she was looking forward to meeting me because she had heard from a mutual friend that I was very clever at laying the cards.

I was so nervous that my voice stuck in my throat, but I answered as naturally as possible and invited her to tea the following afternoon.

When the princess was announced, she was so beautiful that I forgot my fright in admiration. She was a woman of perhaps thirty-five, slim but delicately rounded, with an exquisite oval face, languorous eyes, and a most charming voice. Her sarong was of the finest batik, and of a design worn only by the Sultan's family. Diamonds glistened in her ears and on her fingers. She was one of the most truly elegant women I had ever met in Java. She held out her hand, and her smile and friendly manner put me instantly at ease.

Inviting her to a chair on the balcony I settled her for a long conversation. We talked about life in the kraton, or Sultan's Palace, and about life in Bali. We compared the culture of the two countries, Java and Bali. She asked me questions about America, and told me she longed to go there. Then we talked about the Indonesian Revolution—those dreadful hysterical days and times. Soon we were chatting like old friends.

"You must have a very dull life here," she said. "What in the world do you do all day?"

I said I walked and rode, and played cards and sometimes even told my fortune.

"With cards?" she asked quickly. Here was my opportunity to tell her about the Kempetai and the Surabaya prison and how I had made cards from strips of palms, cut from my sleeping mat, painted with soot and brick dust dug with my nails from the prison floor.

"I would love to see those cards," she said. There was excitement in her voice. "I tell fortunes too."

Deliberately I hesitated. These were no ordinary cards, I told her. During the long, solitary hours in prison there was time to search out my soul, and the cards had been part of my spiritual development. An instrument, actually, for penetrating a higher world. I pretended that the cards would foretell the future for other people only when there was a sympathetic vibration between us. I said I thought she was sympathetic, but there were not many people who would understand.

This improvising was exciting. I was tossing in all the scraps of Eastern philosophy I could remember, and she seemed impressed. She told me stories of ancient animistic magic still practiced in Java, and as she talked her eyes became more and more luminous. What a magnificent high priestess she would have made!

As she rose to go she pressed my hands.

"You were an American spy, weren't you? Tell me, my dear. You can be frank with me."

I told her I had never admitted such a thing, not even under torture, and she couldn't expect me to tell her now. She said she could never have endured what I had gone through, and added that she admired my courage. Her next remark, however, put me on guard again.

"How strange that you are allowed to live here in the hotel and go about the streets of Jogja," she said. "You are the only free white person in the city. Do you think it's safe?"

"Safe as the Bank of England," I answered lightly. "At least, I think so while the Indonesians are looking to America for help in their struggle for self-determination. Still, one never knows."

As she left she asked if she might come again, and perhaps I would read her fortune. She would like to bring her husband and a friend. My nerves began to tighten. She was gullible—at least, I thought she was—but her husband? Well, that was the next move in the game called espionage.

"Of course," I said. "But I'd not like telling your fortune in front of others."

"Oh, they'd adore it. And now, before I go, won't you accept this little diamond and ruby ring as a souvenir of our meeting?" I shook my head, embarrassed, and gave her a warm farewell smile. She really was a charming creature.

Soon the major arrived for a report. He listened, then threw back his head in spontaneous laughter. The situation appealed to his sense of humor.

He explained carefully the "fortune" I should tell the princess on her next visit. From now on, he said, I must not try to get in touch with him. He would be briefed about my movements from other sources. Then he left.

When the princess brought her entourage a few days later I took an instant dislike to the husband, a sleek and portly Javanese business-man with a Dutch veneer. The friend looked less repulsive—in fact, almost innocent. After an exchange of introductory courtesies and small talk, I was asked to tell fortunes. I hesitated, pretending reluctance, and then agreed. I told the princess, whose fortune I read from my tiny palm-leaf cards, that she was about to undertake a transaction with a man of another race—perhaps Dutch. This would lead to great fortune and might even make her a power in international affairs. The cards also revealed a white woman with whom she would undertake a most successful venture.

Everybody seemed pleasantly surprised with my performance. The husband begged me to tell his fortune, but I tried to look as though I had been under a great strain—as indeed I had—and said "some other day."

For three weeks we drank tea and told fortunes, sometimes the princess and I, sometimes the friend and the husband. At last the long-expected happened, over cups of tea. After the usual polite talk the husband leaned over and pushed aside his cup.

"We have had a very pleasant time playing cards, K'tut," he said. "Now let us really put our cards on the table. We can do a lot for each other if you want to play our game. First, we know that you are an agent of the American government."

"How do you know that?" I hedged, leaving the impression that I was.

"Oh, you're not such a good actress as all that, you know!"

Perhaps not, but at that particular moment I felt qualified to give pointers to Mata Hari.

Factually, briefly, ruthlessly, he told me they were working in a plot to overthrow the present Indonesian government, and possibly to kill President Sukarno. "That weakling—we must get rid of him." They would make the Sultan of Jogja president.

"But you can't do that," I protested. "The Sultan is an absolute monarch, and this is supposed to be a democracy. The people wouldn't stand for it, and the whole world would laugh at you. Besides, the Sultan and Sukarno are the closest of friends. If anything, the Sultan is heart and soul for the Revolution."

Why not just return the Dutch to power? I asked. They were not so bad, after all. The banker replied that the Indonesians would never consent to the Dutch, so the next best thing was to install someone who would look after Dutch interests.

"What do you want me to do?" I asked.

Could I get information to Washington saying that the people intended to rise against the corrupt government of Sukarno, the Japanese collaborator, and replace him with the Sultan of Jogjakarta? The husband said that several army generals were with him and that whole divisions were ready to rise at strategic points. Sukarno would be forced to abdicate or face a firing squad.

"This is terrific news," I said. "Are you the brains behind the movement?"

The banker smiled like a man well pleased with himself. "Not the whole cheese. The rest is in Bandung. But tell me—could you really get that information to Washington in a manner in which it would be believed by the right people?"

Yes, I said, there was a way. But I must have time to think. I asked them to leave. I promised that I would telephone later and arrange a further conference.

Almost on their departing heels the major arrived. Having heard the full story, he insisted that we go to Sjarifuddin this same night.

Past midnight we slipped out of Jogja and drove to Solo, where Bung Amir lay in a hospital bed, his broken arm in a plaster cast. Quickly he outlined a plan for the major.

Credentials must be faked for me, on an exact duplicate of the stationery of the United States embassy in Batavia. They must take the form of a letter thanking me for my latest dispatches from Jogjakarta, and saying the information was on the way to Washington and would be in the State Department within twenty-four hours. The letter should ask me for a summary of the present situation in Republican territory, mentioning that the messenger to carry it was a trusted diplomatic courier.

For the role of courier the major must find a top-flight intelligence officer able to speak with an American accent. The courier should arrive with his faked letter in the midst of a conference between the plotters and me. He should deliver to us a convincing note and take back with him an incriminating letter from the princess and her associates.

"Keep telling them they must put it all down in black and white—everything, especially names," Sjarifuddin said.

Was it clear? he asked. Quite clear. But could I ever pull it off successfully? That point was not clear.

As we drove back to Jogja, the major instructed me to call the princess three days later. "I need that much time," he said, "to get the letterhead printed and to brief an officer on how to act like a courier."

Having been set in motion, events moved inexorably to their climax. In military parlance, according to plan. At eight o'clock in the evening the princess and her two escorts came to the hotel. An hour later a train from Batavia carrying a "courier" arrived in Jogja.

Although the trio appeared as calm and suave as usual, I could sense hidden tension. The husband's eyes kept blinking rapidly. The princess held her fan so tightly that the knuckles of her hand were white. We sat on the balcony with the jalousies down. My visitors had a paper, all right, addressed to the United States government, Washington, D.C. The husband spread it out on the table. It was written in Malay. A quick scanning showed me that it was a good brisk summary of the plot. But it named no names, incriminated no individuals.

"I am afraid that this will never do," I told them. "This won't convince Washington. It won't mean a thing unless you tell the State Department exactly who is in this with you. To give your plan any logic, any meaning, you must provide the names of the officers on whom you can rely, and the disposition of the troops at their command. That is the only way the Americans can determine whether this is a serious countermovement—a venture worth supporting—or just a small-time thing with no chances of success. They will want facts."

The husband began to argue, but the friend cut him short in a voice that made the other man cringe. Miss Tantri was right, he said. Of course the Americans would have to have facts. He took the document to my desk and began writing down the details.

The husband, meanwhile, pulled out a revolver and laid it on the table, its muzzle pointed toward me. I tried to push it away. "I don't like guns," I said. He removed it, only to keep it in his hand, waving it at me. "This is what will happen to you if anything goes wrong," he said. "I mean—if we are double-crossed."

When the friend came back with the document and I saw what he had written, my scalp began to tingle. It was all there, just what the major wanted. The people involved, and how they planned to go about ousting Sukarno—bloodily, if necessary—and seizing control. Now, if only I could push the traitors out and lock the door! But the husband was talking prices, offering me a hundred thousand guilders if the coup d'état succeeded.

"What!" I exclaimed. "For a job like this?"

"But all you're doing is sending this letter on to Washington!"

"All I am doing is signing my own death warrant if anything goes wrong," I replied. "It's worth a hundred thousand dollars, not guilders."

Arrogantly he agreed to payment in dollars. "If this succeeds, you can name your own price," he said.

The bell rang. Although I had been expecting it, I jumped like a frightened rabbit.

"It may be the courier from Batavia," I said. "I didn't expect him until tomorrow."

Going to the door, conscious of that gun at my back, I opened it. "It's the courier," I said over my shoulder, and to the man, "Come in quickly and shut the door."

The man started to enter, and at sight of my other visitors drew back. "Come in," I said. "These are our friends. Don't be afraid. You can say what you have to say before them. They are with us, and are giving us some important information to take back to Jakarta."

"What! You've told them everything?" His accent was perfect; listening to him, he might have been straight from San Francisco or Chicago. "You mean, I should give you the usual stuff?"

I nodded. Playing his role most convincingly, he stepped into the bedroom a moment, and then emerged with a large envelope in his hand. I tore it open, glanced at it hurriedly, then tossed it onto the table near the banker. The sheet of paper lay open, the letterhead and address plain to be seen, and the body of the letter itself easy to scan. I stepped into the bedroom for a bottle of whiskey and stayed long enough for the banker to have a good idea of the letter's contents. The major had done a beautiful job; it was as official looking as anything I had ever seen.

On my return with the whiskey I asked the courier, "How was the trip? Were you examined?"

"Oh, I got through all right," he replied. "Yes; they looked me over, but they never find anything. They are not experienced searchers." He brushed dust from his soiled white suit.

"I'm sorry that I must send you back to Batavia tonight," I said, handing him in a sealed envelope the material I had received from my three co-schemers.

"Tell them in Batavia that everything is ready for an uprising. You see here we have on our side General _____ and Colonel _____." I went over the list; it would help to have a verbal witness if something happened to the letter. "The plan is to make the Sultan the new president, and his army will fall in line."

The courier took the letter for Washington. "I'll be on my way now," he said. "All's safe."

The princess spoke up. "But where are you going to hide our letter? Are you sure it will be safe?"

The courier was truly nonchalant. "Maybe in America or England, where they read detective stories, it wouldn't be safe." He smiled. "But no Indonesian soldier would ever think of looking where I hide it." With that he leaned over and unfastened the sole of his over-sized shoe. The others watched, pop-eyed.

"Good night, folks," he said. "I've just got time to catch that midnight train." He closed the door softly after him.

When he left we stared at each other, with nothing to say. I was terrified. Suddenly it occurred to me that they could easily do away with me, now that they believed their appeal for support to be on its way to Washington. In a panic I exclaimed, "Isn't it hot?" and ran to the jalousies, pulling them up. There was just a chance that some of my friends across the courtyard might be alerted if my associates in the room became menacing.

The friend was right behind me. "Be careful," he said. "We don't want to be seen." Looking at the street, he added, "I'm worried about that courier. I think I'll follow him to the station and see that he gets safely on the train."

As he left I almost screamed. The courier probably would go directly to the major's office, and the whole deception would be exposed. Why didn't the princess and her husband leave? If they stayed another minute I would surely give myself away!

At last they departed. It was as though tight bands around my temples had suddenly relaxed. . . . An hour later the major was dancing around the room and I was dissolved in tears.

"There, there, K'tut," he soothed. "Cry all you want to. You have done a wonderful service for Indonesia Merdeka. I was in the room next to you on one side and the military police were on the other side. Nothing could have happened to you."

"The courier!" I cried. "The princess' friend has followed him to the train. They will know by now that he didn't get on it."

"Oh, but he did," the major said. "That was taken care of, too.

We do things properly, à la Scotland Yard—or FBI. We'll get the courier off the train a few miles up the line and have him back here with those papers in less than half an hour.

"Cheer up, K'tut. Go powder your nose. We are going to Solo to see Sjarifuddin."

Bung Amir was upset when he read the list of the Indonesians involved in the plot. Some of the high-ranking officers implicated were among his most trusted friends. He gave orders for their arrest, and for the arrest of the princess, her husband, and her friend.

"I am a little concerned now for your safety, K'tut," Sjarifuddin said. "For a while you must leave the Merdeka Hotel and go stay at the house of Colonel X. That is one place where we know you will be safe. And from now on you must have a military escort wherever you go."

The thought of a constant guard was extremely irksome to me. For a small place like Jogjakarta, it was much too conspicuous.

We called on President Sukarno and told him the whole story. He was much amused at our descriptions of the princess. "You should have brought her to see me," he said, his eyes twinkling. "What a chance I have missed! I love having my fortune told."

"Bung Karno," I chided him, "I will tell your fortune. You will be much safer with me!"

We went also to the Sultan of Jogjakarta and told him of the plot to make him president. He was amazed and horror-stricken. "The Dutch are behind this—using my name for their own ends," he said. "It is good that the plan was exposed before it progressed any further."

A few months later a similar plot was flowering when intelligence officers again uncovered it. This one, also, named the Sultan as the new president. In neither case was there any reflection on the Sultan, but only on the misguided people who thought he should be at the helm. The Sultan of Jogja was a sincere revolutionary, and so much a friend of the President that he later became minister for defense. If the cloak-and-dagger undercurrents of trouble-torn Java seemed at times bizarre—well, that was life in the time of Merdeka! Truly, there was never a dull moment.

7

SOME HARDSHIPS AND A TOUR

P. S. Gerbrandy, Holland's wartime prime minister, in his book *Indonesia* said the Indonesians had one asset, one idea—"a clarion call Merdeka! even if it were a bit cracked." He conceded that the Republicans were constant in their faith and in their belief that Indonesia was now a sovereign state. He added that he found their pose ridiculous. "They believe Sukarno was right," he said. "Such was their childish faith, that if we ourselves [Hollanders] enjoy freedom why shouldn't they have the same right."

It was evident that the Dutch would never willingly give Indonesia recognition as a sovereign state. The Indonesians had no choice but to fight in order to hold on to their new-found freedom.

Waves of hate were sweeping over Java. The British were bringing thousands of Dutch troops back into Java in spite of the protests of President Sukarno. There was now fighting on three fronts, and the situation was daily getting worse. White people had disappeared from the streets throughout Republican Java, with the single exception of myself. Some even doubted that I was safe in public places, at the time that I moved back from Colonel X's house to Jogja's Merdeka hotel.

I found the hotel overcrowded with military personnel. But for Amir Sjarifuddin's thoughtfulness in reserving my room during the time I was away I never could have found accommodations. The lobby was jammed with young men just returned, weary, worn out, from the eastern front. With no bedrooms available, they simply collapsed on the floor or in chairs and slept from sheer exhaustion. They were in rags, many of them, and gaunt and thin. Some plainly were on the edge of starvation. But all held grimly onto their rifles or bamboo spears.

My heart went out to them. These boys were not the regular army troops, but peasants and students—the guerrilla fighters who had held back the mechanized army of the British, Dutch, Gurkhas, and Japanese. They had shown great courage and had sacrificed much.

I looked around my large and comfortable room and felt ashamed.

Two oversized beds in the main room, and a couch bed on the veranda. Each of those enormous beds could easily sleep four of these little people. I could not give up my room. There were no other women in the hotel; I had nowhere else to go. But I could share the room with the battle-weary freedom fighters. So before I could change my mind or think what I was doing, my bedroom contained ten very grateful warriors, blissfully asleep—eight on the beds, two on floor mats.

When he heard, Bung Amir looked at me with grateful eyes. "You are a real Indonesian, K'tut," he said. "It is hard to realize that you are of a race that has brought us much sadness."

Perhaps because I had cleared my conscience of its feeling of guilt, I slept very well that night and for the following two nights that the guerrillas were my guests. And for three days at least they had plenty to eat.

My life at this time was very busy. I was broadcasting every day, sometimes from Jogjakarta and sometimes from Solo. I wrote my own broadcasts in English. Later I broadcast also in Balinese, sending a special message of hope to the people on that island. For Bali was now in the hands of the Dutch. Not until 1948 were the people of the Netherlands government forced out of the island.

The magazine, *The Voice of Free Indonesia*, was now in circulation. It was published in Jakarta (Batavia), which was still in the hands of the British and Dutch. A reason for this was that the foreign correspondents were in Jakarta, and so could read the magazine regularly and pick up items from it. Every issue contained one or two articles by me. If the Dutch were not furious with me before, they certainly were now.

One article in particular, which questioned their right to reinstate themselves in Indonesia—I titled it "Lest We Forget"—aroused their rage. In it I reminded the Dutch of their shameful behavior at the time of the Japanese invasion, of how they actually collaborated with the Japanese, and of how army officers had escaped from Java by stealing Australian planes, leaving the Australians behind to meet the enemy. The Dutch were so infuriated that they raided the printing offices of *The Voice of Free Indonesia*, destroying part of the machinery and confiscating all the copies containing my article. Nevertheless, the issue was distributed widely and was widely quoted.

On our side of the lines, in the Republican capital of Jogja, and in other parts of Java too, serious food shortages were developing. Shortages of rice especially. The Dutch had imposed a very strong blockade around the island, making it almost impossible to import the many necessities usually acquired from other lands. Many Indonesians had died in attempts to sail through the blockade.

Chinese merchants owned most of the food shops in Java, and many of them were profiteers of the worst sort. They closed their shops and hid rice in warehouses, waiting for prices to rise. At last the day came when not one kilo of rice could be purchased in any shop or market place in Jogjakarta. Even at the Merdeka Hotel we could not buy a meal or a spoonful of rice. The restaurants and even the fruit stands had to close. The people were hungry, and I was hungry too. Three days passed without any food.

An intelligence officer came to me to say that I was to go to the palace of President Sukarno for meals until the Chinese reopened their shops. (Amir Sjarifuddin was away from Jogja at this time.) He confided that the Indonesians were planning to raid the Chinese warehouses and force the Chinese to open their shops. The price of rice would then be set by the government so that there would be no black market in food.

I could not go to the palace to eat when so many of my friends were starving. It was common knowledge that the President was feeding as many people as possible, but that even he was no longer able to find enough rice to keep the palace kitchen going. I thanked the officer and said I would find some other way to get food for myself.

The streets of Jogja were empty. With nothing to buy, people were staying in their homes, growing weak from hunger. I walked through the deserted streets and came to the Kohinoor, the art shop of a wealthy Indian trader of my acquaintance. This shop too was closed, but I hammered on the door. At last the owner peered out. Recognizing me, he smiled broadly and opened the door.

I came to the point immediately. "Friend, I am hungry," I said.

"Friend, come in," he said warmly. "I will share with you what little we have." Indeed it was not much by the old standards, but to me it was a grand meal, in very good company.

That night the Indonesians raided the shops and storehouses of the Chinese and helped themselves to rice. The Chinese lost everything, but they learned a lesson. They never closed their shops again.

It was dangerous to be abroad in the streets of Jogja that night, for the people were like hungry wolves.

When Sjarifuddin returned from his trip he informed me that President Sukarno would leave within a few days on a tour through East Java. He would be accompanied by Vice-President Hatta and most of his ministers, and by the top officers of the army, navy, and air force. The purpose of the journey would be to enlighten the people as to what was going on in the rest of Java, and to prepare them for the worst in the event of a Dutch attempt to retake East Java. It was also to be a propaganda tour, to let the world know that seventy million Indonesians were behind President Sukarno and would never surrender their freedom.

Mrs. Sukarno and Mrs. Hatta would accompany their husbands, and I also was to be a member of the party to broadcast in English.

I shall never forget that trip as long as I live. We boarded the President's luxurious air-conditioned train—once the crack train of the Dutch—at Jakarta. Several of my army friends were aboard, and in particular a colonel, an aide to the President, named Radin Susatyo. Radin in Javanese means lord or count, but Susatyo preferred to be called by his military title. We became great friends, and have remained so through the years.

At that time the colonel was attached to army intelligence. He never failed to amaze me, for he spoke beautiful Churchillian English, and yet he had never been out of Java. There was hardly a classic or any of the great biographies that he hadn't read. He was familiar with Western painters from the time of Giotto until the present. He was very handsome, had charming manners, and was excellent company.

I remember one incident with particular vividness.

On the long train rides between towns Colonel Susatyo and his friends usually whiled away the time in my compartment. When one of the officers mentioned in Susatyo's absence that the following day would be the colonel's birthday, we decided to give him a surprise party—and managed during a stop at Kediri to buy a bottle of Johnnie Walker Red Label Scotch for the occasion. The bottle was entrusted to my care until we would reach Banjuwangi, where we planned to have the party. The bottle was precious, for it was very expensive and obtainable only through the Chinese.

Colonel Susatyo and two other officers were sitting in my compartment when Bung Amir walked in. The whiskey lay wrapped on the seat, so I pushed it over to make room for him. We talked until it was time for lunch, then the company separated. Arriving at Banjuwangi late in the afternoon, we prepared to go to the home of the local rajah, as we customarily did on stopovers. The President was to speak in the evening, and afterward we would have our birthday party.

But on leaving the train I discovered that the Scotch was missing. I searched everywhere, and then confessed to the officers that it had disappeared. We thought at first that Colonel Susatyo had taken it as a joke, but he insisted that he hadn't. We all felt badly about the apparent theft.

That night, as at every previous major stop, thousands of cheering Javanese assembled to hear the President speak. He used one technique in particular that had proved highly effective.

"I shall never settle for anything but 100 per cent merdeka," he told his rapt audience. Then he asked, "Shall I settle for 90 per cent merdeka?"

As always, the people shouted "No!" at the top of their lungs.

"Shall I settle for 99 per cent merdeka?"

"No!" the people thundered, delighted.

"How about 99½ per cent merdeka?"

The audience was enjoying itself to the limit. "No! No! No!"

"Then what shall I settle for?" the President asked, in mock perplexity.

"One hundred per cent Merdeka!" The roar of approval came straight from the heart. In this childish way President Sukarno won constant reaffirmation of public support. The Javanese adored him.

The Vice-President followed Sukarno to the microphone. Dr. Hatta's speech was more scholarly than that of the President, and was effective with the sophisticated and educated people. For the peasants, however, he had little appeal.

Others spoke in their turn. Then Sjarifuddin, who rarely addressed a mass meeting, being shy of personal publicity, stepped forward saying "I should like to speak a few words."

The President and Vice-President stared at him in astonishment. This was unheard of.

Bung Amir strode onto the platform, rolled up the sleeves of his khaki tunic, and began expressing his views on the Revolution. He spoke of serious matters in a light vein, sprinkling his remarks with jokes and witticisms. The people loved it. "More, more, Bung Amir!" they chorused.

Sukarno smiled indulgently at the spectacle of his scholarly minister for defense in such a relaxed mood. Leaning over to me, he whispered, "I wonder what got into Bung Amir? I have never seen him like this before."

At that moment the light dawned for me. I told the President, "Johnnie Walker got into him," though I am quite sure Bung Karno did not understand.

Bung Amir was in such good humor that he had all of us on the speaker's stand laughing with his vast audience. When he returned to his seat he winked at me and said, "That was good whiskey. Just what I needed for my cold!"

In these hard days there was not much time or cause for laughter. We treasured such funny incidents. As Sjarifuddin said later, half in apology, "The world has been ruined by men who took themselves too seriously."

Indonesians are unpredictable. Everyone who knows them will vouch for that. They do things, and say things, on the spur of the moment. And the educated are almost as impulsive as the unlettered. That even the President shared this national trait was most disconcertingly revealed to me at Malang, the largest city and most important stop on our tour.

Thousands of people had come to see and hear Sukarno. Many had slept on the grounds the night before to make sure of a good position. It was the greatest gathering of people that I had ever seen anywhere.

The applause that greeted the President's speech was tumultuous. Then Bung Karno held up his hand. When the people had quieted, he said: "I have one more thing to say before I leave you. You see on the platform with me tonight a white woman. Many of you may have wondered what a woman of the race that is fighting to deprive us of our freedom is doing in the company of the President of Indonesia. Allow me to introduce Sudara K'tut Tantri, from the island of Bali.

"Now, the name K'tut means fourth-born of a Balinese family. I am sure you all know what the name Tantri stands for in our folklore. Sudara K'tut is a British-born American citizen, but she is more Indonesian than she is either British or American. She is the one and only foreigner to come openly to our side. She has done everything in her power to help us in our struggle for independence.

"Now, I want every man, woman, and child here tonight to look on the face of K'tut Tantri and remember it well. I want that no harm shall come to K'tut Tantri from any of our people. You must do all in your power to protect her, for she probably will be in Malang many times before our struggle is through. Remember that sudara means sister, and remember that my own mother is a Balinese woman. I commend Sudara K'tut Tantri to your care. Guard her with your life if it is necessary."

I was caught completely by surprise, and the deafening applause that followed touched and embarrassed me to tears. I had to fight to regain my composure.

That journey through Java gave me a wonderful insight into the character of the top man in Indonesia. No other Westerner, I suppose, has ever been so close to him and his work—certainly not in a time of stress. I observed him closely as, on our homeward journey, our train moved slowly from town to town. At every village they surged around him, men, women and little children in from the jungles and down from the mountains, a flat sea of eager brown faces. Many times barriers thrown across the rails forced us to make unscheduled stops at tiny settlements, so that the insistent people could do him honor. At every village great banners proclaimed MERDEKA ATAU MATI, and everywhere there were cheers for merdeka and Bung Karno.

A part of his amazing power to sway the people came from his ability to tell stories. No one loves a story better than does an Indonesian. For example, he would tell of the famous ride of Paul Revere, embellishing it with the lush figures of Oriental speech and driving home his point by admonishing his listeners: "When Paul Revere knocked at the doors of the people of America, they heard him. See to it that when our own Paul Reveres knock at your door you will answer and be ready to defend your country."

By nature Sukarno was a great psychologist and an even greater actor. At each stop he would say to the people that he would soon return, and would be accompanied by foreign correspondents. "I want you to tell these newspaper- and radiomen from all over the world, in their own language, that all is running well in Indonesia."

"Now, repeat after me and don't ever forget it—ALL IS RUNNING WELL!"

When the phrase had been repeated many times, he would then ask his audience, "Now, tell me what you are going to say when I return with the correspondents."

"ALL IS RUNNING WELL IN INDONESIA!" the people would shout, as though it were a football cheer.

When the correspondents did eventually visit Java with the President, they heard the yell from thousands of throats and they were impressed.

Over the years Indonesia's Cabinet members have risen and fallen. But always there has been the one President, a humble and kind man. We who knew him in those early days agreed that he was Indonesia's greatest man.

8

THE SPICE OF DANGER

The daily routine of life during this period was spiced with more danger than I liked to admit. On the insistence of Amir Sjarifuddin that I have an armed guard at all times, two little soldiers with rifles bigger than themselves followed me everywhere until I could stand it no longer. I went to Bung Amir.

"I have no fear of being killed by any Indonesian," I said. "Those guards are making me nervous. Not only that, they make me much too conspicuous. And psychologically I think it is wrong. I should not have a guard."

I told Bung Amir of the admonition of the American colonel at the bombing of Surabaya. "Never be afraid, K'tut," he had said. "If a bomb has your name on it, it will find you no matter what you do or where you hide."

Sjarifuddin laughed. "That colonel was right," he said. "We Orientals believe that what is to be will be. Man cannot escape his fate." The bodyguard was removed, and I felt more natural again.

Nevertheless, little incidents occurred. One day I was shot at while riding in a betja, or tricycle rickshaw. The bullet whizzed right past my face. Neither the rickshaw driver nor I was hurt, but we were badly frightened.

Another time I was riding down the main street of Jogja in a dokkar, a light carriage pulled by a small horse. An automobile containing two men came roaring down the street and tried to force us off the road. The dokkar was hit on one side and turned over, throwing the driver and me into the ditch. Then the motorcar raced away without stopping. I realized at once that this was no accident, but was a deliberate attempt to ram us. Luckily I was unhurt. The poor driver suffered a rib fracture and had to be taken to the hospital.

It did not take the military long to find the motorcar. Automobiles were very scarce, and not in the possession of private citizens. Investigation revealed that the two men who had tried to run us down came from Bandung and were members of the same ring of traitors as the plotting princess.

It seemed that, like Bung Tomo, I led a charmed life.

The dangers that menaced me were often in disguise. There was the time that an Indonesian woman whom I knew well invited me to go to Solo. She was charming. We got along together very well, and I trusted her thoroughly.

"Two important gentlemen have to go to a very hush-hush political meeting in a mountain village outside of Solo," she said. "I thought you would find the meeting interesting and instructive—something about which you would want to be informed."

I readily accepted the invitation and made arrangements to broadcast from Solo that evening instead of from Jogjakarta. By leaving Jogja in the afternoon around three, we would arrive at Solo at five, rest at the hotel until eight, then start off for the mountains to hear her friends speak.

Before I left Jogja I wrote a note to Bung Amir, telling him I had gone to Solo and explaining why. Much to my surprise, when we arrived at the Solo hotel an army officer was waiting for me with an urgent message to call the defense minister, not from the hotel but from the privacy of military headquarters. I excused myself and went with the officer to make the long-distance call.

"Thank heaven we caught up with you before you went to that meeting," Sjarifuddin said.

I replied that I saw nothing wrong in going to a political rally.

"There is plenty wrong," Bung Amir said. "I want you to return to Jogja immediately. Two officers have already left here and will escort you back. You are in danger of being kidnaped, or even killed."

"That can't be so. I am with friends," I said.

"Friends!" he exploded. "Do you know who the men are?"

I had to admit that I had never seen them before and that I did not get their names when we were introduced. We had had little chance to talk on the drive to Solo, because the men sat in front and my friend and I chatted together in the rear seat.

"I'll tell you who they are!" Bung Amir thundered. "One is certainly Tan Malaka, the number one Communist of Java. The other is one of our former officials who is working hand in hand with Tan Malaka. They are holding some kind of secret meeting in the mountains, and they are not taking you along just for the pleasure of your company. They will try to make use of you some way, and if you don't go along with their plans they will detain you."

"Why in the world would they detain me?" I asked. "I couldn't help them. I am not a Communist. I know nothing that could possibly interest them, because it is well known that I do not interfere in the internal politics of Indonesia."

"Listen, K'tut; be guided by me in this matter," he pleaded. "Return to Jogja immediately. Wait at the hotel until the two officers arrive."

Back at the hotel I told my friends that an important matter had come up and I must return to Jogja at once. The two men tried to persuade me to change my mind, and gave up only when the officers arrived.

The incident remained a mystery to me. Even if Tan Malaka and the ex-official were Communists, they were still Indonesians fighting for merdeka, as were the Socialists of Bung Amir's party and members of the President's Party National Indonesia. I personally could not believe I had been in the slightest danger, and Sjarifuddin would never enlighten me. When I joked about the matter he said only, "If you don't believe me, ask Bung Karno or Bung Sjahrir. They will tell you I did the right thing in getting you away from those men."

It is ironic that Bung Amir was later executed as an enemy of the Republic in company with Tan Malaka and Communist Leader Moesoeh.

Although I was friendly with the leaders of the Revolution, it was the simple peasants and artists whom I most enjoyed. Daily I received letters from soldiers at the front and from ordinary people throughout Java. Young Indonesians called at the hotel and many confided to me secrets that, had they not trusted me, could not have been beaten out of them.

It did not surprise me, then, when one day two young men called at the hotel and asked to speak to me in private. The story they told made my blood run cold. Were the plot they described carried out, it would have serious consequences for the Republic.

In brief, the plan was to kidnap Sutan Sjahrir, the prime minister. The men behind the plan were Tan Malaka and his followers. The kidnaping would take place three days hence. The young men told me where it would happen but could give me no definite hour.

Though the kidnaping of ministers and army officers was a commonplace these days, it was incredible that anyone should wish to kidnap this ardent revolutionary dedicated to merdeka and the new Republic. It seemed downright silly.

"We personally are against the kidnaping, and that is why we are letting you know about it," my informants said. "Most of our people oppose Sjahrir because they resent his policy of conciliation with the Dutch and British; they do not like any part of the negotiations now going on in Jakarta. They say that negotiation is a betrayal of the principles of the Revolution. But we think that a kidnaping would be political suicide for our party and very bad for Indonesia in the eyes of the world. We know that this move is only a part of the struggle for power between the two parties."

"Why didn't you go to the military authorities?" I asked.

"We don't dare to be connected with this leak of information," they explained. "We belong to the group that is planning the kidnaping. If we went to military intelligence we would have to give our names and addresses. Even in the military intelligence department there is bound to be a Tan Malaka follower. The word would get out, and we would be killed."

"Then why not go directly to Sutan Sjahrir?" I suggested.

"We would surely be recognized by someone," they said. "That is why we came to you. No member of our group will be suspicious, because you are not even remotely connected with Tan Malaka. And there would be nothing strange about you dropping in on Sjahrir. You are the only one who could warn him without being suspected."

After further objections on my part and pleading on theirs, I agreed to tell their story to Sjahrir, without confiding in anyone else —and they left me. I was not at all sure that the story was true, that I was not being led into a trap. But the worst that could happen would be for the prime minister to have a good laugh at my gullibility.

I learned that Sjahrir had gone to Solo, so it was six-thirty the next morning when I called on him. Indonesians are very early risers and I was not surprised to find him on his veranda having coffee. He greeted me without any show of surprise, as though he had expected me, and offered me coffee. Between sips I told him the story of the plot.

He listened attentively, and then had a hearty laugh. "Ridiculous!" he said. "Why should my own people want to kidnap me? If it were the Dutch, I could believe it." But he asked many questions nevertheless. Apparently he believed the story in part, at least.

When at length I excused myself, Sjahrir thanked me graciously for taking the trouble to come and see him. "I still think it's some kind of hoax—perhaps someone with a poor sense of propriety, trying to test your sincerity to the Republic," he said.

Back in Jogjakarta, I dismissed the whole incident from my mind. I had fulfilled my promise to the young men. It was now up to the prime minister.

Two days later the news swept over Java: SUTAN SJAHRIR HAS BEEN KIDNAPED. He was being held prisoner by parties unknown. The people were shocked, and all the ministers extremely upset. The Dutch were rejoicing, and making much propaganda of the incident. It was only the impassioned pleas of President Sukarno over the radio, begging the captors to free Sjahrir immediately before any further harm was done to the Republic, that brought about his release. Such was the power of President Sukarno, such the respect and affection, that even the opposition parties could not hold out against him. Sjahrir was turned loose, none the worse for his brief internment. Easygoing, lenient, and good natured, he dismissed the kidnaping as childish. Nothing was done about it.

I wondered what the young men from Maduin were thinking of me. They must have been disappointed, assuming that I had failed to warn Sjahrir. I never had a chance to let them know otherwise.

Such was life in Jogja. Interesting, and now and again spiked with peril.

9

PITO BRINGS A LETTER

My watch told me it was 3:30 A.M. when the room boy in the hotel pounded on my door and said a young officer who would not give his name was demanding to see me immediately. The visitor insisted that it was most important.

I had learned from experience not to be surprised at anything the Indonesians might choose to do. Their code of convention was their own. If something were really important, then 3:30 in the morning was as good a time as any in which to take care of it.

I asked the room boy to show the officer to the veranda and to bring kopi tubruk. Then I dressed hastily and walked out to meet my early-morning guest. He was seated with his back to the door and did not see me enter.

"Selamet pagi, bung," I said. Good morning, brother.

He jumped up from his chair and turned around.

"Pito!" I cried, in utter astonishment. "I can't believe it's you. You're back from Bali! Allah be praised for your safe return."

Then I turned off the flow of words, for his face told me plainer than anything else that something was wrong. He appeared to be very tired, and his brow was wrinkled in pain.

"Are you ill, Pito?" I asked. "Come; sit down and tell me all about it."

He sat down and put his head between his hands and started to sob.

A chill . . . a foreboding . . . a presentiment of disaster crept over my heart. I was afraid to say anything.

Finally Pito gazed at me with stricken eyes. I stared at him, and felt the color draining from my face. Suddenly I knew what he had to tell me.

"Go on, Pito. I think I know. It's Anak Agung Nura, isn't it?"

"Yes," he whispered. "He is dead, K'tut."

Suddenly I felt that I was no longer part of this world, that I had been transported into outer space where all was dark. I saw the beloved face, smiling at me with mysterious eyes. I could not move; I could not cry.

After some time I asked Pito how it had happened.

"He was shot by a band of irresponsible permoedas." The permoedas were a youth organization.

"Permoedas! Do you mean Dutchmen?" I asked. "The young Dutch toughs in Bali?"

"No, not Dutchmen. His own countrymen."

"I can't believe it," I cried. "I won't believe it. It couldn't be. His people loved him."

Pito told me the whole dreadful story. A band of young extremists went to Anak Agung Nura's chalet in the mountains and awakened him by pounding on the door. They said they had something important to tell him. Unsuspecting, he opened the door and was shot down before he could say a word. The assassins escaped in a car that was waiting for them on the main road. They must have driven toward Negara, for the car was found abandoned near Djembrana.

"There are many conflicting stories," said Pito. "Some say it was the work of Dutch agents. We do not believe this to be true. It was the work of irresponsible guerrillas, either Balinese or Javanese, who took the law into their own hands. As you know, Anak Agung Nura was against all forms of violence. He did not believe in indiscriminate retaliation—an eye for an eye, a tooth for a tooth. He would not condone the cold-blooded murder of private citizens, even if they were Dutchmen. To the illiterate mountaineers who had suffered much at the hands of the Dutch this could mean only one thing. Anak Agung Nura was working with and for white people, or at the very least was pro-white."

I shook my head. "Surely, Pito, that would be no reason to shoot him down in cold blood."

There were many factors to be considered, Pito replied. The permoedas had been emotionally upset, and their feelings outraged, by one of the most brutal atrocities yet committed against the natives by the Dutch military in Bali. A young guerrilla had fallen into the hands of the Dutch, and a sadistic Dutchman had ordered his head shaved, and then half the head scalped until it was red with blood. The other half was to remain white to produce the colors of Indonesia Merdeka—red and white. The tortured youth was then wheeled through the streets of Den Pasar as an example to his countrymen, as a warning not to resist the return of the Dutch to Bali.

As could be expected, the permoedas of Bali went wild. They called for the massacre of all the Dutch in Bali. Nura, greatly upset, pleaded with the permoedas not to take drastic action. Two wrongs would not make a right, he told them, and he urged them to have patience. The hour of their delivery from the Dutch was near, he said; but it must be brought about without violence. A small band of roving fanatics, misunderstanding his motives and assuming that he was trying to save the Dutch, carried out his execution.

The story left me stunned, speechless. "Why don't you let yourself go, K'tut?" Pito said softly. "Let the tears come. Don't hold back. Cry. It will be a relief."

"No, Pito, I will not cry, nor give in to my feelings," I said. "If I do I shall not be able to endure staying in Indonesia another day. Agung Nura would not want me to grieve. I shall carry on as he would have wished. Anything I can do for Indonesia Merdeka will be, somehow, a tribute to the memory of the most gentle Indonesian that ever lived."

Pito told me that the Balinese prince had been buried temporarily. When freedom had been won at last, his body would be removed from its grave and cremated in the Balinese fashion, in royal style. Thus would his spirit be released to join his ancestors.

"One day he will be reborn," said Pito. "And you, K'tut, will meet him again in a free and happy land, where there will be no slavery and no violence. Who is to know, K'tut, but that you in your next reincarnation will be a true Balinese? We believe in such things."

We fell silent, each lost in his own somber thoughts.

"By the way," Pito said after a while, "Agung Nura left a letter for you."

A letter? He had no warning that he was to die. Why would he have left a letter?

"It was found in his bureau drawer, with orders that it be sent to you in Java. They gave it to me to deliver. Shall I open it for you?"

"No, Pito dear," I said. "I shall open it when I am alone."

Pito said he had been traveling for three days and nights with almost no sleep. There were, as usual, no vacant rooms at the hotel, so I told him to rest in the spare bed in my room, and said I would call him in time for lunch. He was soon fast asleep.

I sat on the veranda with a heavy heart, Anak Agung's letter un-opened in my lap. I was afraid to open it; if I made any contact now with Agung Nura, even in death, it would be the end for me. I could not face the pain of his written words. Not yet. I dropped the letter unopened into the drawer of my writing desk, and silently left the veranda.

It was still dark, and Jogja was fast asleep. I walked down the main street as in a dream, and came finally to the market place. The early-morning peasants were trickling in from the hills and outlying kampongs with their heavy loads strapped to their backs or balanced on their heads. They were dressed in rags or gunny sacking. The Dutch blockade around Java had cut off the supply of cloth; and even if clothing materials were to be had, these poor people had no money.

The women greeted me with shy smiles, and the men stoutly called, "Merdeka, K'tut Tantri." "Tetap Merdeka, bung," I said in return.

They all knew me well, for this was not the first time I had sat in the market place at dawn watching these industrious folk set out their wares. They had suffered much for merdeka. Many had lost homes or loved ones. But they were of a brave and fatalistic stock, and went about their chores with a smile. They understood that merdeka meant sacrifice on their part, and they were willing to make the sacrifice. I learned from them patience—patience and courage.

Pito and I lunched together on the veranda. He had much to tell me of Bali, and especially about the old Rajah, who had taken to his bed at the news of Nura's death.

What of Wyjan, Maday, Njoman? They were all safe, and living in their respective kampongs. But they were very poor, for they had lost much to the Japanese. They had been told that I had been killed by the Japanese, and were overjoyed to learn that I was alive. They were hoping that I would return to Bali, to build again our moon garden on the ashes of our dead dreams.

As Pito unfolded the story of the reoccupation of Bali by the Dutch I became more and more depressed. As long as the Dutch remained in Bali, I could never go back.

"The Dutch are like leeches," said Pito. "Once you get them on your body they never let go, and it is difficult to remove them. They have reinstated themselves all over the island except in the mountains, where the guerrillas hide out. There really is not much the guerrillas can do, for they have very few firearms and can only get more if they are smuggled in from Java."

Den Pasar, Pito said, was crowded with Dutch military. All that the Balinese could do for the present was to smile, and wait. Dutch government officials were busy with plans to set up a puppet government to be called the East Indonesian States. It would embrace all the Indonesian islands east and north of Java: Borneo, Celebes, Ambon, New Guinea, and hundreds of smaller islands. An Indonesian would head the government, but the Dutch would keep full control of defense, foreign affairs, finances, and trade transactions. The new president would be purely and simply a puppet of the Dutch. He would have no power whatsoever.

"It is the old policy of divide and rule," said Pito.

"And who is to be the Indonesian head of these puppet states?"

"A Balinese friend of yours, K'tut. The Rajah of Sukawati, Tjokorda Gde Rake Sukawati!"

"Tjokorda Sukawati? I can't believe it!" This was stunning news, indeed. The Rajah was a good friend, a man I liked very much. He was European educated, charming, a linguist, and one of the most intelligent Balinese I had known. Many pleasant days had I spent in his company, and in the puri of his brothers. They had patiently taught me to write in the Balinese characters. Countless evenings I had listened to them translate the Indian epic poems, and afterward explain the dignity and beauty of Hindu literature. What could have induced a man of his exalted caste to forsake his own people to become a puppet of the enemy? It was unthinkable.

"Are Tjokorda's brothers and his son in this betrayal with him?" I asked.

"No," said Pito. "The son broke with his father over this move, and is a hundred per cent behind the Republic."

Pondering the riddle, I recalled that he had married a French woman, and it seemed probable that pressure had been put on him. Whatever the reasons behind his decision to serve the Dutch, his ultimate fate was one of the many tragedies of merdeka.

For when the East Indonesian States collapsed, as could be expected, Tjokorda Sukawati's career was finished.

And what of Pito's plans for the future? He confided that he was on his way to troubled Bandung, carrying important messages to the guerrilla chieftain of that area. He would go also to see his father, for he had heard that the old man was not well. After that he would return to Surabaya to confer with Dr. S. and Bung Tomo. A plan must be developed to help the guerrillas in Bali.

I suggested that Pito stay on a few days in Jogja to rest. "Duty first," he replied. "On my way back I shall stop, but now I must be on my way."

I hated the idea of Pito's going to Bandung. It was full of the Dutch military, as were Jakarta and Surabaya. Dreadful stories were beginning to come through to Jogja.

Pito assured me that the way he traveled he would be under no suspicion. "I am the original Invisible Man," he said playfully.

Once more I said, "Selamet djalan, Pito." Once more he answered, "Selamet tinggal, Sudara K'tut."

I waved, and then he was gone. And I was left alone with my gloomy thoughts.

10

OLD NICK REJECTS ME

The Indonesians, awakened from three hundred years of sleep, were bursting with energy, avid for knowledge and education. Day and night I was besieged by young Indonesians begging me to teach them English. But there was so little time. Fierce fighting was going on in every town and village where the British and the Dutch had entrenched themselves.

Repeatedly President Sukarno asked the British to stop bringing Dutch troops into Indonesia. But his pleas were ignored. Thousands upon thousands of Dutch military personnel poured into the islands, and trigger-happy patrols were creating so many "incidents" that Sukarno had to order all Indonesians off the streets at dark to prevent major trouble.

From the words of Major F. E. Crockett, the United States military observer at Batavia, writing in *Harper's Magazine* of March, 1946, there seems little doubt that the British were fully aware of Dutch intentions:

> It seemed clear to me from what I had seen that the Dutch, in view of Britain's political noninterference pronouncement, would try and were trying to involve the British inextricably by provoking unrest among the native population. I could see no other reasonable explanation for the brutal conduct of the Dutch patrols. What they would gain by such tactics was obvious: they would keep the British too busy to disarm the Japanese (which was their primary reason for being there) and they would force the British to commit more and more troops to the area, which would mean more and more involvement.

At long last, of course, the British did come to see that they had been duped.

Since learning of Agung Nura's death I had kept myself very busy, traveling all over Republican Java. Often I wished I had been born an Indonesian, so I could look upon death in their philosophical way, without long grieving.

I visited Bung Tomo in Malang. I went to the mountain stronghold near Modjokerto where I had lived with the guerrillas, and they begged me to stay. I would have remained had I been able to follow the dictates of my heart. But now I knew the time had passed for that. On returning to Jogja I learned that I was once again to accompany the President on a tour, but this time to the West instead of the East.

More and more I found myself attached to the Ministry for Defense, and to Amir Sjarifuddin—in quite an unofficial way, of course.

One day my old friend, the major from army intelligence, came calling. I had not seen much of him since the arrest of the plotting princess and her accomplices. He had been away on a mission to West Java.

I could tell by the gleam in his eyes that this was not just a social visit. He had something up his sleeve, very plainly. Before he could say a word, I told him, "Now, Bung, I am warning you in advance. I am not going to get mixed up in any more cloak-and-dagger dramas. If that is what you are about to suggest, the answer is no. I could not stand another plotting princess. My nerves are still shattered from that little deal."

The major laughed. "Nothing like that this time," he said. "This will be an adventure, but not what you think." He paused and grinned, thoroughly enjoying my suspense as he walked up and down my veranda. Suddenly he said, "How would you like to go to Australia on a mission?"

Whatever I had expected, this was not it.

"There's that little matter of the Dutch blockade, major," I said with a bit of sarcasm. "Our merchant fleet isn't exactly operating a regular schedule out of Java these days. Submarines and long-range airplanes are small luxuries that we have never permitted ourselves."

"Ah, but we do have a plane," said the major. "It's a leftover from the Japanese—prettiest thing you ever saw—and we have it hidden at Malang. Certain repairs were necessary, but we were able to get the parts from the Philippines. We think that after we attach extra gasoline tanks it will be able to reach Darwin, if not Perth."

Extra gasoline tanks! The idea of trying to stretch out the range of an airplane by adding fuel tanks was not an appealing one to me, a layman. And what of a pilot, and navigator? Such a flight, across 1,400 miles of water, would require an experienced crew.

"We think the chances of arriving safely in Australia would be about fifty-fifty," said the major.

I told him acidly that it would take a safety factor of about 95 per cent to interest me in a flight to Australia. "Besides," I said, "I have no passport or identification papers. The Japanese Kempetai took my American passport and destroyed it so far as I know. And we would have to have visas."

"Don't let the little details bother you," he replied. "This is a revolution, and we have to take our chances. We'll just fly into Australia without passports and papers. The Australians won't shoot us, that is sure. They are sympathetic, and already they've helped us very much with their union ban on loading Dutch ships with firearms. We'll be able to tell our story all over Australia. And we'll see that you are provided with identification papers and a passport claiming you as a warga negara, an Indonesian citizen."

"I'd consider it a high honor to be a citizen of Indonesia, have no doubt about that, major," I said. "But officially we are still a colony of the Netherlands. We are not recognized by Australia or any other country. An Indonesian passport would be honored nowhere."

"Rubbish!" said the major. "We no longer belong to the Netherlands. In any case, you are British, and Australia is part of the British Commonwealth. It seems to me you should have no trouble."

"But I am not British now," I reminded him. "I am an American citizen."

"Nonsense! You can only be what your parents are. You are British."

"All right; so I am British. So what then?"

"It makes it much easier if you are British. You needn't advertise the fact in Australia that you are an American citizen. You do not speak with an American accent. You can become an American again when we send you to the United States."

"And if you send me to China, do I become a Chinese?" I teased.

"Oh, no; that won't be necessary," he said seriously. "You will go as a warga negara."

"Who cooked up this Australian trip?" I wanted to know. "Army intelligence? Amir Sjarifuddin?"

"No. Bung Amir has been away. He doesn't know about it yet. . . . Of course, K'tut, if you do not want to make this trip—if you really think it's too unsafe—forget it. We realize the danger. The Indonesians can go by themselves. The only reason we had you in mind was that you are British, and our party would have a better reception in Australia if you were on the plane. In fact, it would be sensational."

Sensational? Perhaps—if we got there at all! Yes; it had become we, not they, in my thinking. I had been persuaded. After all, I could speak the English language and would be in a position to tell the Aussies the truth about conditions in Indonesia.

The major was pleased at my decision. "You will be leaving a week from today," he said. "Bung Amir will be back from Maduin tomorrow, and I shall inform him immediately." As he started to leave he turned, winked, and said, "Berontak, K'tut."

Berontak means revolt. It was a catchword with the permoedas and guerrillas, shouted with raised fist on leaving each other's company. "Carry on, until we win our fight" was its meaning. The educated classes did not use the word as a parting salutation, so this was just a bit of the major's humor. Well, carry on I would. "Berontak, bung!" I called.

Australia! What next? I asked myself. I retired to my room and laid out the wee cards that I had made in prison. I could see nothing of what might be in store for me in Australia—neither a departure nor an arrival in a strange land. I wondered at this, but put it down to the fact that I wasn't in the mood that day for fortunetelling.

Bung Amir came back from Maduin, and when he heard the plan he was dead set against it. He was extremely dubious that the airplane would be able to make the long flight. However, the major enlisted the help of a top official of the air force. Together they were able to convince Bung Amir that the plane was skyworthy.

Two days before we were to depart I was told that Colonel X would be accompanying us and that the plane was flying in from Malang that evening. On the following day it would make a trial flight over the Indian Ocean, staying aloft until only enough gasoline would be left to get it back to Jogjakarta. This test would reveal how long the plane would stay in the air without refueling.

Early on the morning of the trial flight, Colonel X and the major called at the hotel to ask if I would like to go along, just to get the feel of the plane. I had been working very late the night before, and was tired. "I would rather wait until we set out for Australia," I said.

Hearing my decision, Colonel X told the major that he too had changed his mind. "I will stay at the hotel with K'tut and talk over our plans for Australia," X said.

"All right," replied the major. "I am going to my office now to get the papers ready. I'll meet you after dinner and we'll go to Bung Amir's house to pick up the letters for Australia and to get our final instructions."

The colonel and I dined together, and then waited for the major. He was late. We left a message, finally, that we were proceeding to Sjarifuddin's house and would meet him there.

On entering the study of Bung Amir we found him standing by the telephone. When he saw us he closed his eyes and said, "Thank God!"

He noted our bewilderment. "You haven't heard the news?" he asked.

We shook our heads.

"Is it possible? I thought it was all over town by now. The plane crashed off the coast of Sumatra! Everyone was killed!"

We stared, absolutely thunderstruck. I shivered. The colonel asked, "Was the major on the plane?"

"No, thank God!" said Bung Amir.

We sat in thoughtful silence for a little while. Then Colonel X said, "Come on, K'tut. Let us go home to my house. Evidently Old Nick didn't want us."

We said good night to Bung Amir and walked silently back to the barracks. Our Australian trip was off, of course. Our plans had been kept top secret. No one knew we were supposed to fly away in that plane at daybreak the following day. All that ever appeared in the press and over the radio were the sad details of the crashing of an Indonesian plane on a trial flight off the Sumatra coast.

Colonel X never mentioned the tragedy again. Neither did I.

11

I INTERVENE IN A MAN'S FATE

Pito was back from Bandung, downhearted and upset and nervous. Horrifying atrocities were being committed by the Dutch against any Indonesians caught wearing the Indonesian colors of the badge of merdeka. The swaggering Dutch troopers forced their captives to chew and swallow the bits of red-and-white cloth and the soft-metal badges. Many a young Indonesian thus suffered permanent internal injury. We printed the story of this outrage in *The Voice of Free Indonesia*. The incensed Indonesians tried to retaliate, and many Dutch were killed.

Pito was worried, too, about his father, weakened by recurrence of the malaria and dysentery he had contracted during long years of exile. Pito had tried to persuade his father to leave Bandung for the relative safety of Jogja, but the old man had refused, insisting that he would continue the struggle for merdeka in the town of his ancestors.

"You are too young for this dangerous job of traveling up and down Java on secret missions," I told Pito. "You have never had time for fun. You do not know how to play. You are much too serious, trying to carry the struggle for freedom as a burden all your own. You must take a few days off for once, and let me show you a good time."

Pito agreed so readily that I was taken a bit by surprise. He must have been even more weary than we had realized. For three days we acted like a couple of tourists discovering Java for the first time. We went on picnics, and visited the famous Borobudur and Prambanan monuments to the past. We visited by moonlight these great temples, created long centuries ago by people of a magnificent culture, and we marveled at the delicate beauty of their handiwork.

We visited the Sultan's kraton, and Pito saw for the first time in his life the renowned dancers of Jogjakarta. He sat entranced. "It's like a fairy tale, and the kraton is like a magnificent castle," he said. And indeed it was. There was nothing elsewhere in Indonesia to match the feudal splendor of the kraton.

We called on President Sukarno and attended a reception at the presidential palace. We saw performances by dancers from Sumatra, from all over Indonesia. We visited homes as guests of some of Indonesia's famous artists.

Pito was enchanted. It had been his lot as a child to walk the highways and pick up a living by his wits. He had never had time to enjoy the amazing and beautiful things of mid-Java. Self-trained, without formal education, he nevertheless had managed to learn to speak Dutch almost as fluently as his native Javanese. His English, mostly picked up from tourists, was intelligible, and very picturesque. He was sensitive and refined in appearance, and he walked like a prince, his head held high. I was very proud of Pito.

At last the day came when he must leave for Surabaya. "And from Surabaya I am going to Celebes," he said. He might as well have told me he was taking off for the moon. The island of Celebes was at least three days from Java by native prau. Its people spoke an entirely different language.

"Why Celebes?" I asked.

"I am to go there and learn what I can of Turk Westerling."

Pito was amazed that I had never heard of Captain Turk Westerling. A notorious officer in the Dutch army, reportedly the son of a Dutch father and a Turkish mother—a man known throughout Indonesia as "the Butcher" for his monstrous, sadistic activities, he said.

Westerling at the outbreak of World War II was in Rotterdam. He escaped to England, joined the Dutch forces fighting with the British army, and became a sergeant major. In 1943 he managed to become one of Lord Mountbatten's bodyguards. This did not suit the restless Westerling, so he volunteered for service in Burma. Later he won a commission with the Allied Forces.

In 1945 Westerling parachuted into northern Sumatra and before long managed to establish himself as an absolute dictator. When the British forces reached Sumatra after the capitulation of the Japanese they were surprised to find Captain Westerling in complete charge. He had organized a remarkable intelligence service embracing half of Sumatra. Whenever anything happened in Sumatra, Turk Westerling knew about it a few hours later. A British officer wrote of him in one of the Singapore papers:

I visited Capt. Westerling at his bungalow and we were having coffee. Suddenly Westerling pulled from out of a wastebasket the head of an Indonesian and said, "My intelligence service tracked down this rebel and found out where he was living. I dressed myself up as a native and, covering my face with a demon's mask, entered his house. I hid in the corner of his bedroom and waited for him to return home, and when he did he froze with fright. I took him by the hand and told him this would be his last day on earth. I gave him some rice and locked him in the bathroom. At 4 a.m. I entered the bathroom and told the rebel to turn around, and with one stroke of my sword, I severed his head from his body."

"The Dutch have sent Westerling to Celebes to put down the rebellion of Indonesians fighting for merdeka," Pito told me. "He has been trying to do this in a ruthless and brutal manner. Women and children coming home from the market, men in the streets, have been shot down in cold blood. Some have been dragged from their homes. Men picked at random have been shot as a warning to the others not to try to overthrow the Dutch. A whole village was exterminated. The men were forced to dig a mass grave for the massacre that was to follow."

I shuddered at the idea of sending a young, inexperienced boy to Celebes to investigate a madman. Supposing Pito fell into the hands of Westerling or his gang of murderers. I made a mental note to ask Amir Sjarifuddin to use his influence to see that the assignment be given to an older, more experienced man. But I said nothing of this to Pito, of course.

Once again we rubbed noses in farewell, and Pito left saying that he would stay two weeks in Surabaya before sailing for Celebes. I was not surprised, a few days later, to receive a long-distance call from Surabaya. It was Pito, telling me that his mission to Celebes had been canceled and that an older man was taking his place. I smiled to myself, and silently thanked Bung Amir. Apparently I had intervened in Pito's fate, after all.

The older man who took Pito's place never returned from Celebes.

As a footnote to this incident I might add that in a later phase of Indonesia's struggle Westerling created havoc and terror in Java, particularly in the shooting up of Bandung. Ultimately he was accused of responsibility for the deaths of 30,000 Indonesians and his brutal activities gave rise to world-wide revulsion, requiring the Dutch government to send a parliamentary commission to Celebes. Although the commission's report was never published, the Dutch concluded that Westerling was responsible for "only" 4,000 to 5,000 deaths instead of 30,000. But the Indonesian government insisted that 30,000 was the correct figure. These developments are not a part of my present narrative, however; nor is a later episode when I tipped off the Indonesian government as to Westerling's hiding place and his plans for escaping from Java with the assistance of high Dutch officials.

12

A SENSATIONAL PROPOSAL

Indonesia at this time had two strong friends, Australia and India. Both countries had done much to help the cause of merdeka. The Australians had put a ban on all Dutch ships loading firearms or war material in Australian ports. Prime Minister Nehru of India had asked, "What has become of the United Nations Charter?" and had voiced acidly his opinion of Dutch aggression in Indonesia.

The British were in an unenviable position. Criticized and mistrusted by both the Indonesians and the Dutch, they were under fire also in the United Nations and were being castigated by the world press. Yet there was no doubt that British sympathy and sentiment were on the side of the Indonesians.

The dilemma of the British was understandable enough. If they supported the new Republic openly, they would alienate Dutch advocates in the United Nations, with far-reaching effects on any European alliance.

The British had eventually to change their policy and urge the Dutch to negotiate with the Indonesian leaders. When the Dutch refused, the British put strong pressure on them, emphasizing that a peaceful compromise was the only way out of the situation. In the end the Dutch were forced to agree, but they felt that they had lost face and had been humiliated into dealing with Indonesian leaders whom they had branded as Japanese puppets.

The British then sent two very capable statesmen to Indonesia as mediators, Lord Inverchapel and later Lord Killearn. Lord Killearn came into the interior to talk with President Sukarno, accompanied by several pilots, young men clearly from the cream of the Royal Air Force. I met Lord Killearn and his party at the palace, and it was my pleasant duty to entertain the fliers while Lord Killearn, Amir Sjarifuddin, Prime Minister Sjahrir, President Sukarno, and Vice-President Hatta were in conference. It did not surprise me that they were very sympathetic to the Indonesian cause, which they seemed to understand well. They were on their way home to be demobilized, and said they would like nothing better than to return and join the Indonesian air force, to help carry on the struggle for freedom.

The Indonesian leaders and the British representatives got along very well when they met informally, which irked the Dutch no end. The British pointed out to the Dutch that Britain had walked out of India and Burma leaving good feeling behind, with the result that Britishers were now back in India working side by side with the Indians. But the Dutch were not so subtle as the English and preferred to fight until they were forced into the sea.

When Lord Killearn left Jogja, President Sukarno thanked him for his good offices and expressed the hope that efforts to negotiate a peace treaty with the Dutch would be successful. A truce was effected, and shortly afterward the Dutch and the Indonesians signed the ill-fated Linggadjati agreement. This provided for Dutch recognition of the de facto Indonesian government. The Dutch and Indonesians would be partners in Java, Sumatra, and Madura. The status of the other islands would be negotiated.

The British withdrew from Indonesia. The withdrawal in one

sense was a calamity for the Indonesians, for more than 90,000 Dutch troops were left behind, fully equipped with British war supplies. In the year that they had been in Indonesia the British had suffered many losses. Hundreds had been killed and thousands wounded, and many had deserted to the Indonesian side. But the most surprising thing was the respect the Indonesians had for the British, so totally unlike their feeling about the Dutch.

Prime Minister Sjahrir said, on the departure of the British: "In all circumstances, even in unfriendly contact or in conflict with us, we learned to appreciate and to admire you. You introduced to our country by your personal qualities some attractive traits of Western culture—your politeness, kindness and dignified behavior."

After the British withdrawal from Indonesia the Dutch showed plainly they had no intention of living up to the Linggadjati agreement. The treaty was a farce from beginning to end. It took Indonesia three more years of fighting against the Dutch before freedom was finally achieved.

It might have been expected that after the signing of the agreement the Dutch would at least lift the blockade around Indonesian territory. The native islanders were suffering severe economic hardships, for they could neither sell their produce nor bring into the country the things they needed. But the blockade was continued as before, and the people were reduced to smuggling produce into and out of Singapore. Some were lucky, but most were not.

Now that the restraining hand of the British had been removed, the Dutch diehards in The Hague were planning war. It soon became evident that the Dutch intended to force themselves once again into Indonesia. For several months after the signing of the agreement there was explosive provocation, and a series of incidents. At last the colonial war that the British had tried to avoid in Indonesia broke out, and the Dutch army was on the march. Once again protests came from all over the world.

It was in this period that my friend, the major from army intelligence, telephoned and said he had something important to discuss.

I was not readily taken in. "When you have something important to talk about, my dear major, it is time for me to go into hiding," I told him.

"This time," he said, "it's sensational."

"Sensational!" I scoffed. "Remember, major, the Australian trip was supposed to be sensational. I am not interested in any more sensational schemes. Next thing, you'll ask me to take off in a space ship to enlist the aid of the Martians for merdeka. Is that it, major?"

"Not quite, K'tut—but something like it. It's not Mars. It's Singapore." He said he could not talk further, but would come around to take me to dinner.

I was aware that life in Java was becoming dangerous for me. If the Dutch ever got as far as Jogjakarta, I would certainly be arrested, and probably shot. (In this conjecture I was right. The Dutch did get to Jogja, finally, and they arrested President Sukarno and other leaders. It was my personal good fortune that I was no longer in the city.) But how could anyone safely get to Singapore with a land, sea, and air blockade around Java and Sumatra? Hundreds of Indonesian patriots had tried it and met death at sea. Yet I knew in my heart that the Indonesians could plan their way in and out of Hades if they made up their minds to do it. They had a great sense of adventure, and worried little. This was the spirit that finally won for them merdeka, for certainly they did not outdo the Dutch with guns. It was their willingness to risk their lives for a principle that triumphed in the end, even when they knew without doubt that they would be killed.

The major and I went to a Chinese singsong café for dinner. We did not discuss Singapore, but the latest Dutch maneuvers, and the effect of the blockade around the island. After dinner we went to the home of Colonel Ebanda where he and two other old friends, Colonel Barata and Colonel Sorotiyo, were waiting. The five of us had been through many an adventure together, and the homes of the colonels had been like my own.

We gathered around the dining-room table. There was a certain tension in the air. The major was the first to speak.

"K'tut," he said, "we are meeting here tonight to talk over plans that may bring you the biggest adventure of your life."

Before he could say anything else, I broke in. "I really am getting tired of adventures. I want to do all that I can to help the Indonesians, but there's a limit to what my nerves can take."

Colonel Ebanda spoke up. "Perhaps we should not call this mission an adventure," he suggested. "That may be the wrong word. It is an important project. We are going to call it 'Operation Hide-

and-Seek.' If it is successful, it will be a great thing for us. The publicity in itself will be something to our advantage. It will be very dangerous, and that is why we are meeting here tonight. We want you to listen to the plan. Then, if you don't feel equal to taking part in it, you know full well we will think no more about it."

The major explained. "That plan to fly to Australia was a disaster, a catastrophe. But we have not given up the idea of reaching Australia and of getting our story through to the outside world. Since the withdrawal of the British, things here have gone from bad to worse. We know now that the Dutch have no intention of living up to the Linggadjati agreement. We can hold them back for a while, but not for long. We must have help. The outside world must be made to understand just what the Dutch are up to, now that the British are gone. The Indonesian story must be brought to the attention of the United Nations. This surely will be done by either India or Australia. We have learned that the Dutch are going to try to bring in guns by planes, loading them from an airport in northern Australia. This must not be allowed to happen. The Australians must hear the truth."

I knew, of course, that the situation was more critical as our radio stations were now blocked by the Dutch and it was impossible to gets news through to the outside world. The Indonesians were in desperate need of medical supplies. Hundreds were dying every day for want of the proper medicines and drugs, even bandages.

"The Australian Red Cross would fly in aid, if they understood our need. No one can tell them better than you, Sudara K'tut Tantri," the major persisted.

"What is this talk about Australia?" I asked. "I understood the major to say Singapore. Has there been a change in your plans?"

"No," the major said. "It's like this. First we would like you to go to Singapore, and from there to Australia—and maybe to America."

I gazed fondly at the four men. Really, they were wonderful. So casual that, for all the excitement they showed, they might have been discussing a tour around Jogjakarta.

Again I pointed out that I had no passport or documents of any kind, and reminded them of the blockade around Java.

"Supposing I could get through the blockade—how would I get into Singapore? It sounds to me like a plot for a Hollywood movie."

There was silence for a moment. Then the major said softly, "By sailing through the blockade to Malaya, and from there on to Australia."

My heart skipped a beat. I had speculated that he might have another plane hidden away, and I wouldn't have been too surprised had he produced a submarine. But to sail through the blockade—that was unthinkable! Many had been blown to pieces by Dutch patrols by daring such a thing.

Surely, I told the major, he couldn't be serious. The whole idea was preposterous, especially as I could expect no cordial reception in Singapore, a British crown colony, after all my criticism of British policy in Indonesia.

The major had anticipated all my objections. "We'll get you into Singapore by way of the underground. The British won't even know you're in the city."

"And what of the Dutch, who would love to catch up with me?"

"They will not know what ship you are on. No one but the four of us will know that you have left Indonesia until you are safe in Singapore."

And where would they get a ship capable of sailing to Australia?

"We have no ship that could sail to Australia," the major agreed. "But we have a small wooden ship left over from the Japanese that can go as far as Malaya safely. It's about two hundred tons."

When I exclaimed that this was not much bigger than a native prau, he said confidently, "Oh, it's big enough. And it has a diesel engine. True, it has no cabins or toilet facilities. But it will reach Singapore all right—if it isn't ambushed at sea by the Dutch. And it sails under the British flag with a real Britisher for captain—a renegade English blockade buster."

The British skipper was more a blind than anything else. He was too old to be sailing on his own, and besides he was hardly ever sober. The true captain would be an Ambonese, a reliable and resourceful man who knew the Indonesian waters from many years of sailing under the Dutch. Besides the two captains, there would be four deck hands—Indonesian guerrillas from Java Timor. "These young men know you well; you will be looked after most carefully," I was assured. The ship would sail from the small port of Tegal, near Cheribon. The date had not yet been set.

We talked for hours. The officers had thought of everything. All activity at the Tegal docks had been ordered halted, to make it seem that the port was closed down and to lull the suspicions of the watchful Dutch, who had a cruiser outside the harbor waiting like a vulture to pounce. But the little ship was ready to sail on a moment's notice. The captains were aboard, with a plentiful supply of liquor for the Englishman who was in the adventure solely for money; he was brokenhearted to be forced to retire at sixty-five and dreamed of earning enough money by such hazardous enterprises to buy a ship of his own.

The longer I listened the more practical the plan appeared. When we finally parted, it was with the understanding that we would meet again the following day, with Bung Amir, to work out the troublesome financial details.

It was nearing daybreak when I returned to the Merdeka Hotel, and I had difficulty getting to sleep. I realized, suddenly, that I had not promised to undertake the hazardous journey, but that somehow my friends had taken it for granted that I would go along with their plan. I called myself several kinds of a fool. The very idea of sailing through the Dutch blockade with five Indonesian guerrillas and a drunken Englishman made me shudder. Certainly I was not contemplating this venture for personal gain. I had never taken any money from the Indonesian government for help I was able to give. Obviously I was ruled not by my brains but by my heart. And in my heart I knew that I must go, for I had sworn solemnly "Merdeka atau Mati."

I remembered again my mother's saying to me in my childhood, "Remember, you are a descendant of pirates and kings." The pirates I could now believe. About the kings I still had my doubts.

The next evening we met again, this time at Bung Amir's home. As I listened to my friends discuss their plan, I thought what remarkable people they really were—and I found myself wholeheartedly with their cause. Their problems were my problems now, and their joys and sorrows were mine. When Bung Amir asked what I thought of the program I replied, "Others have made it, why not we? If a bomb has my name on it, quismat. If not, I'll get to Singapore. It is as simple as that."

Bung Amir's help and advice were required because the Indonesians had no foreign currency and their own money had no value in the outside world. However, the Indonesians had managed to smuggle tons of rubber and sugar through Sumatra into Singapore, and to sell it to Chinese merchants. The proceeds were paid to the agents of the Indonesian Republic. A number of Indonesians were in Singapore for this activity, most of them highly educated, friends or relatives of the Indonesian leaders. Many Indonesian army officers were there secretly buying firearms from neighboring Asian countries, paying for them with money from the sale of sugar and rubber.

Bung Amir gave me letters to some of these men, and one instructing an Indonesian to give me a certain sum for my expenses in Singapore and Australia. Sjarifuddin also gave me letters to high personages in Singapore and Australia, and to an admiral in Washington. In view of Bung Amir's unhappy fate, I must record here that none of the letters was addressed to an individual Communist or to a Communist organization.

"It is best that you go," Bung Amir said. "I am afraid that if you stay on in Java your life will be in great danger. The way things are going now, it may not be long before the Dutch march into Jogja." Amir spoke truer words than he knew.

There was the problem of a passport for me. When I told Amir with some heat that I had applied for one only recently at the American consulate in Batavia and encountered nothing but red tape, he patted my shoulder and told me not to worry about it. "We will give you an Indonesian passport," he said.

But Indonesia had no passports. It was not yet recognized by any country in the world.

"Do you mean a Dutch passport, Bung Amir?" I asked.

"Certainly not," he replied. "I shall have an Indonesian passport made especially for you. One never knows what may happen in this life. Someday we will be a recognized republic, and then we shall have our own passports. If you ever find yourself in a country without a passport, an Indonesian document may be very useful. You can put our passport away and forget it until such a time comes."

So it was that within a few days I had Indonesian passport No. 1, an impressive-looking paper not unlike the United States passport. The front page was decorated with the red-and-white flag of Indonesia; I smiled to note that the word Republic was spelled wrong. The signature on it was that of Amir Sjarifuddin himself.

To humor Bung Amir I took the worthless passport and hid it away among my things. At least it would be an amusing souvenir of

Indonesia. I could not know how useful this document would some-day prove to be and how fervently I would thank Bung Amir for it. The day came at last when I was to leave for Tegal, there to wait possibly days or weeks for the Dutch cruiser to sail away. Colonel Sorotiyo was to accompany me to Tegal. I made my farewell to Amir Sjarifuddin and gave him a letter for Pito. Bung Amir looked tired and wan, which indeed he was, and it saddened me to say good-by. We were to leave Jogja just after dark. I was ready, for I had nothing to pack. I owned only the clothing I was wearing and an extra sarong and kebaya. After saying adieu to the major and the two colonels, Colonel Sorotiyo and I set out for Tegal in a car that had seen better days. About midnight, before we had covered half the distance, one of our tires blew out. We had no spares, of course; tires were hard to come by during the Revolution, and they were more precious, almost, than gold. Here, in the heart of the land of rubber, we were stalled, alongside a paddy field by a road with no traffic. All we could do was sleep and wait for daylight when the peasants would come by on their way to the rice fields.

It was noon before help came, in the form of a military car from Tegal headed back toward Jogja. Colonel Sorotiyo exercised his su-perior rank on the drivers, and they turned around and took us to Tegal, where the military commandant gave us rooms. After a bath and something to eat we went out to look at our ship.

It was now night again. I was shocked to see how small our vessel was, and disturbed to be informed that the Englishman was dead to the world, sleeping off a hangover. On the horizon the Dutch cruiser could plainly be seen, its lights twinkling like rows of stars. Regularly a searchlight swept the waters around Tegal harbor.

Day after day we waited in Tegal. In the second week I was awak-ened long before daylight with the word that the cruiser had lifted anchor and steamed off toward Cheribon. We could not know whether it was bound for Batavia or would merely sail up and down the coast. But this might be our only chance; we must make a dash for it. In less than an hour I was aboard and we were ready to sail.

"Selamet djalan, K'tut," said Colonel Sorotiyo huskily. "May all the gods protect you and sail with you, and bring you back safely to our shores. We shall pray for you day and night."

I could not hold back the tears. "Merdeka, K'tut," he said, softly. "Tetap merdeka, bung," I whispered. With that he was gone into the darkness. Before I knew it our little wooden ship was moving away from shore, putting out toward Borneo.

As the profile of Java faded from sight, loneliness swept over me. I was a ship myself, an insecure one without a rudder, drifting into an uncharted future. I could only hope that the Dutch had no knowledge I was aboard, yet I realized that in Indonesia secrets were hard to keep and this one might have leaked out in spite of our precautions.

My thoughts turned to Bali, and the Rajah, and Anak Agung Nura, and the letter that I had not read. I had brought it with me, and I decided to read it now by the dim, curtained light within the ship:

Beloved Sister K'tut Tantri:

If this letter reaches you, then you will know that I no longer walk this earth. But before I join my ancestors I should like you to know that my last earthly thoughts are of you.

I heard your brave voice over Radio Pemberontakan, and later over the Voice of Free Indonesia, and it brought me great joy to know that you were still alive. I had long mourned you for dead. That you had been arrested and tortured by the Japanese Kempetai I knew, for friends had sent me word. But later it was reported that you had been put to death. It is a great miracle —and a tribute to your courage—that you survived.

You are safe, and it is now clear to me why you were spared, and the purpose of the gods when they led you from a foreign land to my father's puri.

Yes, dear K'tut, I was especially proud when you broadcast to the Balinese in their own language. I would have thought that the years of imprisonment would dim your memory and cause you to forget our tongue. But one cannot forget what is written on the heart.

Dear Sister, the wolves of the Netherlands are prowling our beautiful land, killing and destroying as they roam. Can you remember the night I read Vergil to you, at the time we were in the Kintamani mountains?

"Had I a hundred tongues—a hundred mouths
A voice of iron—I could not compass all
Their crimes."

That is how I feel now. I could not tell you the atrocities that the Dutch are inflicting on my people. But as long as we have Merdeka in our hearts we have hope. Merdeka is the light that will lead all mankind out of the darkness. I know, dear K'tut, that you will keep that light burning in your heart until our country is free—and even after. You will never shut your eyes or still your voice against the voice of freedom. And after we are free we must turn the light inward and search our souls, so we can cast out of our hearts any selfish or base thoughts—then we may be able to walk among men with heads held high, and be not ashamed.

Grieve not for me, K'tut. Though my spirit has left its earthly body, it will still be with you. It will protect you in the hard days to come, and lead you to the door that opens the way for Merdeka. And it shall guide you back safely to the shores of Bali, and to the people you love. Sometimes I fear that the great love you bear for my people will not be fully understood by them, or by your own countrymen.

For the last time, beloved sister, adieu—and may the gods protect you always. I shall love thee through all eternity. I know we shall meet again in another time.

Nura

After I had finished reading the letter I wept as I had never wept before and shall never weep again.

With the waning of the moon I fell asleep on the deck, on a tikar —a woven mat of palm leaves. I was secure in the thought that Anak Agung Nura was sailing with me, and all the gods of Bali were aboard. I would reach the shores of Singapore safely. This I knew.

13

OPERATION HIDE-AND-SEEK

It was a fine morning when I awoke, and the sun was high in the heavens.

The Ambonese captain introduced himself, and then introduced the other four Indonesians. Three of them I recognized as friends from Modjokerto. It was much later in the day that the English captain staggered onto the deck, bleary-eyed and unshaven, plainly just recovering from a long drinking spree.

From the first I felt sorry for him. He was a lonely old fellow who had spent most of his life sailing the seven seas. With forced retirement at sixty-five his world had blown up; there was nothing left for him. He was basically a very decent sort.

The sea was in an angry mood, and our little ship bounced up and down like a ball afloat on the ocean. We were camouflaged to look like a native fishing yawl—a precaution lest an inquisitive Dutch plane should fly low over us. The decks were covered with fish nets and dead fish which smelled to high heaven.

There was only one tiny toilet aboard, and no bathing facilities. But the crew had thoughtfully stretched a large piece of canvas across the aft of the ship, and had placed a bucket, attached to a stout rope, behind this improvised wall. I could draw water from the sea and bathe in complete privacy. I quickly became used to the primitive conditions aboard ship. After my years in a Japanese prison, this was relative luxury.

For two uneventful days we sailed along peacefully, but in the evening of the second day we sighted a vessel on the horizon. We had been zigzagging all over the Java Sea, first to the north, then to the west, and then to the south.

The Ambonese captain, whom we shall call Captain Ambon, looked grimly at the distant ship and said, "We must run for the shore. I know a cove about two miles up the coast. It will make a perfect hiding place until those Dutchmen sail out of sight. They can't follow us into the shallow water. Luckily they are so far off that we have the time we need to get there."

The crew gave the engines full steam, and the boat shivered and shook with the strain of the added power. We made our dash to the secret cove and hid there, in a tiny palm-fringed bay. The Dutch ship sailed back and forth for a while and finally took itself off. Its commander may have concluded that we were a fishing boat from one of the villages strewn along the Sumatra coast.

When it was dark we pulled out of the cove and puffed our way up the coast, keeping as close to shore as possible. The next morning we were out at sea again, but once more we had to run to the shore when another Dutch ship came over the horizon. This time we hid behind a jutting point of rock and watched the visitor cruise up and down for hours, and thanked our lucky stars that ours was a small ship, able to go places that were barred to larger craft.

We thought the Dutch ship would never leave. Several times Captain Ambon mentioned his fears that they might send a launch to investigate us. But they didn't, and some hours later they steamed off to the east. At dusk we ventured forth again and once more were on our way north and west. This running to shore and hiding was wearing on the nerves, but we could only resign ourselves to the need for it.

Bangka island, north of the western tip of Java and just off the southeastern flank of Sumatra, lies across the southern approach to Malaya. There are numerous sand shoals, and the currents are treacherous, so that sailing the Bangka Strait is dangerous at all times. I must say that Captain Ambon was a dexterous and fearless mariner and appeared to know the Sumatra coast from one end to the other. He had nerves of steel, and plainly was enjoying this game of hide-and-seek from the Dutch. I thought what a wonderful painting he would make, standing at the helm like a handsome Asian pirate of days gone by. Watching his bronzed face, his gleaming white teeth, his overlong black curly hair with a red-and-white scarf wound around his head, I was reminded of heroic Prince Diponegoro—with a wooden ship and primitive compass in place of a black horse and jeweled sword. The two men were born a hundred years apart, but essentially they were the same. Both had nobility in their faces and dedication to Indonesia Merdeka in their hearts.

We had been four days at sea now, and the strain was beginning to tell. Captain Ambon and his crew of four were busy constantly, but time hung heavy on my hands. The Englishman I hardly ever saw. On the first day, when we met and he learned I was British born, he was curiously uninterested. All he said was, "Jolly, what! We will show the Dutch blighters that they can't fool around with we British." When he was sober he could be very funny, with his frightfully British mannerisms and his typical English clichés. Usually he would come on deck already half drunk. "Hello, old bean, what's up?" he would inquire. "How many knots has our jolly old tub done today?" And when we told him we had been chased into hiding by a Dutch ship he would reply, "Silly old blighters, the

Dutch. Wasting their time. Can't the blighters see we are flying the British flag? Silly bawstards." He would stumble back to his bunk, and Captain Ambon and I would exchange smiles.

Near sundown of the fifth day once more we sighted a ship. The captain soon identified it as a Dutch destroyer, steaming full speed toward us, and I could see that for the first time he was really worried.

"If they keep bearing down on us, we will have had it," he said. "There are no safe places to hide for the next fifteen miles. The best thing I can do is to head for the shore; they can't follow us into shallow water. But the sand shoals are especially bad in this area. We can't afford to get stuck on one, and become a sitting target for the Dutch."

Captain Ambon took another sighting on the destroyer, and then sent me to wake up the Englishman. "We might be fired upon," he warned. "When you get the captain up, come to the wheelhouse. But keep off the deck."

He ordered the British flag raised, but remarked that it probably would not do much good. "The Dutch are wise to us," he said. "They know that the Chinese are registering ships in Singapore, signing on English captains, and then running the blockade under the British flag. It may not actually help us, the British flag. But it can't hurt us either."

I tried to awaken the Englishman. "Get up, captain; get up," I said. "The Dutch are practically on top of us. Captain Ambon is worried. Get dressed quickly and come to the wheelhouse."

He looked at me dazedly. "The Dutch again?" he said. "The silly blighters. Have they nothing better to do? They are like a whale chasing a sardine. To hell with them." He rolled over and pulled the covering around his shoulders.

I joined the Indonesians in the wheelhouse, and sat quietly on the floor. There was nothing I could do.

It was about six o'clock in the evening. The sea was very rough, and the skies were black and threatening. Tropical lightning streaked across the skies, but so far no thunder or rain. It had been like this most of the afternoon.

Captain Ambon pointed the ship toward the coast and ordered full steam ahead. And then it happened! There was a sharp jolt, a lurch, a slight listing, and we were dead in the water. We had jammed onto a sand shoal fairly close to shore.

The captain strained at the ship, trying to move it off the barrier, but it was impossible. Finally he had to give up that effort, for the ship was listing to starboard at about forty degrees. I was frightened almost to the point of tears, sure that we were about to capsize. We might be able to swim for shore, but I doubted it. And there would be sharks to contend with.

It was now quite dark. The destroyer had come as close as it dared in the shallow waters, and evidently had cast anchor. The Dutch fired a few shells across our bow, apparently to frighten us. The explosions were terrific, and I was thoroughly shaken.

Captain Ambon, noting my terror, looked over and smiled. "Berontak, K'tut," he said. I had to laugh in spite of myself, for I hadn't heard that expression—the guerrilla term for revolt—since the major had used it when I was supposed to fly to Australia. I was able to respond to the Ambonese, "Sure, captain—sure. Berontak teroes! Berontak to the end!"

It was too dark now for the Dutch to determine whether we were an authentic British trader or just an Indonesian tramp under false colors. Knowing that we were lodged firmly on the shoals, they apparently decided they would wait until daybreak to look us over. Captain Ambon removed from a locker a couple of Tommy guns, two or three rifles, and a couple of pistols. He handed me one of the pistols.

"I don't know how to shoot," I told him. He stared at me with surprise.

"I thought you lived with the guerrillas in East Java," he said. "Didn't they teach you?"

I shook my head. "I have never had a gun in my hand. I never will."

He gave me a resigned look, and said, "All right, then; if shooting starts stay directly behind me, and stay there until I fall. After that, may Allah protect you, K'tut! But don't be afraid. It may be that they will not take the chance of shooting up a ship flying a British flag."

At this point the Englishman staggered into the wheelhouse and looked around. "What the hell's going on here?" he bellowed. "Why the guns?"

Captain Ambon pointed to the Dutch ship, dimly visible and ominously close.

"Silly blighters!" the Englishman jeered. He looked down at the deck. "Am I drunk?" he asked. "What is the matter? We are about ready to capsize, by the look of it."

Captain Ambon explained about the sand shoals. "The tide is out, and there's not enough water to float us even if we could get off the shoals," he said.

At once the Englishman became sober. His eyes cleared, his shoulders straightened, and he said, "Hand me one of those Tommy guns, old bean. I haven't handled one of these since the war, but I can still blast the blighters if they attempt to board this ship."

He looked over at me and smiled. "Cheer up, old bean," he said. "Don't look so scared. Don't forget—there'll always be an England as long as this tub is flying the jolly Union Jack and as long as there is one Englishman aboard. This is British territory, and no Dutch son-of-the-bitch is going to board this ship until we are all dead. We will show the blighters what an Indonesian and an Englishman can do when they stand together. We'll put up a jolly good show."

The unexpected spurt of spirit and humor delighted the Indonesians. Like me, they had lost hope that the Englishman might be relied upon in an emergency. Now Captain Ambon had a bold, determined partner. Suddenly the whole atmosphere aboard had brightened. We all felt better.

And then all hell broke loose. Lightning flashed and thunder pealed. The rain came down in torrents. Between the blinding flashes it was pitch-dark and we could no longer see the lights of the Dutch ship. It was as though the heavens had opened and put a solid sheet of water between the two vessels. This was a tropical storm, the likes of which I had never seen. It seemed the gods were protecting us by making us invisible to our enemy.

The tide had turned, the water started to rise. I was startled to see the crew members dive overboard, and feared for a moment that they had become panic-stricken and were deserting us. Then I saw that they carried crowbars and shovels, and were working under the ship. Repeatedly they dived and came up for air, and dived again, struggling furiously to get us off the reef.

The Englishman was at the wheel and had started the engine. The continuous peals of thunder drowned out any noise. Still the rain poured down, furiously. Bit by bit the ship began to right itself, until at last we were level again and bobbing up and down in the turbulent waters. "It's coming in to high tide," Captain Ambon observed. The storm grew worse and the winds raged against the rain. And we sat around in the wheelhouse waiting . . . waiting.

At last the Ambonese turned to the Englishman and said, "Captain, what do you say to giving the Dutch the slip? In this rain and pitch-darkness they can't see us. There are shoals for another fifteen miles, but they'll be no more dangerous than sitting here waiting for the Dutch to come at daybreak."

"Now you're talking sense," the Englishman agreed. "It's no jolly good to be a sitting duck. Pull up the anchor. Turn out all the lights except in the wheelhouse. Cover up the portholes. We'll give those Dutch bawstards the old disappearing act!"

Then the Englishman did something most considerate. He took up the Indonesian flag and spread it on the table, and placed the charts on top. "Just so we don't forget merdeka!" he said. Captain Ambon, touched and pleased, patted him lightly on the shoulder.

At midnight we sailed, a little black ghost ship, Singapore bound. The rain was still coming down in torrents, and the wind lashed at the sea, and all was black outside. There was no reaction from the destroyer, unseen out there in the dark.

The Englishman actually appeared to be enjoying this harrowing escapade. As I watched him curiously I realized that he was living again the exciting times of his past, remembering perhaps the blackouts and the submarine threats when he had commanded a large merchant ship in the World War. Now he seemed contented, at peace with himself. He bantered with the crew, and after a while improvised a song.

"There'll always be an England. Heave-ho, heave-ho, heave-ho."

He repeated the line several times in his deep voice. Captain Ambon, not to be outdone, interrupted him by singing at the top of his voice, "There'll always be an Indonesia, no matter what the Dutch may do. Heave-ho, heave-ho, heave-ho!"

The Englishman smiled approvingly, and started again. "There'll always be an Indonesia, with England by her side. Heave-ho, heave-ho, heave-ho."

Captain Ambon turned to me and said, "Come on, K'tut. It's your turn now." The two men were for all the world like a couple of youngsters out on a lark, and I was disposed to humor them. "There'll always be an America," I sang. "As long as we have England and Indonesia by our side." The two men chimed in on the heave-hos, and the crew joined us in laughter.

As usual aboard the ship I fought sleep, for I was afraid of sailing into the unknown in the dark. At last I dropped off to the tune of heave-ho, heave-ho. When I awakened it was almost dawn. I walked out on the deck, to be greeted by a sky of crimson, purple and gold, the magnificent and mysterious sunrise of the tropics. The sea was purple and gray, and very calm. I scanned the horizon. There was no sign of a ship.

The Englishman was at the wheel, and Captain Ambon was sleeping nearby. The Englishman looked worn out, ready to drop. It had been a tough night negotiating the shoals in the dark and in the rain, he said. Several times it appeared that the ship had run aground. In each case they worked her free, without damage. We still had two days to go to reach the Malayan coast, but if we could get through this day safely all would be well. We would then have sailed beyond the reach of the Dutch and would be nearing Singapore.

I went aft, stripped behind the canvas, hauled a bucket of water from the sea and bathed. No bath ever seemed sweeter. A bit later we all sat on deck and watched the beautiful sunrise as we sipped our coffee, and we talked of our miraculous escape from ships and shoals.

For the next two days we sailed blissfully along. Early on the second day the Malayan coast line came into view. About noon, some three miles offshore, we dropped anchor. We dared not venture into Singapore harbor—not with me aboard, to say nothing of two of the crew members who had no passport or papers. Captain Ambon would have been all right, for he had a Dutch passport.

A couple of hours passed with our ship at rest, just bobbing peacefully up and down on the calm water. "What are we waiting for?" I asked Captain Ambon. "Why don't we try to find a lonely place along the coast, and go ashore?"

"That won't be necessary," he said. "We are expected. Some friends will discover us soon and send a launch out to meet us."

Again I marveled at the unruffled thoroughness with which my Indonesian friends accomplished risky missions. Sure enough, later in the afternoon a motor launch with two Indonesians and a Chinese drew alongside. They immediately boarded the ship and went into the wheelhouse for a conference.

The Englishman was asleep in his bunk with a bottle by his side. I felt differently about him now, as did the Indonesians. He had been great in the hour when he was needed most.

Captain Ambon informed me that he would go ashore in the launch to make arrangements. "We have to work out a few details of getting you ashore without the knowledge of the English immigration and customs officials," he explained.

I sat on deck and worried about what might happen next. Surely the British would find out about me, I thought. Would they jail me? Turn me back to the Dutch? In every direction the outlook was unpleasant. Then it suddenly came to me that we had already accomplished the impossible by sailing safely through the Dutch blockade. For the first time since my free-roaming Bali days I was outside of Indonesia, and for the first time in years I was away from the immediate threat of the Dutch. Nothing could stop me now.

Captain Ambon returned to the ship about six o'clock, bringing with him a very handsome and elegant young Chinese gentleman. He was, the captain told me, the nephew of a well-known Chinese, the richest man in Singapore. It was immediately apparent that he was well educated and of good family. He wore the uniform of an officer of the merchant marine, but this was only a blind.

"We have decided to let you go ashore with our friend here in a sampang," Captain Ambon said. "You will land right in Singapore. You'll be wearing his topcoat, as a cover-up, and you must act as though you were drunk, and a—well, how should we say it?—a woman of loose morals. You'll pull up brazenly at the Singapore jetty and roll ashore as though you had been spending the night with him on one of the merchant ships in the harbor. And you must cling to him as though you couldn't walk under your own steam. The British officials are accustomed to this sort of thing."

I was horrified and disgusted. "How can I do this?" I protested. "I couldn't fool anyone. I'd only be foolish and conspicuous, and give everything away. Why can't I go ashore with the Englishman? That wouldn't seem nearly as strange, and it certainly would be less noticeable."

"The British know the captain too well," the Ambonese said

quietly. "They are quite sure he is a blockade runner, and they suspect him strongly of smuggling activities beyond the reasonable needs of the Indonesians. If you were with him they'd be sure to interrogate you, and they probably would detain you. We can't take that chance."

The Chinese looked amused and said, "With me you will be safe. The British will not be in the least suspicious, and will only take it for granted that you are one of the waterfront women."

Reluctantly I agreed to go along with the plan. There was simply no alternative.

The two men discussed the problem of my red hair and my light skin. Not many European women visited the ships. Mostly they were Chinese women and half-castes, and sometimes a few degraded Malayan girls. I must look as un-Caucasian as possible. A scarf could hide my hair and much of my face. The officer's coat would help my disguise.

The Chinese smiled at my obvious agitation. "Relax, Miss K'tut," he said. "Just act natural. I will make it easy for you. I will do all the work. You just follow my cues and play along. It will come out all right. Don't worry."

"Relax! Act natural! Don't worry!"

The Englishman had come on deck now, and we said good-by. He was in danger of arrest himself and not eager to go ashore. I promised to meet him as soon as it was safe for me and safe for him. I also said my thanks and farewell to Captain Ambon and the crew and arranged to see them later at the house of the Chinese in Singapore. I regret to say, however, that I never saw them again, for they sailed two days later. The Englishman, I was told later, did not even go ashore.

The sampang was barely large enough for my Chinese friend, a native boatman, and me. As we neared the Singapore jetty the Chinese took my hand and whispered, "Have courage, Miss K'tut. It will soon be over."

We stepped ashore and immediately began our little drama. I discovered, suddenly, that I was really drunk—drunk with fear. The Chinese began singing loudly, and I joined in. We staggered along the dock quavering, "London bridge is falling down." He stooped down and kissed me, roughly. I kicked at him and told him not to be so realistic. He responded by trying to kiss me more. I became infuriated, and tried to break out of his embrace and run away.

We were now in the middle of the jetty. He caught up with me and swept me into his arms, shouting drunken endearments. I fought him off, and the British immigration and customs officials stood laughing at the lovers' quarrel. They had no idea it was a real battle and not an amatory disagreement.

I gave the Chinese such a push that he almost fell over backward, and I started to run from the pier. He caught up with me again and led me possessively past at least six Britishers watching the scene with amusement. He pushed me into a waiting automobile. Once inside I broke down and sobbed. I was so hysterical, so upset that I could not say a word.

The Chinese patted my shoulder. "Don't cry, Miss K'tut," he said. "It's all over now. I was only acting my part. I thought you might have guessed that."

My nerves eased and I daubed my wet cheeks with a handkerchief.

"And now you are free and in Singapore," he continued. "In a little while you will be safe with my family."

We rode through the beautiful city of Singapore. In the suburbs we turned off the main road into a driveway that led to a lovely Oriental house among trees and flower gardens. At the front entrance two attractive Chinese women met us. My companion introduced them as his sister and mother.

I laughed and cried at the same time as they greeted me. "Welcome to our humble home, K'tut Tantri," the older woman said. "We are proud to have you as our guest. We have heard much of you from our Indonesian friends."

We had a delicious Chinese dinner together. My escort had cast off his uniform and put on a long black silk Chinese coat lined with turquoise blue, so that he looked like a mandarin of the olden days. He told his family of my confusion when he tried to kiss me at the dock and how I struggled against his advances. They laughed at the account, and before long I was laughing too.

"You know, Miss K'tut, that scene at the dock would not have had the same realism if we had planned it in advance," he said. "Because the whole affair was unpremeditated and your indignation genuine, it worked out fine. It was most convincing."

"I couldn't act that scene again if I tried," I agreed.

My new friends informed me that tomorrow some Indonesians would bring me money for clothing. My hostesses would go shopping for me, since it would be unwise for me to walk about the city. I must have dresses, high-heeled shoes. It would be much too conspicuous for a white woman in Singapore to be seen in a sarong and kebaya. The wearing of native-style clothing by whites was simply not done.

I retired early to a luxurious bedroom. In spite of dangers, in spite of hardships, Operation Hide-and-Seek had been accomplished. I was through the blockade and inside Singapore, and now I could relax. Exhausted from the nervous strain, I fell asleep immediately.

14

I AM DISCOVERED IN SINGAPORE

It was late in the afternoon. I wakened from a long, dreamless sleep. After taking a shower I was surprised to find that I was still very tired. I dressed and strolled into the garden, where a sweet-looking Chinese maid brought coffee and rice cakes. She informed me that my host and hostess had gone into town, but would be back for dinner.

I was half asleep when I heard a car coming up the driveway. Not wishing to be seen by strangers, I ducked quickly into the house and to my room. After a few moments I was startled to hear a male voice calling my name. Someone knew I was here; it was no use to hide. I walked into the sitting room and stopped, not quite believing my eyes. There on a sofa were two Indonesians, and one was Colonel X.

"Bung, what a wonderful surprise!" I cried. "What are you doing in Singapore? I understood that you had returned to the eastern front at Surabaya."

Colonel X smiled. "Yes," he said. "That was the general impression. But I did not go to Surabaya; I came to Singapore. I have been here for over two weeks."

He was in Singapore, he said, to purchase firearms and small ships, if he could get them. "We have to do our buying through other Asian countries, of course, and it has to be done very secretly. We are able to get some firearms from the English. Not officially, of course, but under the table, as the Westerners say."

Questioning disclosed that he had entered Singapore legitimately on a Dutch passport and expected to stay for some time. For privacy he had rented a large villa which Major Abdul shared with him.

"As soon as we feel it is safe for you to leave this place, you will stay with us," he told me.

"And how did you know I was in Singapore?" I asked.

He laughed. "Oh, we were alerted to be on the lookout. Captain Ambon came to my house the day you arrived, and it was I who made all the arrangements for you."

Colonel X introduced me to his companion, his aide-de-camp, a rather young lieutenant, and we talked for quite a while. Then they left, saying that I could expect other Indonesians to call, for there was a small colony of Javanese in Singapore.

This last bit of information left me uneasy. Too many people were in the know, it appeared.

More than a week went by and I was beginning to tire of the inactivity and uncertainty. It had been good to have plenty of rest and nourishing food, but after the first few days these too began to pall. My hosts were charming and gracious, and had purchased quite a little wardrobe for me. But somehow I got no joy out of my new clothes. European-style clothing made me feel uncomfortable and did not suit me. I felt out of character. My Chinese hosts took me often on long drives in the country, especially in the evening. Still I was often homesick for Indonesia.

The day came at last when my host said it was safe now for me to go into Singapore town, if I wished. So one morning I got up early and had the chauffeur take me to Raffles Square, where he would pick me up again in two hours. I did not want to stay too long in the town, only long enough to get my bearings and have a look around. I did not feel at all conspicuous, for there were many Europeans on the streets. I looked no different from anyone else. Yet it was strange, after all these years, to see so many white people about.

In Singapore, as elsewhere, newsstands try to stimulate paper sales by the use of large posters with glaring headlines. Strolling idly past the Capitol Theatre I noticed one that proclaimed, "Surabaya Sue in Singapore." Elsewhere similar posters were fastened to walls or propped up against newspaper kiosks.

I wondered casually who Surabaya Sue could be and why she should be given headlines. I was curious because I was from Surabaya and had never heard the name. I bought a newspaper, and after reading just a few lines my blood froze. They were referring to me. I was Surabaya Sue.

I had disappeared from Java some time ago, the article said, and it had now been learned from authoritative sources that I was in hiding in Singapore. I had earned the name of Surabaya Sue because of my broadcasts from the East Java city, on the Voice of Free Indonesia, and from the revolutionary radio in territory near Surabaya. The writer went on to say that my broadcasts for the Indonesians had been noted with concern in The Hague, in Whitehall, and in Washington. The rest was speculation as to how I eluded the Dutch blockade and was admitted into Singapore.

I was shocked and indignant. That silly name—a handy label invented by some newspaper correspondent, obviously. Patterned after Shanghai Lil or Tokyo Rose, definitely. I felt like buying up all the newspapers and destroying them. Instead, I took the more practical course of finding my chauffeur and returning quickly to the house, to tell my host. My friends were out, however, at a Chinese wedding.

How did the story get out? I wondered. Did the information come from Indonesians in Singapore or had there been a leak through Indonesia? Either way, the British authorities would soon find out now where I was staying. I was especially worried because Colonel X was out of town and I could not turn to him for help. I must move out of this house tomorrow, at any rate, to avoid involving my Chinese friends.

Late in the afternoon a jeep drove up to the entrance, and two white men stepped out. I concluded immediately that they were either officials from the CID—the Civil Intelligence Department, the British equivalent of the FBI—or detectives from the police force. They were neither.

They came up to the veranda where I was sitting quietly, with my heart in my mouth. "Hello!" one said. "Are you Surabaya Sue?"

I winced and said, "No. I know no one of that name."

"Well," the man drawled, in what sounded like an Australian accent, "are you by any chance K'tut Tantri, the English broadcaster for the Indonesians? We have been tipped off that she is staying here. Since this is a Chinese house, we presume that you are Surabaya Sue."

"Who are you?" I asked. "And by what authority do you come here?"

They smiled and introduced themselves. Earle Growder and Eddy Dunstan, both of the *Singapore Straits Times*.

It was useless to deny my identity.

"Yes, I am K'tut Tantri," I said. "I didn't know until today that you call me Surabaya Sue—and I do not like it. What do you gentlemen want?"

"We want the whole story," they said. "We want to know how you got out of Indonesia, how you evaded the Dutch blockade, and how you entered Singapore. And we want to know what you are doing here. The British officials still evidently are unaware that you are here. This story ought to rock Singapore."

"You don't mean to tell everyone where I'm staying, and all about me?"

"Damn right we will. And why not?"

"Because I would be arrested by the British for entering Singapore illegally and would be sent back to Indonesia to the Dutch. Because you are both British, and I am your countrywoman. Because you wouldn't betray your own countrywoman to an enemy just for a scoop that would be forgotten day after tomorrow."

"We can't kill a story just to save you from trouble you got yourself into," they said. "That's too much to expect."

Tears welled into my eyes. They looked uncomfortable, and one said, "But what can we do? It is our job."

We sat silently for a few moments, then I said, "Let me make a deal with you. If you will withhold this story for twenty-four hours, I promise faithfully I'll give it to you and you alone. Only wait until this time tomorrow."

"How do we know you'll even be here tomorrow?" one asked. "You could easily disappear, and hide out somewhere else."

"I promise you I shall be here."

"Why do you want twenty-four hours? If you will tell us the story tomorrow, why not today?"

"Because now that you have discovered me and know who I am, it is necessary for me to go as quickly as possible to the immigration officials and to the CID and give myself up. If I do this now it will be more to my advantage than if I wait until they start looking for me. I shall go immediately and inform them who I am, and that I entered Singapore without the proper papers."

After a little more hesitation, they agreed.

With that settled, we sat down together and had a drink. I learned that an Indonesian had told them my story with great pride, confiding in them because he believed they were sympathetic toward the Indonesians. During my stay in Singapore I was to see a great deal of Dunstan and Growder, and came to regard them as real friends.

After they left me I called a taxi and went to CID headquarters, and asked to see the chief. When he entered the room with a "Good afternoon, young lady, what can I do for you?" I knew my luck was holding out. I could tell by his brogue that he was a Scotsman.

I told my story, withholding nothing except mention of my Chinese friend. I said only that I came ashore in a native sampang, and that was the truth anyway. As the ship on which I fled from Java had sailed many days ago, there would be no trouble for Captain Ambon or the Englishman.

When I had told my story, the Scotsman called in other CID officials and the immigration officers, and had me repeat it. They were frankly amazed, and more than embarrassed. "Well, I'll be damned," said one. "An English girl and a few guerrillas sail from Java right under the noses of the Dutch. What a joke on them and their impregnable blockade!"

"Scotswoman, if you please," the Scotsman jested. "And it may be a joke on the Dutch, but what about the British? This is supposed to be the strongest patrolled, best policed coast in Asia. We should poke fun at the Dutch!"

With typical British sportsmanship, the officers had a hearty laugh. "Only a Scotch lassie would try such a thing and get away with it," said the Scotsman.

I did not tell him that my mother was Manx and so was my natural father, even though the only father I ever knew was a Scotsman. I was satisfied to know that being born in Glasgow of British parents could have some influence on British officials in Singapore, and confident now that the British would not deport me or hand me over to the Dutch.

Before I left the CID headquarters I was not only forgiven, I was handed landing permits, an identity permit, and permission to stay in Singapore. The British could not have been more courteous and gallant, although they needled me a bit about my broadcasts criticizing the British during the Revolution in Indonesia. I found that most of them agreed with me and were decidedly more sympathetic toward the Indonesians than toward the Dutch. And they resented the false position in which the Dutch had placed them.

When I returned home my Chinese hosts were in a state of much agitation. They too had seen the posters and were wondering if I had been arrested. When I explained, they were so happy that they insisted on a celebration. We all had a big night at the most famous night club in Singapore.

A free woman, I moved the next day to the villa of Colonel X and Major Abdul.

15

SOME SWINDLERS AND THEIR VICTIMS

News that I had been given permission to stay in Singapore spread quickly through the Indonesian colony. Before I had been installed at Colonel X's villa more than a couple of hours, a stream of visitors began to call.

I was anxious to keep faith with the two reporters who had been such good sports in holding up their story until I reported to the CID. But they were not to get the exclusive information after all. They were not in their office when I called to confirm our appointment. And, unknown to me, a press conference was arranged for that evening by an Indonesian who was not aware of my pact with the Englishmen. When I protested, I was told that to cancel the conference and give exclusive information to one British-owned newspaper would deeply offend the Malayans, Chinese, and Indians and would make for bad propaganda for Indonesia. Though I felt miserable about breaking my word, I could not cause dissension between the Indonesians and the other Asian population of Singapore. Happily, the Englishmen were good sports and forgave me.

The press conference turned out to be a hilarious affair. Champagne flowed and everyone was happy, seemingly enchanted by my adventure. The following day the newspaper comments were everything we could desire and warmly favorable to Indonesia.

There was in Singapore at this time a highly connected Indonesian who had been entrusted with several thousand tons of sugar which had been smuggled out of Indonesia to a small island just off Singapore's coast, for quick sale to a Chinese merchant. It was to this man that I had brought letters from Java instructing him to turn over to me money that would enable me to go to Australia and America. When I presented the letters, he told me he had sold the sugar to a merchant who promised to pay for it as soon as he had disposed of it to wholesalers in Singapore. Now the Chinese had disappeared, he said, along with the sugar. He had tried hard to find the man and was greatly concerned because the loss to the Indonesian government would be more than $150,000.

This was shocking news to me. Aside from the substantial financial setback to the Indonesians in Singapore, it meant that I could not proceed to Australia. It would be difficult now to get a letter to Bung Amir unless we could find a courier with a Dutch passport.

"Have you notified the Singapore police or the CID?" I asked.

"Heavens, no! How could I complain of being swindled by the Chinese when we ourselves are guilty of smuggling? Even though we are forced into this ridiculous situation because of the Dutch blockade."

"Just the same," I said, "you should inform the CID. They seem to be a very understanding lot. I'm sure they would be able to round up the Chinese in no time."

The Indonesian demurred, but in the end he agreed on my promise to bring the English official to his house so that the story of the theft could be kept private.

The Englishman listened gravely as the Indonesian unfolded his story, then said: "Don't worry. We should be able to pick up the swindler soon. Sugar is very scarce here, and going at black market prices. He won't be able to dispose of it without our knowledge."

He added that the Indonesians henceforth must beware of strangers, and especially of Chinese merchants. Many such men were on the alert for Indonesians with money, knowing that where smuggling was involved the victims would be afraid to go to the police. He said nothing of the Indonesian's part in the smuggling of sugar into Singapore, but there was no doubt that the English officials were well aware of what was going on. Nelson-like, they looked through a blind eye and said, "We see nothing, nor have we heard anything."

Some days later the CID official informed me that a thorough investigation had been made, and all the evidence indicated that the Indonesian was lying. "We do not believe that he was swindled," the Englishman said. "The Chinese merchant paid for the sugar, and we are quite positive that the money was deposited in a foreign bank to the credit of a private individual, not to the credit of the Republic of Indonesia. It is your Indonesian friend who has been doing the swindling."

During my stay in Singapore I was to hear of many such cases of corruption. The Indonesians had never handled so much money and the temptation was great for men so young. A shocking number of them lived in splendor and luxury beyond all common sense, driving handsome cars, and spending government funds recklessly. All this greatly saddened me. I could not help but think of the thousands of poverty-stricken Indonesian peasants lying in muck at the front, dressed in rags, defending the nation's freedom with bamboo spears and machetes. There they were, sacrificing their lives, while here in Singapore the men entrusted with government funds to buy firearms and needed supplies were living like lords and squandering the money on Chinese dance-hall girls and other pleasures. I had now been in Colonel X's house for several weeks and knew every Indonesian in town. There were two groups, the very rich and the very poor. I saw for myself that the sincere Indonesians were the ones who had no money.

Time passed slowly waiting for news from Java. We had managed to send a courier with a letter for Bung Amir, but since he had to travel by way of Dutch-held Batavia there was no knowing if he would be able to get through to Jogja and Republican territory. Meanwhile I must be patient, for I had no money whatsoever. I spent my time writing articles for a Singapore paper on Indonesia, its leaders, and Asian politics in general.

The sugar swindle was the first of several outlandish incidents which made for liveliness and kept me continually embroiled with the CID. The second, the affair of the Admiral's yacht, had nothing directly to do with me and so has little place in this story—though it did provide comic relief.

According to my Scots friend, some Indonesians had stolen the British Admiral's yacht, anchored just outside the Navy Basin, from under the very eyes of the CID. "A most brazen and outrageous act," the chief declared with considerable temper. He wanted the hiding place of the vessel discovered before his department was made a laughingstock and he thought I—or Colonel X—might have some secret knowledge of the culprits. We didn't. However, Colonel X succeeded in enlisting the aid of a Javanese general newly arrived in Singapore, and after a series of telephone calls that went on for hours this missing vessel was restored to its rightful owners. It turned out, as the British suspected from the first, that guerrillas from Sumatra had made off with the yacht and had hidden it cunningly in a small cove along the Sumatra coast. No charges were pressed, British honor was saved, and the CID officials even managed to find amusement in the disgust of the sailor guerrillas deprived of what they called "the best little ship we could have got hold of for smuggling our goods past the Dutch blockade into Singapore."

Shortly after the affair of the missing yacht the Indonesians were involved in another boat story, one that shook Singapore with laughter. British faces had been red before, Indonesian faces were red now, and the reddest of all was the face of my good friend Colonel X.

It was an amusing story, but it had its pathetic side. Knowing the Indonesians as well as I did, watching their superhuman struggle against overwhelming odds, it was not easy to laugh at their failures. The Dutch had provided them with little or no education, and no experience in business matters. It could not be expected that the inexperienced Indonesians sent to Singapore by their government and entrusted with large sums of money would be able to match wits against the shrewd Chinese merchants, or English and American confidence men. They were natural targets.

Colonel X certainly had no business experience, and he was much too young for his rank. At this time he could not even speak English well, and he was no judge of human nature. He was jolly and good-natured, and if people were polite to him he thought they must be good. He overrated his ability to judge the businessmen with whom he came in contact, and he could not judge Westerners at all. All was gold that glittered to Bung X. More than once he had been swindled by Chinese merchants, but he never learned to tell diamonds from paste—until the affair of the British torpedo boat.

"Two high-ranking British naval officers are coming to the house for cocktails," Bung X informed me one day, with such pride in his voice that one might have thought the Duke of Edinburgh and Lord Louis Mountbatten were calling.

"Who are they?" I asked. "And where did you meet them?"

The colonel said he had been having lunch at a Chinese restaurant. The officers came to his table and introduced themselves. They said they had heard that he was in Singapore to buy ships for the Indonesian government. When X admitted that such was his purpose, they asked permission to join him at lunch to explain a proposal that might interest him.

"They told me the British navy intends to dispose of several obsolete ships," Bung X said. "War surplus vessels, for which they have no further need. They offered to sell me a small torpedo boat for $50,000. The British have declared it outmoded for their use, but it has many years of service left in it, and would be just the thing for Indonesia. It cost millions to build, they said. And, you know, I even bargained them down to $30,000! And they agreed to throw in a torpedo free, as a bonus. It's a real giveaway."

The colonel clapped his hands together in excitement. "It's the greatest stroke of luck! Even in my wildest dreams I never expected to be able to buy any sort of warship, especially a torpedo boat, for such a ridiculous price."

It must be remembered that Colonel X was an army man. He knew virtually nothing of ships, and had no experience in buying anything but firearms and ammunition. He saw nothing strange in the fact that two British naval officers of high rank should approach him in a restaurant to peddle torpedo boats. All X could see was that it would be a feather in his cap to sail a British torpedo boat back to Indonesia, and hand over to the Indonesian navy its first combat craft. It would be a great day for Indonesia, and an even greater one for Colonel X.

I listened worriedly, finding the story hard to believe. "Have you already paid for the boat?" I asked.

"Not yet," Colonel X said. "I want to look it over first. This is a very important matter, and I want to make sure that everything is right. I agreed to pay them tonight, after we have made our inspection. The plan is to have cocktails here and then go to the Navy Basin to look the ship over. Later we'll all go out to dinner to celebrate."

The guests arrived. Bung X introduced me proudly, and immediately began to sing my praises. The officers looked at me curiously, undoubtedly wondering what a British woman was doing living in the villa of an Indonesian officer. They smiled covertly, and I knew that they imagined the worst. This didn't bother me much. I set myself out to be a good hostess, and I must say they reacted in a courteous and even gallant manner. It was not until Bung X mentioned that I was known as Surabaya Sue that they finally placed me. After that they seemed to relax.

They were good-looking men, tall and well set, their uniforms immaculate. As they talked to Bung X about the torpedo boat I studied them carefully and wondered why I mistrusted them. It was not their appearance, nor their manners, nor their uniforms, but something else. Could they be British spies? Had they some other ulterior motive? But their story must be true. They would hardly take us to the Navy Yard if it were not.

I watched and listened, and then it flashed over me. Their voices —that was what was wrong! Both voices were extremely common, like those of Lancashire millworkers, certainly not public school.

Almost at the same moment I dismissed the idea as snobbish. Times had changed since I was last in Great Britain. During the war many Englishmen rose from the ranks to become officers in the army and the navy without public school or university education.

At the Navy Basin the Malayan police and British servicemen guarding the gates, the sailors patrolling the yard, all showed great deference to the two officers. We were saluted right and left and were not stopped for questioning.

We boarded the torpedo boat. No one except the watchman was on the ship, and he did not question our right to be there. The Englishmen showed us around. Everything appeared shipshape. Bung X's eyes sparkled with excitement. "Can you imagine what a sensation it will be when I sail this into Indonesian waters?" he whispered. "A torpedo boat for Indonesia! Our first!"

Somehow I still couldn't share his enthusiasm. My doubts kept returning. Why would the British sell all this for a mere $30,000? When the Englishmen turned their backs I mentioned my suspicions to Bung X and warned him to be careful. He only laughed, and said, "You are much too suspicious of your own countrymen. You have been too long in the Revolution. Now you suspect everyone."

I laughed and told Bung X he was probably right. Just because the old school tie didn't seem to fit the two officers was no reason to distrust them. Even so, I whispered to Bung X, "Wouldn't it be wise to ask the advice of the CID before you pay for the ship?"

Colonel X smiled at me. "I don't think we should run to the British every time we want to buy something," he said. "These officers never could have brought us here if they were not in the navy. Didn't you notice how everyone stood at attention? They have done everything possible to show their good faith. They must be on the level."

Again I conceded that Bung X must be right and that I was unduly suspicious. We left the Navy Yard and spent the evening at the Raffles Hotel, and that finally convinced me that the Englishmen were legitimate officers. Had they been frauds they would hardly have taken us to the best hotel in Singapore, the place where the entire British colony gathered for dining and dancing.

There were many naval officers sipping drinks in the lounge. They saluted our friends and were saluted in return. After that I set out to enjoy the evening. Bung X was in the best of spirits. He wrote out a check for $30,000 and gave it to the Englishmen. They in return handed him a very official-looking bill of sale for the torpedo boat, complete with torpedo. We parted company almost at dawn, and the Englishmen promised to call by again in a couple of days.

On the way back to the house Bung X chattered like a magpie, he was so happy. I fell in with his mood.

"Just imagine what we can do with a torpedo boat," he said. "We can blow the Dutch warship, the *Kohinoor*, out of existence for all the trouble it has caused us. 'Member the *Kohinoor*, K'tut? That's the one . . ." and on and on.

I interrupted Bung X's reminiscences of the *Kohinoor* to ask when and how he intended moving the torpedo boat.

"I have already sent a wireless asking Indonesian naval officers and crew to fly to Singapore to sail the boat back," he said.

"Suppose they are shot down by the Dutch—what then?" I asked.

"Then another crew will try to reach Singapore, and another, until one group makes it. We can sail it to Java with the British flag. We can zigzag our way through the Java Sea as though we were on our way to Australia."

Two days later an Indonesian crew managed to reach Singapore. When they saw the boat they were amazed, and congratulated Bung X. It was agreed that they would sail at dawn the following day.

I arose before daylight the next morning to say good-by to Colonel X and to wish him luck on the journey to Java; then I went back to bed. Hours later, around nine o'clock, I was drinking coffee when a messenger arrived with a letter from the CID chief, asking me to come to headquarters as quickly as possible.

"What do they want?" I asked the young Malayan who delivered the note. He replied that he didn't know the details but had heard that Colonel X and a few other Indonesians had been arrested.

Astonished to hear this, I hurried to CID headquarters. I found the Englishmen, whom I had come to regard as friends, cold and unsmiling now. "What is it this time?" I asked lamely.

"Your Indonesian friends are all under arrest," the Scotsman said. "This time they have tried to steal one of our torpedo boats. We want you to tell us what you know about it. And don't try to plead ignorance. You were seen aboard the boat, in the company of Colonel X."

"And two English officers," I answered tartly.

"Colonel X and his friends have been charged with unlawfully attempting to remove a British torpedo boat from the Navy Basin," he went on. "We have heard his story, and now we want to hear yours. It had better be truthful. You could be charged as an accessory to the attempted theft."

"Rubbish!" I retorted. "You know better than that! If you really suspected me, you would have arrested me along with the others, instead of sending for me."

"Well, suppose you give us your version," one of the Englishmen said. "Then we'll decide whether or not to charge you."

I related the whole story of the torpedo boat and the two high-ranking British officers: their offer to sell a surplus and obsolete craft, Bung X's enthusiasm, my own doubts, and my banishment of those doubts. I told them the price asked and the price paid. I left nothing out. The officers laughed, and the ice in the atmosphere melted.

The boat salesmen were impostors, wearing stolen uniforms, they told me. Colonel X and his crew got past the guard at the gates by showing their papers, went aboard the boat and actually had it moving when the harbor police stopped them. The Indonesians were very indignant. "We bought this boat, and we are taking it to Java," they said. "You British have no right to stop us." And then they showed their bill of sale. The patrol officer took one look and exploded.

"Thirty thousand dollars!" he yelled. "Are you crazy? You couldn't even look at this boat for ten times thirty thousand!" And with that he immediately put them under arrest.

Once again the CID officials were lenient toward the Indonesians. Bung X clearly had been telling the truth. He had been the victim, not the thief. His great sin had been his failure to consult the police or the CID before reaching any agreement. The officials scolded him as though he were a child, but they were sympathetic nonetheless.

We were able to provide good descriptions of the two frauds, and the CID quickly caught up with them. Each received a sentence of five years at hard labor.

For days afterward Bung X was silent and remote. He had been malu (shamed) in front of me, and that was bad enough. But to be malu and lose face before his own countrymen was almost more than he could bear. I tried my best to comfort him, and treated the whole thing as a minor incident; but to Bung X it was no joke. He knew that he would be laughed at not only in Singapore but in Indonesia. He had lost standing, and he suffered.

16

RETURN TO JAVA

Now came one of the most bizarre experiences of all. I had left Indonesia with no intention of returning until merdeka had been won, or until the dangers of travel had been lessened. I had planned to go directly to Australia and America, but this plan had been thwarted as I have explained—leaving me stranded in Singapore without funds. Though I had applied to the United States consulate for an American passport, weeks had passed and I had received no reply.

In desperation I went to the Australian High Commissioner to ask permission to enter Australia without a passport. I told him my story from beginning to end, without reservations. Mr. Massey was most sympathetic and heard me out without taking the position that I had done something criminal in helping the Indonesians. He promised to forward my request to Canberra. So now I was waiting for a decision from two governments, the United States and Australia.

The hospitality of Colonel X's house remained open to me all this while. I was in my room one evening, listening to the BBC news from London, when the maid announced a "foreign-looking gentleman" waiting to see me. Just what might be foreign looking in a city as cosmopolitan as Singapore was not immediately clear to me, but I assumed she meant the caller was neither Chinese, Indonesian, nor Malayan. In any event it was very late for callers. I was curious.

In the sitting room I found a very foreign-looking man indeed, dark, hawk-nosed, and distinguished. He introduced himself as Abdul Monem, the former Egyptian consul general to India but now an emissary of King Farouk of Egypt, representing the seven Arab states. King Farouk at this time was very much a royal ruler. No one could have foretold his sorry future.

The visitor presented his credentials, saying, "The Egyptian government and the Arab League have ordered me to Indonesia to extend formal recognition to the new sovereign state. The Dutch consulate here has ignored my credentials and refused me a visa. The British have refused to help me, and have denied me an exit visa from Singapore if used for travel to Indonesia." He added that the British attitude astounded him at first, but then he saw that it would not be to their interest to have Indonesian sovereignty recognized, because of the British situation in Malaya. They had their own colonial problems to consider.

I nodded, and asked, "But why did you come to me, Mr. Monem?"

"I am told that you sailed through the Dutch blockade from Java to Singapore," he replied. "I wonder if the same journey could be arranged for me in reverse, from Singapore to Java. It is important that I get to Jogjakarta, and now I must do so without the knowledge of the British or the Dutch."

I explained that sailing outward through the blockade with the co-operation and planning of the Indonesians was quite a different matter from sailing through it into Java without the co-operation of the British. The Indonesians had no ships of their own in Singapore. Even if they had, they would be unable to sail without clearance papers from that well-policed harbor.

"How did you get into Singapore?" he asked. "Is it so difficult?"

"I was on an Indonesian-manned ship," I said. "I left it outside the three-mile limit and came ashore with the help of friends in a sampang."

"Could I not get aboard a Chinese-owned ship? I have heard that a number of them sail to Indonesia through the blockade."

"Mr. Monem, the Chinese blockade breakers do not sail from Singapore," I explained. "They operate from small ports along the Malacca coast, or from Bangkok or Saigon. Recently the Chinese have lost so many ships that they are unwilling to take the risks any longer. If you found one to go on you would surely be in danger. The Dutch are showing no mercy to the Chinese blockade runners."

He was so keenly disappointed that I relented. "If you will be patient for a few days, I will consult my Indonesian and Chinese friends. Maybe we can find the way." We parted after I had bound him to the utmost secrecy. "I will get in touch with you at your hotel when I have news," I promised.

It would not be easy to get Mr. Monem to Jogjakarta. Even if he managed to reach Java, there would be the problem of going from the distant seaport to the Republican capital, in a land where the language was unfamiliar, where no private transportation was available, and where road passes signed by the Indonesian military would be required all along the way. Guerrilla guards were trigger-happy. A stranger might easily be shot on suspicion of being a spy.

I knew well what a great boost in morale and prestige it would be for the Indonesians to receive early recognition from Egypt and the Arab League and began casting about for means of transporting Mr. Monem through the blockade. Obviously money was the first essential. With money we could arrange almost anything. It might even be possible to charter a Chinese ship, but that would require a small fortune.

For days on end I interviewed Chinese traders and owners of small ships. All were unwilling to take the risk. I secretly visited Malayan fishermen. Some of them were willing to take a chance on Sumatra, but not one would sail to Java. I searched for derelict English sea captains in the employ of the Chinese, and found none. My guide through the blockade, Captain Ambon, had returned to Amboina. My Indonesian friends could offer no solution because, lacking official recognition in the world, they were unable to arrange anything even from the Java end.

I had all but given up hope when I learned that the British government had given the Indonesians permission to charter a Dakota plane to return the Ramushas to their homeland. Ramushas were slave laborers—Indonesians—dragged from their homes by the Japanese during the occupation, and shipped off to work without pay in Singapore and various Asian countries. Since the surrender of the Japanese the Ramushas had been stranded in Singapore. The Dutch had agreed at last to let the former slaves fly back to Java, to land at Jogjakarta. This seemed to me the opportunity for which Mr. Monem had been waiting.

One dismaying circumstance was that the man in charge of the Ramushan airlift was the same Indonesian who had invented the story of the Chinese sugar fraud. Nevertheless, I went to him and told him about Mr. Monem and his mission to Java. I asked that the Egyptian be taken aboard the plane secretly, in disguise as one of the laborers if necessary. "He is swarthy, and would easily pass inspection if he were dressed in rags like the other Ramushas," I said.

The Indonesian flatly refused. "The British wouldn't like it," he said. "If they found out about it they might refuse to allow us to charter any more planes. And if the Dutch learned he was aboard they might force the plane down at a Dutch airport or even shoot it down."

I insisted that the whole plan could be kept secret, and pointed out the significance and propaganda value of the recognition of Indonesia by the Moslem world. "And it would be a personal triumph for you," I said.

After more argument the Indonesian finally agreed that Mr. Monem could board the plane incognito, that the benefit to Indonesia would outweigh the potential offense to the British. Monem would be provided with worker's clothing, and a car would pick him up at Colonel X's villa at 5 A.M. two days hence, for a six-o'clock take-off from Kalang airport.

Mr. Monem was delighted to hear of the plan, and we both chuckled at the idea of disguising the representative of King Farouk as a coolie. He appeared at my house at four o'clock, a safe hour before the car was to arrive. The Chinese maid was shocked to be asked to serve coffee to a ragged peasant. I am sure I lost face with her for entertaining such a creature in the wee hours of the morning.

As we waited for the Indonesian I briefed Mr. Monem on what to expect in Java. Two hours passed, and we were still talking. I was annoyed. Four hours passed, and I was alarmed. Something must have happened to the plane. I telephoned the Indonesian's house but there was no answer. At last we decided to go to the airport. Monem covered himself with an outer coat. At the airport he remained in the taxi while I went to make discreet inquiries. I was staggered to learn that the plane had taken off on schedule with the Ramushas and the Indonesian. Perhaps by this time it was already in Jogja.

It was painful to tell Mr. Monem that we had been double-crossed. I was both furious and embarrassed. But whatever Mr. Monem thought, he said nothing except "Don't take it to heart so, Miss K'tut. You have done your best. It is not your fault." Still I could see that he was depressed, discouraged.

"We'll find another way," I assured him. "We won't give up now." At the same time I speculated on the motives of the Indonesian. Why was he so trusted by the Jogjakarta crowd? Was it because he was related to one of the most important men in Java? All evidence indicated that he had lied about the shipment of sugar. Now it looked very much as though he were sabotaging recognition of his country. Why?

I went the rounds from one Indonesian home to another and from one Chinese home to another, probing cautiously, questioning, exploring. No transportation to Java was in prospect. Near the end of my rope, I went to an English businessman known to be sympathetic toward the Indonesians and asked how he would go through the Dutch blockade if circumstances should require him to do so.

"I'd charter a plane from the Philippine Islands," he said. "A plane with an American pilot and navigator. It might cost a fortune, but it could be done."

I indicated that I would like to return to Indonesia on an official mission, depending on the cost.

"I will introduce you to the head of a well-known British firm here in Singapore," he said. "He can easily arrange for a plane to fly here secretly from the Philippines, and then on to Java."

I wondered if I was falling into a trap. Why would a British company of any reputation interest itself in my project? I learned later that this was a lucrative little industry, the leasing of Philippine-registered aircraft for assorted missions in the Orient.

The company representative told me that, certainly, a plane would be flown down from Manila, would pick me and my fellow passenger up at Singapore, would go on to Jogja, and would wait there for at least three days to bring us back again.

"How much will this cost?" I asked.

"Ten thousand dollars for the plane, and all expenses for the crew," he said.

I gasped. I couldn't raise ten thousand cents. I promised to think the proposition over, and hurried off to talk to Mr. Monem.

The Egyptian said he had nowhere near enough money at his disposal to finance the flight but was sure his government would approve if he could send through an explanation. He dared not telephone or telegraph, for the British might intercept his message and tip off the Dutch. All he could do was write to Cairo. It would take weeks to get an answer by the time all the red tape had been cut.

Asking him not to write to Egypt for a few days, I then looked into Singapore sources of financial support. But the Dutch had effectively halted the smuggling of rubber and sugar. Indonesian funds were low indeed. At last I went back to the English businessman and asked whether payment could be deferred for two or three days, until the plane returned from Java.

"Who would guarantee the payment?" he asked.

"The Indonesian Ministry for Defense will pay it," I said boldly. My voice shook a bit, for I had absolutely no authority to pledge government funds.

"Would you be willing to sign papers to that effect?" he persisted.

"Certainly," I replied.

I realized that my word was being accepted because of the great amount of publicity I had received and because of my articles on the Indonesian leaders. The British understood that I knew these men well, and was known by them. I wondered what the Indonesians would think of my bold action. Bung Amir would understand and agree, but what of the others? I had no official connection with any Indonesian ministry.

The papers were drawn up and I signed my name to a note for $10,000 to be paid to the English firm by the Indonesian Ministry for Defense. By way of reassurance I told myself that surely it was worth $10,000 to the Indonesian government to have the success of merdeka proclaimed by recognition from the Moslem world.

"How many passengers will there be?" the company representative asked.

"Just two," I said. "My djonges [male servant] and me."

The Englishman told me the plane would swoop down just before dawn and taxi to the end of the field, from where it could take off instantly. The engines would not be stopped. He showed me on a map the exact spot at which the plane would pause, and said we were to be waiting there, ready to board.

I thanked him, and asked him why he was taking this risk. "You must know that I am working in the interests of Indonesia Merdeka," I said.

"I know," he replied quietly. "Maybe I am doing it because you are my countrywoman. Maybe I am doing it for $10,000. In any case, Godspeed!"

On the appointed hour Mr. Monem and I sneaked through the terminal area, carrying our small amount of luggage, and found it all but deserted. No airplane movements were scheduled for that early in the day. The few employees on duty were either dozing or engrossed in their work, and no one noticed us. In a few years Kalang airport would become one of the busiest airports in Asia, but after the war traffic there was extremely light. A few commercial planes, an occasional private craft. Military planes did not use this airport.

We puffed our way to the end of the field. The plane landed on schedule, taxied up, and two white men jumped out. "What's your name?" one asked in a Texas drawl.

"K'tut Tantri," I said. "And this is Abdul, my djonges."

"Right. Climb in. We must get out of here right now."

We hardly had time to get to our seats before the Dakota was down the runway and off the ground. Through the windows we saw two or three airport attendants running toward the field. In a few moments we had left Singapore and were over the sea.

Not until we had flown for some minutes and I had started to relax did I begin to reflect upon the seriousness of what I had done. We had left Singapore without exit visas, and I still had no passport. The British were bound to be angry.

Mr. Monem went to the washroom and changed his clothes. When he returned he was once again the well-dressed diplomat. The pilot came back from the cockpit, stared at Mr. Monem, and asked, "How the devil did you get on? I understood there would be only two passengers."

I identified Mr. Monem as my erstwhile "servant," introduced myself as an American citizen, and told the purpose of our flight. "Well, I'll be damned," he said. "Spirit of 'Seventy-six!'" Then he went forward to tell the rest of the crew.

Thirty minutes later he was back again, this time grim and tense. "We've got some Dutch fighters on our tail," he said. "They're trying to force us to head for Batavia. We heard the Singapore radio announce that Surabaya Sue and the Egyptian consul general had taken off at dawn and were on their way to Jogjakarta.

"Now take seats far back in the plane, away from the windows, and fasten your safety belts. No Dutch plane is going to force an American plane to land in Dutch territory. We are headed for Jogja and that is where we'll land. We didn't tangle with the Nips out in the Pacific for nothing. Those boys can shoot us down but they can't force us down. We'll show them a trick or two."

With that he returned to the cockpit, leaving two badly frightened passengers to sweat out the crisis by themselves. If I live to be a hundred I shall never forget that flight, nor shall I be able to describe with accuracy the action of the airplane. First we seemed to be soaring to the heavens, and the next minute we were diving to the sea. I wondered if we were hit, and found myself clinging to the stoic Mr. Monem. He patted me and comforted me as though I were a child. We dived again, and the water was very close. Mr. Monem held me tight, and I heard him say, "If we get out of this alive and you come to Egypt, I shall see to it that you meet King Farouk and are given the key to the city of Cairo." I laughed in spite of my fear.

The plane leveled off finally, and the radio operator came back to say that the danger was past. "We shook 'em off and now we are over the mountains of Borneo," he said. A bit later we were flying serenely in the direction of middle Java. For the rest of the journey Mr. Monem told me stories of Egypt and talked of King Farouk, who was not, he assured me, all playboy.

There were only a few Indonesian soldiers at the airport when we landed in Java. The crew helped us out of the plane. "Hope you enjoyed the flight," they joked. "We'll try to pick out a smoother track when we go back."

The Merdeka Hotel in Jogja looked much the same. My friends there were surprised to see me, and they had many questions to ask about conditions on the other side of the Dutch curtain.

The next morning Mr. Monem was received in state by President Sukarno, Vice-President Hatta, the ministers of state, and the commanding officers of the military services. There was an impressive ceremony in the magnificent reception room of the palace, with Sukarno and Mr. Monem facing each other. The President appeared calm, but the Egyptian was nervous. His voice quavered and his hands trembled as he read from a parchment that Egypt and the Arab League formally recognized the Republic of Indonesia as a sovereign state and welcomed it into the family of nations.

Mr. Monem had assured me in advance that he would not tell anyone that I had chartered the plane or made the arrangements for the flight. I had insisted on this, knowing that if facts were given out the press would sensationalize my part in it. Such personal publicity would detract from the news value of Indonesia's recognition. Also I was determined to protect the Singapore firm from which I had chartered the plane. To the date of this writing the secret has been well kept. Aside from a few people in the Ministry for Defense and the intelligence department of the Djaksa Agung's office—the CID of Indonesia—no Indonesian, not even the President, has been aware of the part I played.

The pleasure of my return to Jogja, the joy of witnessing the first official recognition of the new Republic, was dimmed by one development. I learned that Amir Sjarifuddin had had a nervous breakdown and had been very ill. He was convalescing at a villa in the mountains behind Maduin, where he was permitted few visitors. Nevertheless, I was allowed to call upon him there.

Bung Amir accepted the news of the plane charter and my signature on the note in the name of the Defense Ministry without batting an eye. "It is wonderful that Mr. Monem could get here to accomplish his very important mission," he said. "You did us a service." With that he addressed to Colonel X a note instructing him to hand over to me $10,000, along with money to cover the expenses of a trip to Australia.

I offered to stay on in Indonesia, to help in any way I could. But Bung Amir said my life would be in danger, with the Dutch moving into Republican territory. "I shall feel better if you are far away when the Dutch come in," he said.

Mrs. Sjarifuddin brought in tea. We chatted of generalities until it was time for me to leave. Bung Amir looked almost his old self as he waved good-by. I never saw him again.

We flew back to Singapore the following day. This time Mr. Monem and I had as traveling companions a number of high Indonesian officials, among them a venerable statesman, Agus Salim, on his way to India for a conference with Prime Minister Nehru. Our take-off time and route had been kept secret, and we flew toward Borneo before taking the skyway to Singapore. The Dutch were nowhere to be seen, and we had a pleasantly uneventful flight.

As I had anticipated, the British authorities at Singapore took a dim view of my Javanese escapade. They said I had embarrassed them, and they were sorry they had been so lenient to me before. But once again they forgave me and granted me access to the city.

17

AUSTRALIA

I did not have long to wait for the word from Australia, and it was good. Canberra said I might enter without the formality of a passport. Wonderful, wonderful Australia!

Before making arrangements for the journey I again approached the American consulate and asked about my passport. Nothing had as yet been heard from Washington. I could stay no longer in Singapore merely to await the pleasure of the passport office in Washington.

A major flaw quickly cracked wide my neat new plans. Colonel X had not enough money to advance me the cost of my trip which Bung Amir had authorized. "I have paid the plane charter and the expenses of the crew, and shared what little was left among the various Indonesian groups working in Singapore," he said. "I am expecting some more money shortly, but I cannot say for sure when it will arrive. Much depends on luck, and whether the next consignment of sugar and rubber gets through safely from Java. It might take a week, a month, or even longer. Under such conditions nothing is certain."

Colonel X had plenty of Indonesian rupiahs, but they were absolutely worthless in the outside world. It had begun to appear that the only thing to do would be to return once again to Indonesia and wait until the government was in a position to finance an Australian venture properly.

Among my Chinese friends in Singapore was a wealthy attorney and restaurant owner named Ho Alim, who had come to the city many years before from Africa. British educated, brilliant and broad-minded, he was considered an anticolonial and was most sympathetic toward the Indonesian question. Although he worked actively for a free Malaya he had never tried to interest me in Malayan politics. "You have lived for many years in Indonesia, know the people and the conditions in which they live," he said. "You are qualified, therefore, to speak for Indonesia. You do not know Malaya, and you would be very foolish to interest yourself in its politics." I agreed wholeheartedly.

When I told Ho Alim that because of financial difficulties I planned to return to Indonesia and forget about the Australian trip for the time being he was greatly disturbed.

"You must not return to Indonesia under any circumstances," he said. "The Dutch are about to invade Indonesian Republican territory, and it is evident that they cannot be stopped. They would kill you, or at least put you in jail for a long time. It is more important now than ever for you to go to Australia and tell the truth of what is going on in Indonesia. It is extremely important that the Australians continue their ban on the loading of firearms on Dutch ships. And the Dutch scheme to bring in guns and ammunition by plane from outlying Australian airports must be stopped."

He pointed out that Indonesian warehouses were stacked with commodities that the Australians needed and couldn't get at any price: tea, coffee, sugar, sago, quinine—and other things. The Indonesians should be trading these for the Australian goods they so urgently required.

"No, K'tut; you must go to Australia. You are a Britisher and the Aussies will listen to you. Because I realize the importance of this I want to finance your trip to Australia and back to Singapore."

I asked why he was willing to do so much for Indonesia.

"Because Malaya and Indonesia are closely affiliated," he said. "They are similar in language and religion. They are cousins, and good neighbors. We in Malaya have the British, with whom we can negotiate independence, and not the bullheaded Dutch. When

Indonesian Merdeka is finally won, it will be only a matter of time before the British give Malaya and Singapore their freedom."

Reluctantly I accepted the aid he offered, saying that I would see to it that the Indonesian government reimbursed him as speedily as possible. He was not content that I should travel modestly. "You need a rest, and you need a bit of luxury for a change," he said. "This time you are going de luxe." Though I protested, I must admit that the comforts of a stateroom and the wonderful food and service on the journey to Australia provided a pleasing contrast to my recent travel experiences.

The ship docked first at Perth, in western Australia. No one was more surprised than I, when the gangplank was lowered, to see so many newspaper reporters and cameramen rush aboard in quest of Surabaya Sue. The dock workers—wharfies, they were called in Australia—swarmed around, too, to shake my hand. Photographers asked that I pose with the men who had refused to load guns aboard any Dutch ship bound for Indonesia. This I was proud to do, even though I realized that the reactionary press might attempt to use pictures in a smear program designed to implicate me in Communist activities. Some of the wharfies were known to be red tinged, and my praise of their work would very likely color me with the same brush.

An amazingly short time later, on the streets of Perth, glaring posters at every street corner announced my arrival, and newspapers bore front-page headlines such as "Surabaya Sue, Mystery Woman from Java" and "Surabaya Sue, Fugitive from the Dutch." In all the stories hardly any mention was made of Indonesia and its painfully slow advance toward freedom. Surabaya Sue—I began to hate the name, and even called the editor of one paper and asked him please to refrain from using it. The response the next day was the headline: "Surabaya Sue Doesn't Like Her Name."

Much was made of the fact that I had entered Australia without a passport and also of the help I had given to an Australian officer whose family lived in Perth, during the early days of the Revolution. For my part, I found the people of Australia uncommonly generous and friendly and openhearted. Everything about them seemed big. They reminded me, in fact, of western Americans.

Melbourne was our ship's next port, and the fuss and publicity there was much as it had been in Perth. Some of the reporters tried to needle me into comment about the "white Australia" policy and to heckle me about entering Australia without a passport. The articles they wrote were so sarcastic that I decided not to meet the press in Sydney at all.

But it is not easy to avoid newsmen. In Sydney I was saved from a small-scale mob by one of the ship's officers, who let me hide in his room until the press got tired of waiting. CID officials came aboard to investigate the reports that I was in Australia without a passport. I satisfied them that I had special permission to enter the country, but the customs officers were more than thorough. They went through my baggage so many times that I asked them, finally, if they were looking for the atomic bomb.

"No," said one. "We are making sure that you have not smuggled amber into Australia."

"Amber?" I was incredulous. "Why?"

"Forever Amber, sister," he laughed. "We don't want anyone bringing that obscene book into our country."

I had never before heard of the currently popular novel of that title and thought at first that he was jesting. I learned quickly that he was in earnest, for he confiscated my large bundle of Indonesian- and Malayan-language magazines and newspapers.

"There is nothing wrong with these," I protested. "You can buy them on any newsstand in Asia."

"We have only your word for that," he replied. "I can't read them. How do we know that they aren't in Russian?"

I stared at him, speechless at such idiotic behavior. "If they aren't Russian—if they are all right—you'll get them back in a couple of days," he said. He did keep his promise. The whole lot was returned to me.

On the whole the Australian authorities treated me very well. This could not be said of the public generally. The newspapers had identified the hotel where I was staying, and I was pestered day and night by autograph hounds and curiosity seekers. Many Dutch people, refugees from Indonesia, telephoned and were most abusive.

A Scotswoman whom I had met offered me a small apartment in her home at King's Cross. For a short time I was able to leave the house without being followed. Then a newspaper columnist discovered my whereabouts, and printed a most insulting article about me. The provocation began in real earnest.

The telephone would ring, often hours after I had gone to sleep. A voice would curse me, call me "nigger lover" or "Indonesian stooge," warn me to get out of the city before something happened to me. I at first attributed all this to the Dutch living in Sydney. When it became unbearable I asked the help of the CID.

The Australian department of investigation tapped my telephone, at my request, and quickly discovered the source of most of the calls. They were coming from a newspaper office. I had my telephone number changed. The calls ceased for a time, then started up again.

The CID advised me not to pay too much attention to the tabloid press of Sydney. But when a newspaper printed that I had kept a house of ill-repute in Bali, my limit was reached. I slapped a slander suit on the paper.

In spite of the newspaper attacks—or perhaps in part because of them—I was invited everywhere in Sydney and was so busy I had to refuse many engagements that I would have preferred to accept. I spoke before most of the labor unions, telling them in simple language the struggle of the Indonesians to become as free as the Australians were free. I described the deplorable conditions wrought by the Dutch blockade, the shocking shortage of medical equipment and supplies, the unnecessary suffering of the innocent. I asked for help in the name of the Indonesian Medical Aid Appeal. The response was far beyond my expectations. Donations began to pour in.

The Indonesian Medical Aid Appeal had been set up by a group of Australian churchmen and business people, including an Anglican bishop, a Catholic priest, and Protestant ministers. The donations went directly to the Appeal. Australians, donating their services, handled the fund-raising campaign. I did not personally collect or handle any money. My part was simply to give lectures.

A Sunday afternoon meeting in a large Sydney theater was particularly successful. Some Australian leaders who had recently returned from Indonesia were on the speaking platform with me. After our talks the audience stormed the stage and began pouring money into our laps. Medical aid for Indonesia received quite an enormous sum of money that afternoon.

I spoke over radio stations also, and to the Australian Women's Democratic party, the Housewives' Union, and many other women's organizations. And then I spoke at Sydney University, in a great hall packed with students. A question-and-answer period followed. The questions for the most part were intelligent and indicative of a strong desire to know the truth. At the same time they were evidence of a shocking lack of knowledge about Indonesia, Australia's nearest neighbor. Bitter and frustrated Dutch colonials had misinformed the Australians all during and since the war. No Indonesians of note had been on hand to counter the vicious propaganda.

Only one outright foolish question was asked. Perhaps, in fact, I misunderstood the questioner. I understood him to say, "Tell us what the Indonesian rabble is like. How do the rabble live?" Later it occurred to me that he may have said "rebel" instead of rabble. However that may be, I angrily replied, "Indonesia has no rabble. They have people who are the same as you and I, with the same hopes and dreams. There is one big difference; the Australians are free, the Indonesians are not. They want to be free. And they look to Australia for help."

"How can we help?" one student asked. "We recognize the right of all men to be free. We would help if you could show us the way."

Other students applauded the idea vigorously.

"I can show you how to help your Indonesian neighbors," I said. "You, the students of Sydney University, could organize a march on the Dutch consulate. You could draw up a petition of protest against any further Dutch aggression in Indonesia. You could send telegrams to the Australian Prime Minister asking him to put the Indonesian question to the United Nations."

"Let's march on the Dutch consulate!" one student shouted. "When do we start?" another asked.

A quickly formed committee came to my apartment, and we made banners with a variety of slogans: Dutch, Cease Fire in Indonesia. Stop Dutch Aggression against the Indonesians. We Want the Indonesian Question Before the UN. No Guns from Australia in Indonesia.

The students composed a long petition of protest. They would hand it to the Dutch consul when they had marched to his office, and then they would return to the university, disband, and go home. "Remember," I told them, "if the march is to be effective it must remain orderly. Nothing must get out of hand."

That was the way it was planned. What happened was quite another matter.

"Will you lead us?" one of the students had asked. I quickly convinced him that this must be a student enterprise and that I must take no active part.

Word of the proposed march reached the newspapers, and one of them printed the starting time and the time of arrival at the consulate. The Dutch offices were several flights up in a building in the center of the city. When the Dutch heard that the students were on the march they locked their doors, to bar the young marchers.

I waited near the office building to watch the developments. With me was one of the most important newspaper editors in Sydney. We noticed that the building was surrounded by policemen and that a considerable crowd had gathered to await the arrival of the protest parade.

The word swept through the crowd, "They're coming. Here they come!" The students marched down the street, hundreds of them—quietly, in perfect dignity. As the first of them neared the building the police tried to force them back. The others pushed on. Before anyone could realize what was happening, bedlam broke loose.

First the police roughed up a few of the leaders. Other students began to shout protests, and the officers swung clubs. Bricks and street debris began to fly. Soon bystanders were joining the students against the police. Within moments the whole street was fighting.

From their offices high above the sidewalk the Dutch tossed out buckets of water, unintentionally drenching the police more than the students. Still the students came marching on, cheering, jeering, defiant.

The girl student who had been entrusted with the petition tried to break through the police blockade to get into the building. She fought valiantly. Her dress was torn and her hair disheveled. She fell down, but she was up again. With almost superhuman agility she was between the legs of a tall policeman and off like a deer, through the hall of the building and up the stairs. The police dashed after her, but were no match for her athletic youth. She made it—but only just. A moment before the policeman reached her she pushed the petition of protest under the door of the Dutch consulate.

By this time police whistles and sirens were sounding all over the area, and students were being hustled into patrol wagons. The young heroine was hurried down the stairs and shoved into one car. More police appeared. But as soon as the students had learned that the petition had been served they disbanded and returned to the university or to their homes. Many students had been hurt, and scores arrested.

The students had been orderly at the start, and had they been let alone there would have been no disturbance. Police interference, at the call of the Dutch, had turned the march into the riot. As it happened, this worked to the disadvantage of the Dutch, for the free-for-all received tremendous publicity, in the press and over the air, throughout the Far East. The Australian papers were scathing in their denunciation of the police for using force against the students. The angry fathers of the students included some of the most important men in the country. They joined in the demand that Australia place the Indonesian question before the United Nations. From India Prime Minister Nehru made the same plea. In their wildest hopes the students had not looked for such a profound effect from their simply planned protest march. Not long afterward the Dutch were ordered by the United Nations to cease fire in Indonesia, and the whole Indonesian problem was set before the UN.

In order to raise money for bail and attorney fees for the students who had been arrested, I lectured before a number of business groups and Labor party organizations, and also to the Australian servicemen. The response was quick and generous. Later the court dismissed the case against the students.

18

MISSION ACCOMPLISHED

The voice over the telephone was deep and guttural. It sounded Dutch. The speaker identified himself. He was Dutch. "I should like to see you on a most important matter," he said.

Could there be in Sydney a Dutchman who had seen the light,

who wanted to help the Indonesian cause? That would be too much to expect. I invited him to come for a talk, nonetheless.

The moment he set foot in my apartment I could identify him: a typical colonial diehard. Pompous, arrogant, brusque. He introduced himself coldly, obviously feeling that he was demeaning the Dutch by condescending to call on an enemy of his people.

He wasted no time on preliminaries. "I represent a group of businessmen who formerly lived in Java," he said. "We are prepared to offer you a hundred thousand guilders if you will leave Australia immediately, go to America or England, and forget all about Indonesia."

I just stared at him.

"Indonesia is none of your business," he said. "You are a foreigner. With a hundred thousand guilders you can live in luxury the rest of your life, or you can use it to start another hotel in another country."

I was still speechless. He went on:

"You should realize that the Indonesians are only making use of you, and will forget about you if they ever get their freedom. Then where will you be? But they will not get their freedom—not the kind they are screaming about. We Dutch will be taking over again one of these days. You may be sure we will never allow you in Indonesia."

At last I found my tongue. "You Dutch must have a lot to lose in Indonesia to try these tactics," I said scornfully. "There are seventy million Indonesians. If you and your associates were willing to put up one million guilders for every man and woman in Indonesia, even then I couldn't be tempted to sell out my adopted land or desert it in its struggle to break the chains of colonialism. The Indonesians may forget all about me when they are free—and why not? I am but a very tiny part of the great, swelling tide toward merdeka. I have lived for many years under Dutch colonial rule. I know the little that was good, the much that was bad. Why is it that the Dutch in Holland screamed with indignation when the Nazis overran their country and plundered it, yet now that the Allies have liberated Holland the Dutch are trying to do the same thing in Indonesia? For three hundred years the great wealth of Indonesia has found its way to Holland. Isn't it about time for that flow to be diverted back into Indonesia, at least in part?"

He looked at me with contempt. "How can you, a white woman,

fight for a race that can never be your equal?" he shouted. "What could you have in common with them? What is wrong with white skin, that you should prefer brown or black?"

I handed him his hat and opened the door. "Being Dutch, you profess to be a Christian," I said. "Tell me, what is the color of the skin of your Creator? Have you never heard of the race of man?

"And as for me—I have always been color-blind!"

I could not help slamming the door after him. Standing there, tears of exasperation in my eyes, I recalled the kindly, tolerant face of President Sukarno and others of my friends in Indonesia—Amir Sjarifuddin, Pito, the guerrillas of Java Timor. I heard their voices, warm with affection and confidence in me. These were my true riches, compared with which a hundred thousand pieces of Dutch silver had no value at all.

There were letters—many, many letters, from all over Australia—to be answered. Some were provocative, some flattering. Earnest citizens asked why I did not open an Indonesian information bureau in Sydney. Businessmen inquired about trade with Indonesia. Several men who had read that I had no passport, and was hampered in my traveling, sent proposals of marriage to give me the protection of Australian citizenship. And among the letters came one from the United States consulate in Sydney. The consul general had been instructed by the State Department in Washington to issue me an American passport! I was delighted.

I hurried downtown to pick up the document I had been seeking so long, only to be informed that a passport would be issued solely for a direct journey from Australia to the United States. I could go to no other country, in Asia or elsewhere. The consul suggested a ship from Sydney to San Francisco.

A passport with strings attached! It smelled of politics. "I cannot go home from here," I informed the consul. "I have a return ticket to Singapore, I am running short of money, and I can only get funds for the trip to the United States by going back to Singapore. I cannot accept a passport under the conditions you impose."

"I do not understand your money problems," the consul said. "You owned a hotel in Bali. You had a house in Surabaya. You have raised large sums of money in Australia through the Indonesian Medical Aid Appeal. Why have you no money?"

I explained again, as I had explained before, that the Japanese had destroyed my hotel and that my Surabaya house had been destroyed in the early days of the Revolution. "The money I raised in Australia was for medical aid for Indonesia, and I received not one penny of it," I said. "This was a labor of love. Nor has any government—American, Japanese, or Indonesian—paid me anything as compensation for the loss of my property during the war."

In the end the consul agreed that I should go back to Singapore, and that he would instruct the American consul there to give me a passport for my return to the United States. I pointed out that I had no permit to re-enter Singapore, only the identification paper given to me by the British when I first went to Singapore from Indonesia. "I shall need a visa to re-enter Singapore," I said. "If you will give me a letter saying that an American passport will be issued to me in Singapore, I can then go to the Malayan government here in Sydney and ask for a visa to enter Singapore."

The American consul refused to go this far and I left his office wondering how I could work things out. I dreaded the thought of boarding a Singapore-bound ship without satisfactory papers, on the slender chance that the British would be as lenient as they had been in the past. I had hoped for once to be in the clear.

I flew from Sydney to Perth to board a ship bound for Singapore. There was some newspaper speculation as to whether the British would allow Surabaya Sue to enter that city again without a passport. Would I become, they asked, a woman without a country, doomed to shuttle back and forth between Australia and Malaya, allowed to land nowhere? I refused to worry, as reluctantly I said good-by to beautiful Australia.

It was a satisfaction to learn, from my friends who had organized the Indonesian Medical Aid, that my speaking appearances had raised thousands of dollars for the cause. All this money would be used to buy medical supplies and medicines to be sent immediately to Indonesia through the Australian Red Cross.

Singapore? That problem would be met if, as, and when it developed.

19

HOME FOR CHRISTMAS

It was no shock to me to see familiar faces from the British immigration forces and an official from the special branch of the CID waiting on the dock at Singapore.

"Well, well, Surabaya Sue again" was the first greeting. "It seems like old times. We are delighted to see you—if your papers are in order this time. You have a visa, we presume."

I shook my head. "You presume too much," I said. "Surely you read the papers—all those stories about Surabaya Sue and her fights with the authorities. I do have the documents you gave me the first time I came to Singapore."

"Those papers were good the first time," one of the men said. "But this is the third time. What makes you think you can come and go without the proper papers?"

"I am not doing this because I like doing it—you know that," I retorted. "I am forced into this ridiculous position. It is not my fault I haven't a passport."

"We know, we know," he said. "But you are becoming an embarrassment to us. The Dutch are complaining that we are helping one of their worst enemies, just because you are British born. What are we going to do with you?"

"Since when has a Britisher been intimidated by a Dutchman?" I asked. "I took a great risk in coming back here because I believed in the tolerance and chivalry of British officials. Where else in Asia could a Scotswoman land without a passport? If you consider me a woman without a country, at least you should give me a document certifying me as stateless. Then I could get a visa, at least to enter Singapore."

"Why didn't you apply for such a document?"

"Because I am not stateless. I am entitled to an American passport."

"What are we going to do with you?" he asked once again.

"I hope you are going to allow me to land, and to stay in Singapore until my affairs are in order, and until I get the passport that has been promised to me."

"Do you really expect us to close our eyes for a third time to let you in?"

"There might even be a fourth time," I said—prophetically, as it turned out. "Think of the headlines it would make in Scotland. 'Scots girl refused admission by brutal British!' 'Former Japanese prisoner tortured by countrymen!' It's reason for an uprising by all the Scots who have so long wished to be free from England!"

The men laughed. "You have a point there," one said. "Looks like you win once more."

Thus once again I was in Singapore.

In the months that I had been in Australia much had happened in the city. Most of my Indonesian friends had been recalled to Java because of the grave turn of events. Even Colonel X was gone. The house was closed.

The news from Java was depressing. The Linggadjati agreement had failed completely, as the Dutch had meant it to fail. Prime Minister Sutan Sjahrir had lost the confidence of the people and had been forced to resign. Even his own Socialist party had accused him of concessions to the Dutch at the expense of merdeka. Amir Sjarifuddin had become prime minister, retaining his portfolio as minister for defense as well.

What the Dutch called a police action following signature of the agreement was in reality a preplanned full-scale colonial war. After capturing many Republican towns and villages, they were approaching the capital city of Jogjakarta and had boasted that victory was only three or four weeks away. Then the United Nations ordered a "cease fire." A United Nations Committee of Good Offices was set up to help arrange a settlement, having as its members Dr. van Zeeland, a former Belgian prime minister, Justice Kirby of Australia, and Dr. Frank Graham of the University of North Carolina.

For want of a more satisfactory place, the committee met aboard an American naval transport, the *Renville*, and talks dragged on for weeks.

During this time I was able, through the help of a sympathetic British official, to telephone Amir Sjarifuddin and congratulate him on becoming prime minister. He was unenthusiastic. "I doubt that I'll last as long as Sjahrir did," he said. Nor was he sanguine about the negotiations. When I asked whether it might be advisable for me to return to Java he said I would no longer be safe there. "In view of the Dutch attitude, it is probably only a matter of time before they attack Jogja," he said. "Even President Sukarno and I may be in danger."

The Renville agreement as finally worked out gave the Dutch control of more than two thirds of Java, leaving the Indonesians far less than they felt was rightfully theirs. Sukarno, Sjarifuddin, Hatta, Sjahrir were all against signing the agreement, but the Dutch said that if it were not signed within five days they would march against Indonesia. The Republic could not stand another "police action." Reluctantly Amir Sjarifuddin penned his name to the agreement.

It took the Dutch only a short time to break the Renville agreement as they had broken the Linggadjati agreement. They bombed Jogjakarta, dropped parachute troops, then marched in and took the city—arresting Sukarno, Hatta, and Sjahrir with other high government officials and the directors of the radio stations.

Another brutal Dutch action was the shooting down of an airplane carrying $10,000 worth of medical supplies that had been purchased with funds raised in our campaign in Australia.

World opinion, as everyone knows, swelled so strongly against the Dutch, and the United Nations ultimately took so firm a stand against them, that they were forced to release the Indonesian leaders and restore the Republican government in Jogjakarta. So what had initially appeared to be a Dutch coup turned into a defeat for them and the triumph of the Indonesians.

In Singapore I went to the American consulate and asked for the passport that had been promised to me. "It will be delivered to you as soon as you can show us that you have made arrangements to leave, and that you are sailing directly to the United States," I was told. In due course I raised $650 to pay for passage on a Boston-bound freighter, and showed my ticket at the consulate. After a frustrating wait of more than two years I was, at last, the owner of an American passport—proof to the world that I was an American citizen.

The money was barely enough for my voyage, with a bit left over for the taxi to Singapore's dock and for tips to the room boy and steward aboard ship. This ship would reach Boston in mid-December. The prospect of returning to America in midwinter, absolutely broke, was worrisome. My plan upon arrival in Boston was to wire the Indonesian office in New York for funds with which to get to the big city. In New York I should be able to find work with the Indonesians.

With most of my Indonesian friends back in Java, and Mr. Ho Alim away in North Malaya, I had relatively few farewells to make. I had a final Malayan dinner with two good British friends, a reporter on the *Singapore Straits Times* and her husband. They saw me off, and were the last familiar faces I could see as the ship drew out of Singapore harbor. It was strange and saddening, after all these years, to be leaving the Far East and all it had come to mean to me.

The cargo ship was small and slow, but comfortable. We stopped at a number of ports in the Red Sea and the Mediterranean, to load or discharge cargo. The only other passenger was a Chinese student going to America to study law. He took his meals with the crew and I did not get to meet him on the voyage.

Across the Atlantic we were lashed for days by a dreadful storm. It made us late into Boston, so that we drew up along the dock about 7 P.M. on Christmas Eve. The families of the ship's officers were waiting at the water's edge. As soon as the formalities of customs and immigration were over, the people hurried off. There were no porters, no taxis—and soon there was no one but me standing there, shivering in the dark. I had just five dollars. I had been away for fifteen years. And it was Christmas Eve.

I found a telephone booth on the dismal pier, and summoned a taxi to take me to the railroad station. This cost three dollars, including tip. I carried my meager luggage into the station, and looked around. The Travelers Aid? Closed for the holidays. My heart sank. I knew no one in Boston—no one anywhere in the United States to whom I could send a wire of distress after fifteen years. Over the station loud-speaker there were chimes and Christmas hymns. I sat on a hard bench and fingered two one-dollar bills—my last remaining funds in this world.

There was a gentle tap on my shoulder. "Excuse me," a voice said. "Are you not the American girl known in Asia as Surabaya Sue?"

I turned swiftly, and saw a well-dressed young Chinese.

"We have been fellow passengers from Singapore," he said. "I have read a great deal about you."

Tears came to my eyes—tears of gratitude that there was another human being at this moment aware of my existence.

"Are you going to New York?" he asked. "That is my next stop."

I confessed that I had planned to go to New York but lacked money even for train fare. I would have no way of getting money until after Christmas.

"Please let me buy your ticket to New York," he said. "It is lonely, and I have never been in your country before. I would deeply appreciate having your company."

I told him I would be forever in his debt if he would lend me the amount of my ticket. I would repay him before he left New York.

He gave me a big, happy smile. "We Asians must stick together," he said.

We arrived at Grand Central Station after midnight. He went to one hotel, and was told there was no vacancy; and to a second with the same result. It dawned on me then that his race might have had something to do with his reception. When I inquired at the desk alone I had no difficulty in getting two rooms.

It was a stimulating experience to be with this young Chinese on Christmas Day, strolling the streets of New York. Up Fifth Avenue, over to Broadway, and down to the Village—everything he saw entranced him. The Empire State Building was a thing of beauty. The United Nations Building, which I considered an enormous tombstone dedicated to the lost ideals of the world, was to him a wonder to behold. The department store Christmas decorations were fairy-tale magic. The city as a whole? "A beautiful forest," he said. "A forest —with stately trees of cement proudly raising their branches toward the heavens."

The next day I was able to get funds with which to repay him, and buy him a briefcase, his first Christmas gift from the West. In the evening I saw him aboard his train for the school he would attend in Indiana. Then I walked away, homesick for Indonesia, missing the sun and warmth and glowing color of the Far East.

Above the city lights the stars were twinkling, and I was reminded of a Chinese story out of my childhood. Those who would find tranquillity must first have the courage to leave all earthly joys and possessions behind, and go search for the land of the purple star. When the search was ended the purple star would reveal itself overhead. But the only one who would see it would be he who had sacrificed much.

I searched for the purple star in many lands, but I had never found it. In the stars above New York, shining so cold and bright, was there a purple star? And would it reveal itself to me? I searched the heavens, hopefully.